FREEDOM AND FORCE

This collection of essays takes as its starting point Arthur Ripstein's *Force and Freedom: Kant's Legal and Political Philosophy*, a seminal work on Kant's thinking about law, which also treats many of the contemporary issues of legal and political philosophy. The essays offer readings and elucidations of Ripstein's thoughts, dispute some of his claims and extend some of his themes within broader philosophical contexts, thus developing the significance of Ripstein's ideas for contemporary legal and political philosophy.

All of the essays are contributions to normative philosophy in a broadly Kantian spirit. Prominent themes include rights in the body, the relation between morality and law, the nature of coercion and its role in legal obligation, the role of indeterminacy in law, the nature and justification of political society and the theory of the state. This volume will be of interest to a wide audience, including legal scholars, Kant scholars, and philosophers with an interest in Kant or in legal and political philosophy.

Volume 9 in the series Law and Practical Reason

Law and Practical Reason

The intention of this series is that it should encompass monographs and collections of essays that address the fundamental issues in legal philosophy. The foci are conceptual and normative in character, not empirical. Studies addressing the idea of law as a species of practical reason are especially welcome. Recognising that there is no occasion sharply to distinguish analytic and systematic work in the field from historico-critical research, the editors also welcome studies in the history of legal philosophy. Contributions to the series, inevitably crossing disciplinary lines, will be of interest to students and professionals in moral, political, and legal philosophy.

Recent titles in the series

Volume 4: Hannah Arendt and the Law
Edited by Marco Goldoni and Christopher McCorkindale

Volume 5: The Logic of Autonomy: Law, Morality and Autonomous Reasoning
Jan-R Sieckmann

Volume 6: Law and Authority under the Guise of the Good
Veronica Rodriguez-Blanco

Volume 7: Shared Authority
Dimitrios Kyritsis

Volume 8: Private Law and the Value of Choice
Emmanuel Voyiakis

Freedom and Force

Essays on Kant's Legal Philosophy

Edited by
Sari Kisilevsky and Martin J Stone

•HART•
OXFORD • LONDON • NEW YORK • NEW DELHI • SYDNEY

HART PUBLISHING
Bloomsbury Publishing Plc
Kemp House, Chawley Park, Cumnor Hill, Oxford, OX2 9PH, UK

HART PUBLISHING, the Hart/Stag logo, BLOOMSBURY and the Diana logo are trademarks of Bloomsbury Publishing Plc

First published in hardback, 2017
Paperback edition, 2019

A catalogue record for this book is available from the British Library.

Library of Congress Cataloging-in-Publication data

Names: Kisilevsky, Sari, editor. | Stone, Martin Jay, editor.

Title: Freedom and force : essays on Kant's legal philosophy / edited by Sari Kisilevsky and Martin J Stone.

Description: Oxford ; Portland, Oregon : Hart Publishing, An imprint of Bloomsbury Publishing Plc, 2017. | Series: Law and practical reason ; volume 9 | Includes bibliographical references and index.

Identifiers: LCCN 2016057106 (print) | LCCN 2016057841 (ebook) | ISBN 9781849463164 (hardback) | ISBN 9781782253075 (epub)

Subjects: LCSH: Kant, Immanuel, 1724-1804. | Law—Philosophy. | Ripstein, Arthur. Force and freedom.

Classification: LCC K230.K364 F74 2017 (print) | LCC K230.K364 (ebook) | DDC 340/.1—dc23

LC record available at https://lccn.loc.gov/2016057106

ISBN: HB: 978-1-84946-316-4
PB: 978-1-50993-216-0
ePDF: 978-1-78225-306-8
ePub: 978-1-78225-307-5

Typeset by Compuscript Ltd, Shannon

To find out more about our authors and books visit www.hartpublishing.co.uk. Here you will find extracts, author information, details of forthcoming events and the option to sign up for our newsletters.

Preface

Kant's political philosophy has been gaining ground. Its main text, *The Doctrine of Right,* was long regarded as obscure and fragmentary and lacking the power of Kant's previous *Critiques*: 'It is as if it were not the work of this great man', Schopenhauer bewailed.[1] Various books and articles today offer a different impression, and prominent among them is Arthur Ripstein's *Force and Freedom: Kant's Legal and Political Philosophy*. Ripstein's celebrated book is the cause of the present volume, which contains eight essays written in response to it, followed by Ripstein's response to these responses.

Force and Freedom locates the force and unity of Kant's Doctrine in its idea of people's mutual independence. It also develops this unifying idea in light of modern political philosophy's questions about the nature of rights and the basis of public authority: rights are embodiments of freedom, not summations of welfare; and public authority is not a means of making people happier but a sine qua non of their being free. *Force and Freedom* thus combines an exegetical with a normative project—a guide to Kant's Doctrine with a political theory tendered as true. The following chapters also make original contributions to one or both of these projects. Most of them contest *something* Ripstein says; all of them attest to the significance of *Force and Freedom* as a paragon of what Kantian political thought might be.

The reader will find here much lively argument, a wide range of views and, as is to be expected, some sharp disagreements. Doubtless, the exegetical and normative questions—what Kant meant and what's right—will continue to be debated. Yet one thing does seem settled, or put beyond debate, thanks to *Force and Freedom* and the present discussions of it. Whatever Kant meant, and whatever is right, Schopenhauer was mistaken.

[1] Quoted in Hannah Arendt, Ronald Beiner ed., *Lectures on Kant's Political Philosophy* (Chicago University Press, 1992) 8.

Contents

Contributors

Katrin Flikschuh is a professor of political theory in the Government Department of the London School of Economics.

AJ Julius is an associate professor of philosophy at UCLA.

Sari Kisilevsky is a professor of philosophy at Queens College CUNY.

Japa Pallikkathayil is an assistant professor of philosophy at the University of Pittsburgh.

George Pavlakos is Professor of Law and Philosophy at the School of Law, University of Glasgow.

Arthur Ripstein is University Professor of Law and Philosophy at the Faculty of Law and Department of Philosophy at the University of Toronto.

Andrea Sangiovanni is a senior lecturer in philosophy at King's College London.

Martin Stone is a professor of law at the Benjamin N Cardozo School of Law, Yeshiva University, and an adjunct professor of philosophy at the New School University Graduate Faculty.

Daniel Weinstock is the James McGill Professor and Director of the McGill Institute for Health and Social Policy at the Faculty of Law of McGill University.

Allen Wood is the Ruth Norman Halls Professor of Philosophy at Indiana University.

Overview

1

Ripstein and His Critics

MARTIN J STONE*

POLITICAL PHILOSOPHY HAS many questions: one idea—*Right-as-independence*—underlies most of Ripstein's answers. As this idea is Ripstein's argumentative starting point, it is also the background, and sometimes the explicit focus, of the following chapters. What *is* Right-as-independence? And does political philosophy *have* to start there? By way of introduction, I address these two questions and—in light of this—sketch the contours of the present controversies.[1]

I. RIGHT-AS-INDEPENDENCE

Each person has an 'innate right to freedom', Kant says; and freedom, he adds, is 'independence from being constrained by another's *choice*'.[2]

In explaining what Kant means by this, Ripstein recalls Aristotle's observation that *choosing*, unlike *wishing*, extends only to things in my power.[3] I cannot *choose* who will win the next election or choose to make a mushroom omelette if I have no workable plan for obtaining some mushrooms. Hence Ripstein says that Kant is talking about my freedom to use the means or powers I *have*. If it turns out that the local mushrooms are all yours and that you've priced them—as it is said—beyond my *means*, that's no limitation of my freedom, on this conception: for you haven't affected my powers of choosing, only—by making choices of your own—failed to create the ideal environment (ie the one I'd prefer) for my exercise of my powers. I'm free to choose in ways that

* Thanks to Chris Essert, Micha Glaeser, Rafeeq Hasan, Arthur Ripstein and Ernest Weinrib for comments on an earlier draft and to Jordon Parker for editorial assistance.

[1] My sketch (starting in Section III) is an elaboration of the issues, not merely a paraphrase.

[2] Immanuel Kant, *Metaphysics of Morals* (Cambridge, Cambridge University Press, 1996) 6: 237 (hereinafter *MM*).

[3] Aristotle, *Nicomachean Ethics*, III.2, trans CCW Taylor (Oxford, Clarendon Press, 2006) 19–21; *cf* Kant, *MM* 6: 213.

create a non-ideal environment for you too. We're both free, in other words, to pursue our *own* ends with the means we *have*, without depending on the leave or cooperation of the other.

Doubtless, this first idea of our *practical independence* is vertiginously abstract. Is it even possible at all? Aren't we all in the same boat of vulnerability to each other's plans? Whether it *is* possible, and if so, how it could be realised is Kant's entire topic: 'Right is the *sum of conditions* in which the choice of one can be united with the choice of another in accordance with a universal law of freedom'—so his Doctrine begins.[4] 'Can be united' means united in principle but also in practice—and (this is to say) *perpetually*.[5] Right isn't merely something to be contemplated, after all: 'wrongs are to be rectified' states what Right *is*, not some exotic development of it. Hence, by the end, Kant's Doctrine expands, from this first and abstract statement of it, to say that 'independence' requires 'conditions' of two broad types: first, there must be various *rights* (personal, proprietary, etc); and second, there must be public institutions exercising rights-determining (and related) powers. These are the doctrines of Private and Public Right.

Right as a *whole* is one part of morality and distinct from a second part (ethics) which concerns the conditions of *self*-unity or self-governance. So described, Kantian ethics manifestly continues the oldest idea of that subject as one concerning 'parts of the soul', their conflicts, and their coalition in a good or just person. This is worth mentioning for the sake of a contrast. Plato affirms that the question of the soul's unity and that of the justice of the state are really the same question or at least co-dependent ones.[6] Kant emphasises that these are separate questions: that 'uniting people's choices' is a moral problem of its own, which presupposes only that there are choosers, however devilish or deformed they might be.[7] The political world—Kant's Republic—appears as his answer to a single question: how (ie under what conditions) is this (social) uniting possible?

To see how practical independence is possible will be, then, just to see what is specifically required for several persons to be free to choose—and this naturally starts with the idea of what choice *is*. Kant mentions two questions that are applicable to any instance of choice among us. First, the *matter*: what are

[4] Kant, *MM* 6: 230.

[5] Unlike concepts, practices are *actual*—they go on. *cf* GWF Hegel, *Philosophy of Right*, trans A White (Cambridge, Hackett Publishing, 2002) s 4: 'The system of Right is the realm of freedom made actual.'

[6] See Plato, *Republic*, trans GMA Grube, rev CDC Reeve, (Indianapolis, Hackett Publishing, 1992) 369, 434–35.

[7] See Immanuel Kant, 'Toward Perpetual Peace', in MJ Gregor (ed), *Immanuel Kant: Practical Philosophy* (Cambridge, Cambridge University Press, 1996) 8: 366; *cf* Kant, *MM*, 6: 231.

you going after? Everyone generally knows the answers (in their own case) self-consciously, ie without observation: these are one's *ends*. Second, the *relational* aspect of choice: how are you affected by my choice? This goes beyond practical self-knowledge or my conception of what I'm doing—it concerns your *suffering*, not just my *doing*.[8] When he introduces 'the concept of Right', Kant says that it applies in questions about 'the *relation* of choices' and, moreover, that these questions concern only 'the *form* of this relation', because—or in the sense that—they ignore 'the end each has in mind':

> The concept of Right … has to do … only with the external and indeed practical relation of one person to another, insofar as their actions can have … influence on each other. But [Right] does not signify the relation of one's choice to the mere wish (hence also to the mere need) of the other, as in actions of beneficence or callousness, but only a relation to the other's choice. … [I]n this reciprocal relation of choice no account at all is taken of the *matter* of choice, that is of the end each has in mind with the object he wants. … All that is in question is the *form* in the relation of choice on the part of both … and whether the action of one can be united with the freedom of the other.[9]

This passage underlies many of Ripstein's distinctive views as well as some of his critics' objections. I'll spell out Kant's main point—namely the point about the '*form* in the relation'—as two theses: (1) Right pays no heed to our ends and therefore—though this may not at first be obvious—(2) it doesn't *compare* you and me.[10] This will furnish a more exact idea of our 'independence'.

(1) Right relates our choices, but not (on the present hypothesis) our ends. As an example, consider that one day I might choose this: to move a certain handle up and down. Strange just by itself, such goings-on are subject to a distinctive form of elucidation, a sense of the question *why*, where answers explain my choices not (just) by relating them to efficient causes but by characterising them more broadly:[11]

> *Why* are you moving that handle up and down?
> I'm operating the pump.—*Why are you doing that?*
> I'm replenishing the house's water supply.—*Why do that?*
> I'm helping out these people's campaign.—*Why*?
> And so on.

[8] I can know that I'm 'using you' just as a matter of my own self-consciousness of what I am doing (eg I'm people-watching in a café). It *defines* Kant's second question to say that it asks about something that can't be known in this way. See Section IV below.

[9] Kant, *MM*, 6: 230.

[10] On 'non-comparative', see A Ripstein, *Private Wrongs*, (Cambridge, MA, Harvard University Press, 2016) 36–38; see also the chapter by Sangiovanni below.

[11] See GEM Anscombe, *Intention* (Oxford, Blackwell, 1957) s 5, whose example I'm borrowing. 'Just': inserted here to acknowledge discussions of whether rationalisations of action *are* causal explanations. The answer doesn't matter here.

This series discloses my ends—that in view of which I'm doing what I'm doing. But it lies in the nature of any such series that it can be reversed, by asking not *why* but *how* I'm doing that:

> I'm helping out these people's campaign.—*How are you doing that?*
> I'm replenishing the house's water supply.—*How?*
> I'm operating the pump.—*How?*
> I'm moving a handle up and down.—*How?*
> And so on.

In one direction, we get progressively wider characterisations of what I'm doing; in the other, progressively narrower specifications of *how* I'm doing that.[12] The present hypothesis (that Right ignores our ends) implies that it relates our choices through the *how* series.

To say *how* I'm replenishing the water supply (or helping out) is to reveal my *approach* to my choice but not to explain it: if you were perplexed to see me pumping ('what are you up to … ?'), my telling you *how* I'm accomplishing this feat won't be responsive. Yet, for this reason, the *how* series is the more basic of the two, for I must have reckoned some approach to my end if there is to *be* an action of mine to explain.[13] *How* is an agent's own deliberative question.[14] And this indicates the basis for a commonplace about Right, namely that it ubiquitously involves claims regarding our *bodies,* whatever else it involves. The reason lies in the way the *how* series must continue. Pumping water by using a handle can only be done by way of further specification of means: by grasping *this* or *that* handle and …—and this implies that I have various physical powers. (It also implies that I have various normative powers, as will emerge.) Of course, there's nothing special about pumping: if I'm to do anything, or even to try, deliberation must disclose something in my power to do now; otherwise, the thing is beyond *choice.* Moving your body is only occasionally your end (eg 'I'm doing yoga—that's *why*'), but it is innate to Right as your means of doing anything-at-all.

If Right ignores 'the end each has in mind'," this doesn't mean that there is some part of choice it ignores; for my *ends* in one series are my *means* in the

[12] This can of course be represented without dialogue: I'm moving a handle *in order to* operate the pump, in order to replenish the water, etc; or I'm replenishing the water *by* operating the pump, by moving a handle, etc.

[13] On the primacy of the deliberative perspective, see A Ford, 'The Progress of the Deed', in R Stout (ed), *Process, Action and Experience* (Oxford, Oxford University Press, forthcoming 2017). Ford points out that 'why' is the question of an observer of action.

[14] *cf* Aristotle, *Nicomachean Ethics*, III.3: deliberation starts from an end and considers 'how and by what means it is to be attained'.

other. Like the road from A to B, choice is the same thing whichever way you're headed. '*Form* in the relation' specifies an interrogative orientation: towards our *final means* (as it might be put), our ways of getting things done. No doubt, it can seem that Right looks in the other direction too, eg when it prohibits choices defined in terms of certain *aims*—taking your things or plotting your destruction. But this is only an effect of the series' reversibility. On closer inspection, it doesn't generally matter, as Kant says (and as lawyers know), what I was after or hoped to gain: taking your thing or injuring you (or trying to) are significant just as long as I was after *something*—ie if acts of this description can be exhibited as part of my deliberation.[15] Right's focus on goings-on like stealing or killing or defrauding is not a matter of these being bad ends—depending on *why* you're going in for them, they might be *noble* ones—but a matter of *how* you mustn't go about things, whatever it is you're about.

How to do things with things has perhaps received less philosophical attention than its venerable identical twin, the question of final ends; yet the unification of choices, on Kant's view, involves reflection on just this. And the answer must naturally start in the sensate world of bodies and materials—with our moving things, or our moving ourselves by means of things (eg in walking), or with our just being on some bit of *ground* (while doing whatever). The reason for such crass materialism can be put like this. I may be pumping for various reasons, and what they are—to keep fit, neighbourliness, general happiness, etc—says a lot about *me*: my widening conception of what I'm doing may or may not be a story about you. In contrast, my narrowing deliberation of how to do any of this discloses an immediate relation to you; or at least it does if we are practically separate, meaning that we have some ultimate *means-of-our-own*.

Tarrying with matters aquiferous, what might my operating the pump have immediately to do with you?

The answer appears in Right's more specific form—*rights*. Property law might debar my whole enterprise, whatever its purpose, if it is *your* pump and you haven't authorised my use; or tort law might make using even *my* pump wrongful if this injures you; or contract law might bring it about that I must operate the pump *for* you. Property and tort specify your rights directly as constraints on my powers of getting things done; and contract builds on this, opening a way, besides beneficence or coercion, for my bodily efforts to become *your means* of doing something. As constraints on how to do things (and their cooperative modification), these laws illustrate the general form of thinking about Right. Right systematically demarcates I/you in its practical aspect: ie mine or yours (to do things with). As Ripstein puts it, we are independent

[15] In law, evidence concerning my ends and motives is used to prove this deliberative aspect.

when you get to decide what to do with what is yours and I get to decide what to do with what is mine.[16] This pithy formula needs a loose interpretation: choices affecting you accidentally (not by decision) are also an ubiquitous possibility about which Right must have something to say.[17] Yet Ripstein's formula conveys the basic idea: when each of us is in charge of ourselves (or our own), neither of us is in charge of the other.

On this conception, you don't *first* have a right to freedom—eg a right protecting your interest in choosing—and *then* I'm required to forbear. Interests are not, as such, your means of doing things; and, on such a two-step account, your freedom would be affected by much besides my choices. As 'a relation of choice on the part of both', your right to freedom is nothing *other* than this, that some ways I might get things done would be a *wrong-to-you*. Hence, it is potentially misleading—though it may be common—to describe Right as marking out spheres of individual 'autonomy'. While autonomy may be a fundamental interest, and even part of an account of what choosers are, this description leaves out the relational aspect. Right concerns not what you are free to do, but what you can constrain me *not* to do. This is a special doctrine: there's no route to it, Kant suggests, from monadic concepts of freedom, however significant these might be.[18]

(2) Since Right doesn't constrain me on account of your freedom in a monadic sense, it doesn't put my wrongdoing into relation with your suffering as *several* different items: the *wrong-to-you* (eg of my taking your thing) is not a matter of anything happening to you (like losing your thing) considered apart from what I'm doing or vice versa. (A friendly neighbour might restore your thing; I've still wronged you.) Wrong-to-you is an unjust *transaction*. The logic of this might be illustrated in two ways: first by contrast with relations that *do* have several parts; and second, by contrast with a different account of rights.[19]

Locke said, 'Relation is a way of comparing, or considering two things together; and giving one, or both of them, some appellation from that Comparison, and sometimes giving even the Relation itself a Name.'[20] Relations of measure or degree inspire this account, for these can be applied to any

[16] See, eg, A Ripstein, *Force and Freedom: Kant's Legal and Political Philosophy* (Cambridge, MA, Harvard University Press, 2009) 14–15.

[17] My affecting you 'accidently' means that *why?* is applicable to *something* I do, but the relevant effect on you does not appear in the resulting series. On Right's doctrine in such cases, see Section III below; see also Ripstein (n 10), ch 4.

[18] See, eg, Kant, *MM*, 6: 231; *cf* 6: 442.

[19] The remarks below are illustrations, not a full analysis.

[20] John Locke, *An Essay Concerning Human Understanding* (Oxford, 1894) 429–30.

relevant pair by first ascertaining, and then indeed comparing, two distinct values. We could discover many relations between *us*—taller, wealthier, nobler, more accident-prone—in just this way. But there are many practical relations we *can't* discover in this way. Matrimony, for (a homespun) example, isn't a comparison, though it also 'joins two together'. Right is like matrimony in two ways: (a) the *relational* nature of the acts involved and (b) the nature of the *parts* related.

(a) Can a combination of thoughts and acts which are yours or mine *severally* suffice to get us married? It appears not.[21] For example, my thought that I am, by a certain ceremony, marrying you (which is necessary for marriage to occur) is only marriage-creating when it is—non-accidentally—the very *same* as your thought that you (yourself) are marrying me. Nor would it suffice, as Michael Thompson has argued, if our thoughts had the right content but rested on independent grounds, each of us coming into them in our own way: eg if my way of identifying that it is *you* I'm marrying were something other than your way of apprehending that you (yourself) were marrying me.[22] Relational thought has taken a special turn here: it is *intrinsically dyadic*, not merely about a pair of things. Such thought features a relation with two poles, where what is to be thought about one is the same (and has the same ground) as what is to be thought about the other. Just so, my obligation to you and your right against me comprise the poles of a single thought.

Here it seems equally instructive to notice a difference. Marrying makes for a transparent case of intrinsically dyadic thought (and for an accessible example) because, here, our joint activity must also be self-conscious. Part of getting married is our both thinking we are doing so: if we don't share the relevant (dyadic) thoughts (about what we are doing)—perhaps I think it's only a rehearsal—the thing isn't actually happening.[23] Relations of Right *can* be self-conscious and often are, but they don't *have* to be in order to be actual.

[21] This paragraph follows M Thompson, 'You and I: Some Puzzles about "Mutual Recognition"', lecture, available at www.pitt.edu/~mthompso/i+you.pdf, which argues for the irreducibility of some dyadic practical thought to a sum of our several propositional attitudes. See also M Thompson, "What Is it to Wrong Someone? A Puzzle About Justice', in R Jay Wallace et al (eds), *Reason and Value: Themes from the Moral Philosophy of Joseph Raz* (Oxford, Clarendon Press, 2004) 333.

[22] As Thompson points out, the philosopher's imaginative hypotheticals can insert themselves into a marriage situation involving nominal or even demonstrative identification, showing that we lack the sort of mutuality needed to get married. On this basis, he argues that 'you' is a form of 'I'.

[23] At least, this is so on the 'liberal' conception of marriage, to which these points may be restricted. See GEM Anscombe, 'On Promising and its Justice, and Whether it Need Be Respected *in Foro Interno*' in *Ethics, Religion and Politics* (Oxford, Basil Blackwell, 1981).

On Kant's account, this reflects Right-as-*independence*: if the reality of your rights required my discernment of them (not to mention my caring about them), your rights wouldn't make a relevant difference, for your freedom would be no less dependent (than it was without rights) on my judgement and will. Hence, for the actuality of Right, though not of matrimony, it is necessary and sufficient that the form of thought described in section 1 be applied through *public* agencies such as a court.[24] Public agency embodies a 'we' consciousness, a 'united will'; it is in court, if not elsewhere, that Right is conscious of itself.

(b) Although the parties to marriage are you and me—we who bear proper names, different origins, singularity in death, etc—the parts of this relation obviously aren't separately determined. Since to get married is not to compare but to share our acts, *my* getting married (and everything this consists in) evidently refers to a transactional whole—to something we are doing together, not in several parts. Anything I might do which has no immediate correlative in what you are doing (eg driving to the place of ceremony) won't be what our marrying consists in, though it might be some antecedent to it. Just so with wronging you: we do this *together*, not because you need to actively participate (though you do need to be an agent), but because a characterisation of something *I did wrong* that doesn't yet have in view your suffering—or that is only a causal antecedent to it—isn't relevant, even if it is morally interesting in other ways.

Perhaps one implication of this seems troubling: a mere *part*—eg my part in the affair—refers to the *whole*.[25] How can that be? A brief answer is that the relevant notion of 'a part' is our transaction *under a certain description*, and that this way of having parts is unexceptional: it is, after all, the way *any* action forms an (articulated) unity rather than being items merely added together. For example, a part of my *sending water to the house* was *my operating the pump* (which itself has parts). But these aren't several different actions: here, parts

[24] See Kant, *MM*, 6: 312.

[25] This has been a source of trouble in the law. The controversy in *Palsgraf v Long Island Railroad Co* [1928] 248 NY 339, 162 NE 99, for example, is partially about whether the defendant's negligence can be treated as a self-standing *part* of the tort relation. In this well-known case, the defendant helped a passenger board the Long Island Railroad and thereby caused injury to the plaintiff (a different passenger standing on the end of the platform) through an unusual causal sequence; the passenger boarding the train was carrying fireworks in an unmarked package which exploded when dropped. On one analysis (that of Cardozo J), the defendant simply wasn't 'negligent in relation to the plaintiff' and there is no such thing as 'negligence in the air'—negligence in a non-relational sense; on a different analysis (that of Andrews J), the defendant had been negligent all right, but liability requires a further determination of the nature of the causal relation to the plaintiff's injury.

and whole are *one* action under different descriptions.[26] In the same way, an unjust transaction (eg my pumping water and thereby injuring you) has many distinguishable parts—my *doing* and your *suffering* wrong (and everything these consist in)—but each of them refers (by way of different descriptions) to an antecedent unity. 'Wronging' involves a special *form* of cognising events (which could, of course, be cognised in other ways); but it is, on this score, just like any action as such.[27]

Rights are sometimes said to protect weighty *interests*—weighty enough to be grounds for another's obligation. Rights will be determinable, at least on one elaboration of this view, in the way we determine which of us is taller, for each has her own interests and her own standing ends. Of course, rights might be comparative conclusions that bring us into dyadic relation once they are determined, by comparison, to exist.[28] The case of marrying makes vivid a different possibility: a relation based on joint practical activity that is (publicly, in Right's case) consciousness of itself as such. On this conception, Right can't be reduced to a comparison of interests because our independence isn't just a consequence of the determination that you or I have a right but the very *basis* of such a determination.[29] Hence, when the law specifies rights regarding your body, this is not because bodily integrity is a monadic interest of yours, or an interest of sufficient gravity to justify restricting my liberty interests, but because my interference with what is yours is a way of wronging you.[30] It is a transaction inconsistent with your independence.

In answer to my first question, I've mainly characterised Right-as-independence as a form of thought, while only alluding to the further conditions (such as rights and various public institutions) which, on Kant's account, it also requires.

II. WHY START HERE?

The second question I was to consider might now be put like this: if interests, even basic ones, are not what makes Right significant, what *is* the point of Right? Doubtless, independence is a basic concern. Other political values—such

[26] This is one of Anscombe's better known teachings in *Intention* (n 11) ss 23, 26.

[27] See ibid, s 47.

[28] There are much-discussed problems fitting the dyadic aspects of obligation—such as its being owed *to someone*—into such two-level accounts, but this may be left aside here.

[29] *cf* Kant, *MM*, 6: 238: the innate right to freedom can be appealed to in cases of disputes about rights, 'as if … appealing to various bases of rights'.

[30] See Ripstein (n 10) 13.

as treating persons with equal respect or advancing welfare—seem to presuppose it in some way, at least if it is independent choosers whose fair treatment or welfare matters. But some think this should be reserved: independence matters because this conduces to our faring well.

Understandably, some have attempted to ground Right in something they take to be more fundamental: eg in the moral law or rational agency or the nature of finite rational being.[31] Besides offering leverage against other views, these foundational efforts are sometimes thought to be required for Kant's doctrine to succeed philosophically. By this standard, Ripstein's account is more juridical than philosophical. He argues that, starting with Right, various features of our political world become intelligible; but he doesn't try to prove that an account of political order must start with Right. Indeed, he develops the grounds of Kant's remark that Right is 'a postulate … incapable of further proof'.[32] Kant evidently isn't hoping to explain why people are in charge of themselves, only to explain how, in light of this, it could be possible for anyone else to be in charge of them—to rule them. Similarly, Ripstein makes no appeal to anything supposed to be more fundamental—more certain or valuable—than relations of right themselves.

Yet to lack proofs of Right is not to be without ways of elucidating its point or value. It is just that not *any* way will do.

It has been said that Right's only point is to be *Right*. That's a vivid rejection of Right-*reductionism*. It is apt to appear in contexts where someone thinks that there are no rights, only monadic interests, at the most basic level, the level at which the point of anything (ultimately) lies.[33] But beyond this dialectic, 'Right is Right' isn't appealing, since this way of defending against reductionism seems to concede that non-trivial accounts of something's value must refer to monadic interests—and that seems implausible. The value of love or friendship, for example, isn't ineffable, even if it is irreducible to more basic goods. Indeed, elucidations of the value of love can be found in the lover's own discourse; the study of love by other disciplines presupposes this.[34] By analogy,

[31] See Allen Wood's essay below, and R Pippin, 'On the Moral Foundations of Kant's *Rechtslehre*', in *Idealism as Modernism* (Cambridge, Cambridge University Press, 1997). On self-conscious being, see JG Fichte, *Foundations of Natural Right*, ed F Neuhouser, trans M Baur (Cambridge, Cambridge University Press, 2000).

[32] Kant, *MM*, 6: 231.

[33] See, eg, E Weinrib, *The Idea of Private Law* (Cambridge, MA, Harvard University Press, 1995), which argues that doctrines of private law are incomprehensible on the basis of monadic features of the parties it relates.

[34] See R Barthes, *A Lover's Discourse: Fragments*, trans R Howard (New York, Farrar, Straus, and Giroux, 1978) where this is the methodological principle.

'Right is Right' really means to say only that elucidations of Right should be of a juridical—ie a non-reductive—kind:

> [*Condition R*]: In explaining the point or value of Right, the concepts which figure in the *explanans* should have the same non-comparative relational structure as the right to freedom.

It would be strange if there weren't more to say, consistently with this, about the point of Right, and *Force and Freedom* says a number of such things.

One refrain, for example, is that Right's point is non-subordination, where slavery is a paradigmatic negation of this value but other (impersonal) forms of dependence are as well.[35] This builds on one of Kant's explanations of innate right: 'a man's quality of being his own master (*sui iuris*)'.[36] This formulation (imported from Roman law) satisfies *Condition R*, since being your own master just means you are not anyone's subordinate; 'master' and 'subordinate' are parts of a non-comparative relation.

Similarly, if Right grounds public authority (as one of its conditions of possibility), this gives it a credential by reconciling us to a problematic feature of political practice: Right answers the anarchist. Or, again, if Right illuminates the form and unity of legal practices—tort, property, etc, or the public law of state and subject—then we might reverse things and take jurisprudential reflection on these problems as an elucidation of Right. The law *is* a theory of Right: ie the interpretation (and application) of Right in various types of cases shows, more concretely, what is at stake.[37] (The law is a *doctrine* but not a *metaphysics* of Right.) Of course, these elucidations move in a circle, revealing Right in terms of its consequences. Perhaps they bring out the value of Right only for someone who already (at least dimly) appreciates it—so they don't ground anything. They might be illuminating nonetheless, by exhibiting how a number of elements—independence, wrongs such as slavery, different types of rights, their doctrinal elaboration, political authority, public obligations to remedy systemic dependency (like poverty)—cohere and support each other. All this is open to criticism; but, as a structure of explanation, does it compare poorly to what other political theories claim to accomplish?

35 *cf* P Pettit, *Republicanism: A Theory of Freedom and Government* (Oxford, Oxford University Press, 1997) and P Pettit, *Just Freedom: A Moral Compass for a Complex World* (New York, WW Norton, 2014). Pettit gives wider application to the idea of impersonal subordination than Ripstein, who treats this concern as a systemic extension of dyadic right.

36 Kant, *MM*, 6: 238.

37 Applications of an idea are one way of explaining it. Law professors often explain the law to their students in this way—by exhibiting how it sorts out real and imagined cases.

To be clear, *Condition R* is not defended but only mentioned here to characterise Ripstein's mode of explanation. If someone were to ask, 'Why is *non-subordination* so important?', various responses might be given in this mode: they would present reasons for thinking about things in Kant's way but not for why one *must* do so. (How *do* we inherit the (non-empirical) idea of another as neither master nor servant?) But, on a different hearing, the question looks for some more basic value—something among 'the permanent interests of a man', in Mill's phrase.[38] The difficulties with 'interest' approaches (in accommodating either rights or political authority) are only incidentally part of Ripstein's topic—only as they illustrate something about the nature of Right. For example, it says something about Right that the following is a structurally open question: whether people will do best, on whatever non-relational measure is chosen, by being in charge of themselves.[39]

Kant's own elucidations of innate right—independence, being *sui iuris*, innate equality, being beyond reproach, the entitlement to do whatever doesn't wrong others—all conform to *Condition R*; indeed, they aren't 'really distinct from' innate right, Kant says.[40] Such language indicates articulated unity and thus characterises Kant's overall form of account.[41] Since his entire topic is how independent choices can be united, the 'conditions' of this are to be understood as increasingly specific determinations of an abstract idea, not as self-standing theses that are somehow added together. Mutual dependency is to be expected in such an account: for example, it is internal to Right that its content be expressed through public laws;[42] but to understand how public law-giving is possible, you must understand what Right is.[43]

Ripstein's project unfolds, then, as an account of Right's conditions of possibility, and the following chapters confront this project at different levels. Some accept Right but question its specifics: eg whether Innate Right involves our having, directly, certain *rights*; whether 'independence' requires property rights; and whether 'mutual freedom' grounds an obligation to obey political authorities. For these critics, abstract Right is a fine idea, but the devil's in the

[38] John Stuart Mill, *On Liberty*, 4th edn (London, Longmans, Green, Reader and Dyer 1869) 24.

[39] Textbooks on Roman law remind us that benevolently governed slaves were sometimes envied by those who were *sui iuris* but poor in the Empire. Perhaps starting with Right does have *this* going for it: it takes rights seriously.

[40] Kant, *MM*, 6: 237.

[41] *cf* Immanuel Kant, *Critique of Practical Reason*, trans MJ Gregor (Cambridge, Cambridge University Press, 1997) 5: 10.

[42] *cf* Kant, *MM*, 6: 312.

[43] *cf* Kant, *MM*, 6: 229–30.

specifications, so to speak. Other chapters raise radical doubts about Right itself, especially about its *formality*. Or they raise neither specific nor radical doubts but ask whether Right can be supported on some independent *ground*, rather than just via mutual dependencies.

III. TWO CONTROVERSIES ABOUT INNATE RIGHT

A. Pallikkathayil

In speaking of the body as a *means* of doing things, Ripstein isn't committed to a suspect ghost-in-the-machine, only to the commonplace that practical deliberation must eventually disclose something to be done with the body, if anything is to be done at all; the body is my practical being-in-the-world.[44] Ripstein thus describes bearers of Innate Right as having bodily *rights*. And he takes this to be Kant's view too, when Kant contrasts 'a wrong with regard to what is *internally* mine' (wresting an apple from my hand) and 'a wrong with regard to what is *externally* mine' (taking my apple when I'm not holding it).[45] The first apple-taking is, legally, a battery, since it upsets something contiguous to my body (even if I make no further claim to the thing); the second taking illustrates the idea of a right regarding something 'outside myself'—a right I must *acquire*. Kant's double contrast (innate-acquired, inside-outside) suggests that everyone already has *something* which is (internally) their own.[46]

Japa Pallikkathayil doesn't exactly disagree with this, but she think it requires further conditions to make it hold good: our bodily rights are not so *immediately* available; they need political institutions to be 'conclusively' established. Kant says that claims to *property* in the state of nature are merely 'provisional': they don't create binding obligations until they are publicly (legally) established.[47] Using Ripstein's account of why Kant holds this view—an account of the defects of property rights without law—Pallikkathayil argues that the same problems affect bodily rights as well.

One problem ('indeterminacy') may be illustrated by supposing that—pumping water again—I *unintentionally* scald you.[48] Although your body is the topic of your complaint, your right remains an abstract one (as lawyers know)

[44] 'Using one's own body' isn't un-colloquial in any case: eg how to spread the caulking—by using the spatula or one's fingers?

[45] Kant, *MM*, 6: 250.

[46] See Kant, *MM*, 6: 248; *cf* 6: 250, 6: 254.

[47] Kant, *MM*, 6: 255–57.

[48] *cf Ferringer v Crowley Oil & Mineral Co* [1908] 122 La 441, 47 So 763.

until a legal authority determines whether, in *these* circumstances, it was actually infringed. Such further determinations seem *inevitable*, moreover, on any Kantian account of what is at issue—a unification of our equal freedom. For various rules that might better settle rights in advance—eg (1) 'My action is wrong if it injures you' or (2) 'My action is all right, whatever happens, unless I meant to injure you'—end up subordinating *one* of us to the other: they sort right from wrong on the basis of some feature of the situation (your welfare, my purposes) that concerns only *one* of us. What other rules are possible? If this problem (of accidental injury) starts to explain why your specific bodily rights await a determination of whether I took 'reasonable care under the circumstances' (the universal legal standard),[49] it thereby also exhibits those rights as *naturally* indeterminate: the specific ways anyone can constrain anyone are available only by way of some constitutive public decision.

Positing purely 'natural' rights seems to face other problems too. For suppose your bodily rights weren't *indeterminate* but merely uncertain—not everyone can discern them clearly; or suppose everyone can discern them, but some people just don't *care*. In the former case, the reality of your rights would depend on my good judgement; in the later, on my goodwill. Either way, your rights depend on *me*—and that's not Right.

There's more. My example raises the spectre of indeterminacy without doubting that your scalded skin is—no-acquisitive-act-needed—*yours*. In fact, Pallikkathayil thinks that this, too, can be doubtful—that the indeterminacy of bodily rights can extend (beyond questions about their specific infringement) to questions about their physical basis or boundary in the first place. To show this, she considers various scenarios of bodily alienation and incorporation—severed or extracted parts, and prosthetic parts. Can rights in severed parts be lost or transferred? Do they need to be claimed or (re)acquired? Is interference with a prosthetic part to be modelled on battery or property? Exploring these puzzles, Pallikkathayil concludes that we need public rules for the classification *internally* mine—for the same reasons we need public rules, on Kant's account, governing the acquisition of apples and the like.

Pallikkathayil thus finds in the problematics of bodily right an alternative argument for political authority, distinct from Kant's argument from notionally special features of property. Of course, she uses Kant's argumentative strategy—of deriving public authority from the nature of private right—but, in doing this, she finds 'an even deeper justification for the establishment of political institutions than Kant himself imagined'. Readers of Kant might

[49] For a Kantian approach to the standard of care in negligence law, see Weinrib (n 33) ch 6.

imagine that independent persons could live without political institutions, were it not that their purposes sometimes involve using objects. They can't, Pallikkathayil argues, because the moral problems of using things without public laws are already present in claims regarding the body. Our most basic rights are ours as *political beings*.

B. Flikschuh

Katrin Flikschuh also finds that rightful 'mine and thine' is a politically meditated achievement. But while Pallikkathayil takes Ripstein to keep faith with Kant's (insufficiently deep) account, Flikschuh thinks Ripstein gets Kant's (deep) account wrong. *No* rights are entirely 'natural', on her reading: Innate Right describes only the a priori *form* of determinable rights, not any 'substantive entitlements'.

Flikschuh thus raises the question: (Q1) 'Can wrongs regarding the body be pre-politically in view?' But she raises two further questions about Innate Right as well:

(Q2) *Value*: is Innate Right supposed to protect some valuable feature of the person—eg their capacity for choice?
(Q3) *Argumentative role*: is Innate Right supposed to provide a 'foundational' justification for public authority?

These questions hang together. If Innate Right *is* supposed to protect the capacity for choice (*yes* to Q2), there's a motive for linking it to the requisites of this capacity, the body (*yes* to Q1); and this makes it a 'natural' foundation for public authority (*yes* to Q3). Affirmative answers to all three questions comprise what Flikschuh sees as a familiar, but mistaken, account of Kant's ideas—a liberalism of private freedom—and this is an account she thinks Ripstein is flirting with, if not fully embracing. To be sure, *Condition R* (Section 2) says *no* to Q2. But Flikschuh finds Ripstein equivocal on this point: doesn't his argument treat bodily rights as requisite to *individual purposiveness*? Doesn't he then treat practical agency as the *point* of Right, notwithstanding his more general dyadic pronouncements?

Perhaps this charge (that Ripstein is trafficking in monadic goods) might be reduced by distinguishing two questions. First, does Ripstein sometimes suggest that 'practical agency' is Right's point or value? Second, does his thesis of the immediacy of bodily right *need* this suggestion: could this thesis flow instead from (embodied) practical agency being merely a *condition* (but not the point) of applying concepts of Right? By analogy, the concept 'shaking hands' applies only among practical agents—that is its condition. But the point of 'shaking hands'—eg to seal a deal—won't appear in materials limited to what anyone is doing alone. Like marrying, sealing deals is a dyadic affair: if we don't do it *together*, there's no deal.[50]

The issues here might partly stem from equivocalness on *Kant's* part. On the one hand, Kant emphasises *distinctive* features of property that render it 'naturally' problematic: in claiming bodily rights, you claim just what I claim; in claiming property you (purport to) unilaterally bind me in non-reciprocal ways.[51] Yet, elsewhere, Kant casts his point about the defectiveness of 'natural' Right more widely, suggesting that 'concepts of Right' only find application by way of public judgement.[52] In different ways, Pallikkathayil and Flikschuh push the latter point.

In any case, Flikschuh's suggestion—that a resolute dyadicism entails negative answers to Qs 1–3—leaves to be considered, as she notes, the question of how Right does become (specific) *rights*. She sketches an alternative answer that refers to regulative values of 'public law-making'; and she suggests that the state would enjoy more robust powers, on this alternative, than those which 'private freedom' accounts can support. Flikschuh is not alone in worrying that 'private freedom' won't support all that we've come to expect from modern states—other chapters raise this question too.

IV. TWO CONTROVERSIES ABOUT FORMALITY

A. Sangiovanni

For Andrea Sangiovanni, Ripstein's starting point isn't too substantive—it's too *formal*. When Hegel introduced 'formalism' as a term of philosophical criticism, he meant that no content could be derived from Kant's moral law without the aid of assumptions about what we owe each another—ie without *Right* as realised in social practices. In a similar vein, Sangiovanni thinks that Right lacks content unless it is supplemented with assumptions about a person's basic *interests*.

On Ripstein's formal account, *wrongs* and *harms* are exogenous categories: harm, a monadic notion, is a setback to your interests; wrong, a subjection of what is yours.[53] Sangiovanni thinks this won't do. Let Right be *non-subjection*, he

[50] On condition versus value, see Ripstein's chapter below; on making deals, see Kant, *MM*, 6: 262.

[51] Kant, *MM*, 6:255–57.

[52] Kant, *MM*, 6: 312.

[53] Hence, trespass to property is a wrong independently of whether it tends to be harmful. See A Ripstein, "Against the Harm Principle" (2006) 34 *Philosophy & Public Affairs* 215.

grants, and let subjection be a choice that *uses* or *usurps* your means or powers. Still, no determinate application of *these* concepts is possible except by way of applying notions of basic interests and their setbacks.

Sangiovanni's incisive argument for this conclusion contrasts a pair of cases: *first*, raping (a wrong); *second*, sketching-someone-in-a-public-place (innocent enough, at least without further complications). If this classification of the cases is a matter of Right, it must be possible to *explain* the basis of our judgements in terms of Right. (Isn't this—namely that it can be explained—just what it means to think that the difference between right and wrong is *intelligible*?) But with resources limited to *formal* concepts, the two cases are structurally indistinguishable, Sangiovanni claims: in each, another's body is *used* for purposes he hasn't authorised. The explanation, Sangiovanni says, must be that our *interest* in 'sexual integrity' is sufficiently strong to constrain the rapist, but no similarly strong interest is affected by the sketcher.

'Using people' *is* both socially rampant and only sometimes wrong: I use you (for my pleasure) when I people-watch in a cafe; I use your parked car to hide from my enemies.[54] A defender of formal Right might say these aren't wrongs because, by going about in public, you've implicitly consented to being used in these ways. But this strikes a false note: these aren't even presumptive wrongs, nor could you make them wrong by withholding your consent. If the formalist is to maintain his claim that 'using people' is a main category of wrongs (and to reject Sangiovanni's account of the cases he describes this way), it seems he must say that the counter-examples aren't *really* instances of what he means by 'using'. Of course, this looks suspect. What could be easier—or emptier—than to defend 'All A is B' by saying of some A (ordinarily so-called) that apparently *isn't* B: 'That doesn't count as A for my purposes.'

But maybe the formalist can do better. What if he said this bit (about such cases not 'counting') but *also* said:

> The moral *point* of Right is non-subordination. So it is only to be expected that Right will ubiquitously apply a distinction between (say) 'Using Another' and 'Merely Taking Advantage of the Choices they Happen to Make.'[55] In watching you or standing behind your car, I'm enjoying the effects of your choices. But I'm doing so only by fitting my activity into them, not by affecting your powers to choose. Moreover, given the *point* of Right, I must have the right to do this as the incidence of my own

[54] I've benefited from a conversation with Joseph Raz about such cases.

[55] This distinction is the *passive* mirror image of one which Ripstein claims is central to judgements of right: namely between interfering with someone's purposiveness and merely unfavourably altering the context in which they act. See, eg, Ripstein (n 16), 16, 39, 41, 45, 47–49, 51, 153; see also Ripstein's response below.

> freedom. If you could constrain me from enjoying the ways you've changed the world (eg if I must lower my eyes as you walk by), I would be your subordinate. Right would be impossible if people couldn't *fit themselves in.*

No longer a simple refusal to count the counter-examples as 'usings', this is an explanation of what counts and why. Equipped with this, the formalist might say: 'The rapist *uses* you, because his occupation of your body, however harmless, affects your powers of choice—you might have other corporeal plans. But *some* cases of sketching (no need here for a general rule) are merely cases of *fitting in*.' Could this be the answer?

Sangiovanni suggests that answers like this beg his question, and perhaps the structure of the issue could be represented as follows. *Using* was already an explanation of what *subjecting* is; it could have been produced—in the face of some earlier counter-example—to avoid the empty answer, 'that doesn't count as *subjecting* for my purposes'. In the formalist's speech above, an account is given of *using* in terms of *fitting-in vs affecting*. But Sangiovanni asks: why does harmless *touching* have significance as 'affecting' but not gazing or sketching?[56] Again, the answer had better not be the empty one (about 'what *counts*…'). Perhaps the formalist could say that sketching isn't *moving* or (non-semantically) *communicating*. But while this probably exceeds the needs of routine legal work, it apparently needn't stop philosophical questions. Structurally, the situation looks like this: The formalist is asked to state his *basis* for 'judging that…', but his replies don't seem to reach all the way to sorting the cases out; so—on the (modest) assumption that sorting right from wrong is intelligible—it is felt that a different form of thought must be operating in the wings.

Could the formalist try again, but this time—having spotted a regress—boldly say that no further basis is needed? This would mean that one of the 'empty' answers is good enough; and that while further distinctions might be drawn—ie as needed in explaining particular cases—eventually something does *count* as an instance of the relevant formal category while something else does not.

At this point, Right's content frankly depends partly on *judgements* that extend or withhold its categories—judgements that *count* something as a case of something. But maybe this is ok: don't we operate with many everyday concepts in this way? Judgements about my obligations as a *friend*, for example, are needed in different situations, and these can't be fully codified. Yet explanations are always available of why I'm obligated *here* but not *there*—these typically

[56] No doubt, merely *thinking* about someone won't be affecting them: it isn't a transaction since such *intentional* verbs allow no inference to the passive: eg if I worship Zeus, it doesn't follow that someone *is worshipped;* but if I sketch you, you've *been sketched.*

describe and contrast various facts of the different cases. My judgement does carry a significant burden here, for such explanations may not suffice to resolve a dispute with someone who doesn't see the matter as I do.[57] Doubtless, this might be less than could be hoped for. Judgement doesn't always bear such a burden: eg in deciding what combination of conflicting activities will maximise their economic value, the verdict can be exhibited (given sufficient information) as one that follows from the stated goal by dint of mere theoretical rationality. Yet if someone were to propose that (eg) a comparative schedule of interests could aid practical thought about friendship (ie reduce its burdens), there would naturally be two objections. *First*, it isn't the demand for intelligibility, but only for a particular kind of it—a route to verdicts from outside the circle of thought in question—that makes such a supplement necessary. And *second*, it is in such ways that the *friend* does *not* think. Application of a schedule of interests won't cure friendship of indeterminacy, though it might cure people of friendship: ie someone who avoids the burdens of judgement in this way is already favouring some value *other* than friendship.

Might Right be like friendship in this regard? If so, the formalist judge must do her best to be a judge. She won't lack explanations of what counts and why: using the local legal idiom, she will (in effect) characterise some defendants as merely 'merely fitting in' or describe the facts of the case in light of previous holdings applying similar distinctions. This might not suffice to settle a dispute with her colleagues. Her opinions will be *interpretive* of Right—in a non-trivial sense, they will be *hers*. But, in judging in this way, she engages the relevant form of practical thought.

None of this argues against Sangiovanni's thesis that interests play an essential role in judgements about rights; it merely casts doubt on one argument for thinking they *must*. And it raises a question: can the relative determinacy of two forms of practical thought be considered, just as such, invidious to one of them?[58] Explanations of how particulars are to be classified must, after

[57] My burden can be represented like this: I implicitly claim to embody the situational judgement of someone good at friendship. John McDowell has pursued this theme in various essays. See, eg, J McDowell, 'The Role of Eudaemonia in Aristotle's *Ethics*', in AO Rorty (ed), *Essays on Aristotle's Ethics* (Berkeley, University of California Press, 1980).

[58] This question may reflect an argument that isn't Sangiovanni's. A classic of 'invidious comparison' is Henry Sidgwick's suggestion that 'ordinary moral knowledge' is defective, given utilitarianism's superior power to codify moral judgement. H Sidgwick, *The Methods of Ethics*, 7th edn (Cambridge, Hackett Publishing, 1981) 421 and book IV, chs II, III. For a similar idea, see also John Stuart Mill, *A System of Logic* (London, Longmans Green and Co, 1889) book VI, ch XII, s 7; John Stuart Mill, *Utilitarianism* (London, Longmans Green and Co, 1901) ch V, paras 26–31. For a contemporary version, see L Kaplow and S Shavell, *Fairness Versus Welfare* (Cambridge, MA, Harvard University Press, 2002).

all, end *somewhere*.[59] So there is a sense in which Right *does* (on any account) ultimately depend on *counting as*—all thinking does. This is why I'm imagining the formalist to ask: 'Must there be some further account of classifying judgment to be given here? Isn't it enough that (1) the moral point of Right is accessible; and (2) jurisprudence *does* work out Right's content—with explanations as needed and with appropriate authority—through thinking that involves (burdened) judgements about particulars?' It is partly around such questions—about the nature of determinative judgement—that the issue between Sangiovanni and Ripstein seems to be joined.

B. Julius

AJ Julius argues for a different anti-formalist thesis: namely, that Right is possible only if people act in view of certain *ends*. Ultimately, this would put into question Kant's division of Right and Virtue.[60]

Following Ripstein, Julius takes the target notion ('Right-as-independence') to be that of being free to choose for yourself (where to *choose* is to be *able* to realise your ends: Section 1). This immediately suggests a difficulty. Since anything I might choose to do (eg standing here now) might collide with something you might choose, how is it conceivable that each of us could be free to set ends independently of the other's choices? The solution previously sketched—people having rights to means of their own (Section 1)—Julius finds inadequate.

All solutions to the 'independence' problem—Julius observes—must (in the nature of the problem) lie in my rightful ends being conditioned *in some way* by your freedom. Indeed, he takes this to be Kant's doctrine at its most abstract: the Universal Principle of Right protects my action as rightful *if* it can coexist with everyone's freedom. Hence, if I set the *absolute* end of being in a determine region of space-time, this cannot coexist with your setting the end of occupying that same region; our choices are mutually dependent. But if I make my end *conditional* (eg to occupy that region *if* it is not already occupied), I do not hinder your similarly described action (nor you mine). When some rule or policy conditions our rightful choice of ends, our choices can be independent.

[59] This is one of the upshots of Wittgenstein's reflections on 'following a rule'. See Ludwig Wittgenstein, *Philosophical Investigations*, 2nd edn, trans GEM Anscombe (Oxford, Blackwell, 1958), ss 185–201; *cf* Immanuel Kant, *Critique of Pure Reason*, trans P Guyer (Cambridge, Cambridge University Press, 1998) A133/B172.

[60] 'Virtue' as a doctrine of mandatory ends: see Kant, *MM*, 6: 380–81; 6: 384–85.

Generalising from this, Julius's considers three rules of freedom-consistent action, three versions of what abstract Right might mean, at least for the case of our using external objects and spaces:

1. *The Law of Property*: I have the Right to set out to [E *if I have or come to own the means to E*].
2. *The Law of Usufruct*: I have the Right to set out to [E *if you aren't already using the means of doing so*].
3. *The Maxim of the Virtuous*:[61] I will set out to [E *if it is consistent with your freedom*].

(1) and (2) instantiate the Kantian schema, 'a right to [E consistently with others freedom]'. Our choices are made consistent by my using either (1) only *what I own* or (2) only *what you're not already using.* In contrast, (3) determines no rights, and no specific way of not obstructing one another, in advance; instead, it finds a solution in our cooperative adjustments to each other's purposes. But any solution arising in this way—ie one of us yielding to the other—preserves our independence, according to Julius, because each of our choices bends to no *alien* purpose.

To show this, Julius focuses on the everyday situation in which, moving about the world on some collision course, we *work it out.* (A traffic law could have given one of us a *right of way*, but, by hypothesis, no such thing applies here.) How is *working it out* to be regarded? If the only possibility is to think that one of us must eventually yield *because* of what the other is doing, then the situation is no doubt one of subordination. Kant thinks of 'lawless freedom' in this way—a law of the jungle. But, according to Julius, there is another possibility. I might yield not out of a mere collision-avoiding motive but out of a freedom-regarding one. Being virtuous, my end was never *simply* to get from A to B, but rather: to get from A to B *consistently with your freedom.* If you've also set such an end, then our convergence on a solution preserves independence because it is a realisation—it is rationalized by—our ends of freedom-consistent movement: each of us does what he set out to do.

In light of this, Julius sees property and usufruct not exactly as alternatives to (3) but as specific forms of it—forms of social cooperation-for-freedom. But they are, he argues, defective forms. For under both, my choices are shadowed by something alien. For example, if I decide not to make a mushroom omelette

[61] This is my terminology, not Julius's.

because you've acquired all the mushrooms and put them beyond my rightful means, I may be making a *concession* to your choices rather than realising my purpose as it previously existed; your choices operate as givens, not as realisations of my ends. In this way, Julius doubts one of Kant's central claims: that wherever people have object-requiring purposes, property rights are essential to their independence. Given the possibility of *working it out*, property isn't necessary for independence. But neither is it *sufficient*—on Julius's argument, a certain practical attitude, a will to act for freedom, is also required.[62]

Such a conclusion doesn't seem unheard of—at least not to students of post-Kantian philosophy. Actualised freedom, on Hegel's teaching, is a will that is *with itself*, not dependent on something alien;[63] and since this requires practical mutuality (or *Sittlichkiet*: 'an I that is we and we that is I'),[64] Abstract Right is, by itself, only one of freedom's defective forms. Julius reaches this conclusion, moreover, as Hegel would recommend—via *immanent* critique: he questions Kant's specific idea of Right (as something realised in enforceable obligations), but he questions this on the grounds of the *point* of Right in the first place ('independence'). He suggests a way to ask: does Right depend on *rights?*

V. TWO CONTROVERSIES ABOUT PUBLIC RIGHT

A. Pavlakos

Rejecting 'lawless freedom', Kant avers that overcoming it requires no special virtue: even 'a race of devils' may enjoy just relations in a legal state.[65] Thus, he can be found asserting what Julius denies: life without law remains sunk in dependence and violence, 'however well disposed … men might be'.[66]

Remarks like this are based not on Kant's observations of human nature, but on his cognisance of a defect that conceptually characterises private Right: without law, 'each has its own right to do *what seems [to him] right and good*'.[67] This sentence means to express a contradiction. If the actuality of Right rests on

[62] Could I cooperatively work anything out with you if I don't already have *some* means which are exclusively mine to decide about? That is, does an argument such as Julius's touch Kant's argument that Right requires rights (enforceable obligations) with respect to the *body*?

[63] Hegel (n 5) s 23.

[64] GWF Hegel, *Phenomenology of Spirit*, trans AV Miller (Oxford, Clarendon Press, 1977) s 177.

[65] Kant, 'Toward Perpetual Peace' (n 7) 8: 366.

[66] Kant, *MM*, 6: 312. Or compare Julius's 'right obligates me to act for freedom' by making 'consistency [with your freedom] my maxim' with what Kant says at *MM*, 6: 231.

[67] Kant, *MM*, 6: 312.

what *seems* right (*in foro interno*), then—even with universally good intentions—each would *depend* for their rights on everyone else. Right-as-independence thus requires procedures for adjudicating rights which are themselves *rightful*—ie dependence-free. This implies that some agent is to decide about rights who isn't *me* or *you* or any other party. That could only be *us*: Right requires a common or 'omni-lateral' will—*public* agency.[68]

George Pavlakos approaches this Kantian thesis with one of contemporary legal theory's problems in mind: are legal obligations a *special kind*—not necessarily moral obligations but not merely putative moral obligations either? Some say *yes*, adding that legal obligations also enjoy a special *normativity*—neither moral normativity nor the mere 'obliging' of coercive threats.[69] Pavlakos worries that Ripstein too is making a 'special kind' claim: 'omni-lateral' willing as a distinctive *ground* of legal obligation. He finds this both implausible and inconsistent with Kant's own story about obligation: *implausible*, because the mere say-so of a collective agent can't create genuine obligations (it is an 'open question' whether any putative obligation survives rational reflection); and *inconsistent* with Kant's story, because this *is* a story about my rational reflection and endorsement.

Two discourses meet here: the post-positivist explanation of legal obligation and the Kantian explanation of political authority. Could Ripstein renounce the suspect (special kind) thesis of the first discourse while continuing to think of public authority as a condition of Right? Pavlakos himself wants to affirm a view like this—public authority as (what he calls) an 'enabling condition' of legal obligation—but he suggests that this view has first to be won by disentangling it from the suspect thesis.

To this end, he offers a diagnosis of how the suspect thesis comes to seem compelling. It is product of a framework in which:

1. an explanation is sought of how legal directives can create genuine obligations, consistent with:
2. a 'standard picture' of all obligation as grounded in acts of willing; and
3. the commonplace that legal obligations, unlike moral obligations, admit of coercive enforcement.

Since the person who is legally *compelled* to act does not make obligation his incentive, (3) entails that legal obligation couldn't be grounded in *individual* acts of willing. So it comes to look like the only alternative (for success with 1) must be for some *other* kind of willing to play this grounding role. Pavlakos would

[68] See Kant, *MM*, 6: 256–57, 6: 26–66, 6: 306–13.

[69] See, eg, HLA Hart, *The Concept of Law* (Oxford, Oxford University Press, 2012) ch 1.

discard (2) in favour of what he takes to be both Kantian and common sense: obligations are grounded in rational reflection. How, then, do public authoritative directives make a difference to our obligations? Here Pavlakos applies the distinction between *grounds* and *enabling conditions* of legal obligations; and as an example of the later, he suggests that authorities often concretise our obligations or give them a particular instantiation from among a number of possibilities.

B. Weinstock

Kant stressed the moral impossibility of revolting against public authorities: beyond the duty to leave the 'state of nature' (to create an 'omni-lateral' will) there is a duty not to *regress* from a political state (no matter what).[70] Daniel Weinstock recalls why Kant held this view, before challenging Ripstein's defence of it.

Locke's 'right to revolt' accompanied his idea of the state as the instrument of rightful proprietors: their antecedent rights—the state's raison d'être—could also be grounds for dissolving it. A doctrine like Kant's, which views public authority as a precondition of Right, obviously can't follow Locke. Similarly, 'the will of the people'—the idea invoked by the French revolutionaries—affords, for Kant, no ground for revolt, since only public law can determine what counts as a *people's* acts or views. Kant also stresses (as I might put it) that the state, despite its name, isn't 'static': it is a public *act-in-progress*, and, as such, something reformable. Weinstock's criticism of Ripstein puts this last point to use.

Kant's argument against revolution presupposes one thing: that public authority *exists*. Suppose, in the state of nature, a small band exploits others for their own purposes. Perhaps they follow rules of procedure (as efficient exploitation requires) and call themselves the Governing Authority (since ideology helps). Since this is only a more organised structure of private subjection, one's duty would be to *resist* the Governing Authority if that is a way out of the state of nature. Kant's argument, we may say, requires application of a distinction between the *constitutive* and *regulative* conditions of public order: the former say when public order *exists* (the rule of law, public offices, etc); the latter describe its *justice* and its mandate (innate right and its 'authorisations').

[70] See Kant, *MM*, 6: 320; see also Immanuel Kant, 'On the Common Saying: "This May be True in Theory, but it does not Apply in Practice"', in MJ Gregor (ed), *Immanuel Kant: Practical Philosophy* (Cambridge, Cambridge University Press, 1996) 8: 299.

Corresponding to this distinction—according to Ripstein—are two kinds of political privation: in a *despotism*, public authority exists but acts unjustly; in *barbarism*, public authority is absent, so the argument gets no grip.[71]

Is this distinction sharp enough to sort out historical cases?[72] Unless it can be applied without asking whether things are *bad enough* so that people should revolt if they can, the categories aren't doing the right sort of work. Weinstock's objection is different: he thinks Ripstein's account *does* sort out particular cases—*unpalatably*. In particular, he finds that Ripstein's *constitutive* conditions for public order allow for a particularly bad possibility: namely, a *hopeless* despotism. Here, the regulative ideals of justice aren't just publicly violated but also publicly unacknowledged. In short, the state *has* become static; or, if it is going anywhere, it is likely going backward, to barbarism.

Weinstock is troubled by the thesis that revolution would be morally wrong in such terrible conditions, and he proposes a solution: understand the Kantian argument as presupposing not merely the *existence* but the *progressive* character of public order. I take this to be a claim about what *really matters* about public order: namely, its being an act-in-progress, and not, apart from this, its comprising various institutional structures *as such*. Ripstein's categories of political defect only roughly track what matters: judging by the possibility of progress, despotism can be as bad as barbarism.

Weinstock is a reformer in the Kantian realm, not a revolutionary. He would continue to distinguish despotisms from barbarisms, but among despotisms, he would distinguish regimes that realise the social contract imperfectly (this characterises all historical regimes) from those that fail to recognise the contractual ideal they fall short of. In such *unenlightened* despotisms, citizens considering revolt will weigh the risks to Right against the prospects of something better. On some Kantian views, this would be to compromise morality with exigency or enthusiasm; on Weinstock's view, a revolt from hopelessness can be just *right*.

VI. RIGHT AND ETHICS

A. Wood

Can duties of Right can be derived from (some formulation of) the Supreme Principle of Morality or Categorical Imperative (CI)? Some say they *must* be

[71] This follows Immanuel Kant, *Anthropology*, trans RB Louden (Cambridge, Cambridge University Press, 2006) 7: 331.

[72] J Weinrib, *Dimensions of Dignity: The Theory and Practice of Modern Constitutional Law* (Cambridge, Cambridge University Press, 2016) offers some helpful guidance on issues of classification.

derived if Kant's doctrine is to succeed philosophically; others, like Ripstein, say they *can't* be. Both views have their motivations.

On the one hand: Kant distinguishes between legal obligation (which depends on coercive enforcement: external law-giving) and ethical obligation (which depends on free self-constraint: internal law-giving); the former concerns the formal unification of our choices, the latter, my self-governance and mandatory *ends*.[73] Now suppose that the Principle, 'Choose only consistently with the equal freedom of others' *could* be derived from the CI. Arguably, this is no derivation of *Right*. For it only shows that the other's status as a chooser makes a dent on a good person. She might decide against making lying promises, as Kant says.[74] She might even decide that she must carry out her *sincere* promise, whatever the circumstances. But even this (which is implausible) falls short of showing that anyone has a power externally to constrain her. The point is simple: the CI describes my self-conscious principle of action; but Right isn't, in the first instance, about 'how I *myself should* limit my freedom'[75]—it's about how *you* may do so. Indeed, this is just what Kant says when he presents the Law of Right as a 'postulate incapable of further proof': following directly upon a contrast between Right and *virtue*, this assertion registers the lack of an inferential route from internal to external morality.[76]

On the other hand: Right and Virtue are divisions of a higher category—Morals (*Sitten*). If only *one* of these divisions (Virtue) is grounded by the CI,[77] what is this higher category about? There is also the trouble raised by Pavlakos: all genuine obligations should be able to appear *as such* in rational reflection—but doesn't the CI purport to describe the shape of any such reflection? Last but not least: if Right isn't grounded in the CI, it risks being an unsupported, further principle—and Reason wants more than that.[78]

[73] On these contrasts, see especially Kant, *MM*, 6: 218–21, 6: 239, 6: 380–83, 6: 395–96, 6: 406–08.

[74] See Immanuel Kant, *Groundwork of the Metaphysics of Morals*, trans MJ Gregor (Cambridge, Cambridge University Press, 1998) 4: 402–03.

[75] Kant, *MM*, 6: 231.

[76] The summary nature of my discussion shouldn't be taken to minimise the controversy that exists about these arguments. Considerations in favour of derivation have been advanced by Paul Guyer, Otfried Hoffe, Wolfgang Kersting, Mary Gregor, Leslie Mulholland, Bernd Ludwig, HF Fulda, Roger Sullivan, and Onora O'Neill among others. On the other side (non-derivation), Wood, Ripstein and Marcus Willaschek have made important contributions. For a brief but helpful overview, see R Pippin, 'Mine and Thine: The Kantian State', in P Guyer (ed), *The Cambridge Companion to Kant and Modern Philosophy* (Cambridge, Cambridge University Press, 2006).

[77] Kant earlier seemed to say that the whole of Morals is grounded: eg *Groundwork* (n 74) 4: 391–92.

[78] Not that grounding Right in Morality would remove all given-ness—according to Kant no deduction of *Morality's* principle is possible—but it would remove it for Right. See Kant, *Critique of Practical Reason* (n 41) 5: 46–48.

Allen Wood guides the reader through this dense region, in part by prising apart and then answering *three* questions: that of Right's *derivation* from Morality, that of Right's *foundation*, and that of the *unity* of Morals. *Derivation*: Right's property of coercive constraint makes it underivable from moral self-governance. *Foundation*: yet this needn't mean that Right has no supporting ground—it is grounded in the nature of rational agency. *Unity*: although there is no route from internal Morality to Right, both (1) are grounded in rational agency and (2) employ a concept of obligation as conformity to universal law; this is what makes each a branch of Morals.

Among these points, Right's *foundation*—a problem 'not explicitly solved by Ripstein', Wood says—is the most intriguing:

> The foundation of right … consists in a rational ground that all rational beings have for requiring the protection of external freedom of all according to universal law. What could such a ground be? It is this: As a rational being, I necessarily set ends. This implies a rational requirement that I be free to choose the actions by which I pursue those ends.

Does Wood mean to derive Right from monadic features of my own case? If not, how might his argument be further articulated?[79] Say that I'm rationally committed to being free to choose for myself—this is a 'rational interest' of mine, as Wood also says. I grasp this and so do you, and we grasp that we grasp it. Does this way of figuring in each other's thought mean that we apprehend ourselves as standing in relations of Right and not just relations of potential conflict? After all, in grasping your rational interest, I grasp that you *won't* be interested in leaving me free to choose when this limits you. Prudence might get us to relations of Right from here, but that's of course not what Wood is suggesting. By what steps does my rational commitment to choosing my own actions rationally commit me to *your* being able to *constrain* me from doing this very thing?

Foundations aside, Wood also asks whether the powers of modern states can really take root in Kant's abstemiously unmixed soil of mutual independence. Answering *no*, libertarians have found an ally in Kant; champions of the 'welfare state' have found an objection to his doctrine. Both are mistaken, according to Wood: Right incurs no commitment to a minimalist state, because economic inequality threatens people's independence, not just their welfare.

As an example, consider the homeless. They do not *fare well*. But this is also an effect of a property system under which the homeless need the leave of

[79] The present paragraph may articulate part of Ripstein's concern below.

others—and this characterises what they *are*—to be in a place and to do many other things as well. The latter description roots public action in 'independence', not monadic needs, and it shows why private charity couldn't solve the problem.[80] Similar points can be made about poverty.[81] In this way, the Kantian state has a duty, according to Wood and Ripstein, to remedy poverty and homelessness (and to support health and education and much else) precisely as part of its mandate to sustain the conditions of reciprocal freedom. This argument suggests that while Right *begins* with dyadic thought, the conditions of sustaining a *public system* of Right bring in considerations that are not immediately dyadic. How are these further considerations constrained by their origins in Right, or how far do they go? Since 'independence', for Wood and Ripstein, is a broader idea than the absence of *personal* subjection, there is room for the 'social-democratic' state; but since the state's powers originate from dyadic Right, Kantian political thought must spell out the transition from personal subjection (whose paradigm is master and slave) to its systemic analogues.[82]

B. Stone

I agree that Kant can be liberated from libertarianism, but I still wonder if he can go as far as embracing *discretionary* public powers, like supporting the arts, developing parkland or preserving history. These are good things for a state to do, but they don't seem to be requisites of equal freedom: if they were, they would be *mandatory*.

My main focus, however, is on one aspect of Right's independence of ethics. Political philosophy has often begun outside the *political*, with values that are supposed to be self-standing—ie fully there to be engaged-with, even with no political practices in view. On such accounts, legal and political thought is to *apply* these standing values to our circumstances;[83] the values are the external touchstone of what political institutions should be. Right is *not* self-standing in this way: It is useless apart from its realisation in public institutions; and it is *proprietary* to such institutions—it has no other use.[84]

[80] See C Essert, 'Property and Homelessness' (forthcoming).

[81] Besides Wood's chapter, see Ripstein (n 16) chs 8, 9; see also E Weinrib, 'Poverty and Property in Kant's System of Rights' (2003) 78 *Notre Dame Law Review* 795.

[82] Here I have benefited from an exchange with Rafeeq Hasan.

[83] See Ripstein (n 16) 1, 23–24, 28.

[84] Right does have the *philosophical* role of exhibiting the grounds and unity of these institutions. But this becomes important—on Kant's view—only because Right, like morality more generally, gets dialectically obscured. Philosophy is defence. For this point in relation to practical philosophy, see especially Kant, *Groundwork* (n 74) 4: 403–05.

The most prominent version of 'law as applied ethics' brings the structure of Right into bold relief. For the *utilitarian*, whatever specific value is supposed to be morally relevant to choice (eg preference-satisfaction, wealth, etc), it:

1. is *self-standing*: grasping its content doesn't require law or legal rights to be in view.
2. *fully determines* what we are to do: limitations lie only in uncertainty about what will lead to what.
3. involves *no essential* role for law: whether following legal authority is the best way to realise this value is a contingent matter, not basic to the theory. A book on morality is complete without mentioning law.
4. can determine what our laws should be without need for thinking of a distinctively *practical* kind—merely by predictions of what will lead to what.

In contrast, Right-as-independence:

1. is *not self*-standing: its content isn't fully available without public laws.
2. is *indeterminate*: it can be realised in different ways, so some public, constitutive decisions are needed.
3. involves an essential role for *law*: the most direct (and indeed the only) way of complying with Right is to follow public laws and procedures.
4. is made more concrete through practical specification in different circumstances—not just by reckoning how particular rules might bring about a value that is fully graspable on its own.

Institutions of Right, in sum, *express* or *interpret* an abstract part of morality—they don't bring some self-standing value about.

Item (3)—to comply with Right is to follow what is publicly *laid down* as Right—is apt to suggest that Kant is a 'legal positivist' in contemporary terms. Something seems right about this suggestion but something doesn't. Legal *positivity* must play an indispensable role in any account of political life, like Kant's, that views law as a concretising expression of an (abstract) part of morality. But *positivism* is something else, and Kant's idea (that a part of morality is proprietary to law) doesn't fit the prominent versions of it. Today there are three much-discussed positions about the nature of law: Either self-standing moral truths (1) *do* or (2) *might* play a role in determining the content of the law-in-force, or (3) morality is external to law and never determines its content. Since Right is internal to law but not *self-standing*, none of these positions captures Kant's view: (1) and (2) describe how the-law-in-force might depend on *morality;* but for Kant, one part of morality (Right) depends on *law*.

* * * *

Ripstein's response to these chapters presents a doctrine of Right that is formal and involves coercible obligations (not virtue); that affirms the immediacy of bodily right and emphasises the role of property in grounding political authority; that restricts the right to revolt beyond what some find palatable; and that grounds many of the familiar powers of the 'social-democratic' state. Is this Kant's doctrine of Right? Is it the right doctrine of Right? This volume reflects the present state of these questions and invites the reader to join in.

Part I

Innate Right

2

Persons and Bodies

JAPA PALLIKKATHAYIL[1]

ON KANT'S VIEW, property rights in the state of nature involve certain defects and these defects render such rights merely provisional.[2] Conclusive property rights can only be established through political institutions and this consideration is the basis of the duty to establish those institutions. Property rights are thus politically constructed. Kant, however, treats one's right to one's body differently. He seems to move directly from the claim that we each have an innate right to freedom to the claim that we each have a right to our own bodies. He then proceeds as if bodily rights are largely immune to the problems faced by property rights in the state of nature. Arthur Ripstein's new interpretation of Kant's political philosophy affirms Kant's claims about bodily rights and attempts to motivate these claims far more explicitly than Kant himself does.[3] I will argue that, even with the help of Ripstein's reconstruction, Kant's treatment of bodily rights remains problematic. Our rights to our own bodies can be defective in many of the ways that our rights to property can be. These defects in our rights to our bodies would be sufficient to ground a duty to establish political institutions even in

[1] I am indebted to Kyla Ebels-Duggan, Michael Joel Kessler and Arthur Ripstein for helpful comments on earlier drafts of this essay and to Sari Kisilevsky and Martin Stone for organising the workshop at the Cardozo School of Law, for which it was written. I am also indebted to audiences at the Princeton Center for Human Values, UCLA Legal Theory Workshop, and the University of Pittsburgh for many helpful comments and questions.

[2] Kant develops this view in *Metaphysics of Morals* (hereinafter *MM*). For all citations of Kant's work, I give the page numbers of the relevant volumes of *Kants gesammelte Schriften* (published by the *Preussische Akademie der Wissenschaften*, Berlin), which appear in the margins of most translations. All quotations from Kant's work are taken from Immanuel Kant, *Practical Philosophy*, ed and trans MJ Gregor (Cambridge, Cambridge University Press, 1996).

[3] A Ripstein, *Force and Freedom: Kant's Legal and Political Philosophy* (Cambridge, MA, Harvard University Press, 2009) (hereinafter *FF*).

the absence of Kant's arguments regarding property. I will conclude, therefore, that Kant's political philosophy suggests an even deeper justification for the establishment of political institutions than Kant himself imagined. And this justification suggests a surprising conclusion: we are thoroughly political beings; even our rights to our own bodies are politically constructed.

In arguing for this view, I will *not* be arguing that our rights to our bodies are just property rights. Although I hold that Kant did not properly appreciate the similarities between bodily rights and property rights, I will argue that important differences remain between these two kinds of rights. Unlike property rights, bodily rights are not directly transferable.[4] This has important implications for the possibility of selling or even donating parts of our bodies to others. I will explore these implications and argue that an attractive view of the complexity of bodily rights emerges from this investigation.

I. PROPERTY AND THE STATE[5]

Kant's practical philosophy focuses on developing an account of how action can be free, ie self-directed. Kant uses the distinction between 'internal' and 'external' freedom to capture two respects in which action can be self-directed. The distinction between these two kinds of freedom can be best understood by considering the different threats to self-directed action to which they are meant to respond. Internal freedom, ie autonomy, consists in directing oneself rather than being directed by one's inclinations. External freedom, ie independence, consists in directing oneself rather than being directed by other agents.

While Kant's moral philosophy is largely occupied with the examination of internal freedom, Kant's political philosophy focuses on external freedom. The foundational claim of Kant's political philosophy is that we each have an innate right to freedom (*MM* 6:237). One is free in the relevant sense if one is one's own master, ie if one is independent from the constraint of others'

[4] While I will argue that bodily rights cannot be directly transferred, I will not argue that property rights must be essentially transferrable. It is sufficient for my purposes to claim that a property right is the sort of right that the state may in principal make transferrable, though it may not do so in all cases. I am indebted to Seana Shiffrin for pointing out this distinction. Furthermore, if the innate right to freedom were to ground inalienable rights to external objects in the world (a possibility I describe in the text to n 30) like, for example, air, these rights would represent a new category of rights in the Kantian scheme and would not be best understood as property rights. I am indebted to Seana Shiffrin for also prompting me to consider this possibility.

[5] In this section, I draw on my work in Japa Pallikkathayil, 'Deriving Morality from Politics: Rethinking the Formula of Humanity' (2010) 121 *Ethics* 116–47. There I develop an account of the relationship between Kant's moral and political philosophies.

choices. When does one count as independent in this sense? I take it that Kant eschews any attempt to develop a non-normative characterisation of independence. Instead, Kant's view suggests that in order to make sense of being one's own master we must identify a domain that one has the right to control. The extent of this domain is only limited by the equal claim of others to be their own masters as well.

Which rights comprise the domain within which we are each our own masters? Most basically, one needs to be an individual who is entitled to make one's own choices. In other words, one needs a right to oneself. As embodied beings, this seems to amount to a right to one's body. Some kind of right to control over one's own body is thus a precondition for engaging in independent action. This thought seems to underlie Kant's apparent assumption that the innate right to freedom necessarily involves a right to one's own body. Indeed the connection here is so close that, as Ripstein puts it, for Kant 'your person is your body'.[6]

Ultimately, I want to call into question Kant's assumption about the nature of bodily rights. But for now, I will begin by taking this view on board in order to lay out Kant's view on property rights. So, let us suppose that independence straightforwardly requires the right to control one's body. What about rights to control other parts of the world? Our rights to our bodies give us a derivative right to anything that cannot be moved without moving us. So, if I am holding an apple, my right to my body prevents you from snatching it from my hand. But this falls short of a property right in the apple. A property right includes the right to control the object even when one is not in physical possession of that object. Recall that the extent of the domain within which we are each entitled to be our own masters is limited only by the equal claim of others to be their own masters as well. The right to acquire property rights is one that we can all have. From this, Kant concludes that there can be no justification for restricting the possibility of acquiring property rights.[7]

Nonetheless, property rights suffer from three kinds of problems in the state of nature. First, consider the indeterminacy problem: there is indeterminacy regarding what one must do to acquire a property right and indeterminacy regarding what counts as an interference with a property right. As an example

[6] Ripstein, *FF*, 177.

[7] This step in the argument is more difficult than I have indicated. Indeed, I worry that Kant's argument here may not work. But if my arguments regarding bodily rights succeed, we may be able to sidestep Kant's focus on property rights in his justification of the establishment of the state.

of the first kind of indeterminacy, consider the problem of specifying what kind of sign one must give to others that one is appropriating an object. As an example of the second kind of indeterminacy, consider the problem of specifying what counts as damaging another's property. May you, for example, set up a fan on your land that will blow over the daffodils I have planted on my land?[8]

However detailed the principles devised to resolve these indeterminacy problems, there will remain cases in which there may be reasonable disagreement about how these principles apply. This brings us to the second problem facing property rights in the state of nature: the problem of adjudication.[9] Third and finally, in order to be truly independent from the choices of others, one must be able to rely on one's rights. Now, of course, in the state of nature I can have very good reason to believe that you will not violate my rights. Perhaps I have ample evidence of your good will. Or perhaps I know that you are exceptionally prudent and that prudence dictates respecting my rights. But your unilateral will is the source of either of these kinds of assurance. As long as I can rely only on the unilateral will of others for the security of my rights, I am still dependent on their choices. Call this the problem of assurance.[10]

[8] Ripstein seems to argue that this problem is at least somewhat more tractable than I am indicating here. Ripstein gives the following pair of examples. Suppose that I grow porcini mushrooms on my land in the shade of the garage that you have put up on your land. If you take down your garage, my mushrooms will die. But I have no claim that you give my mushrooms the shade that they need. Likewise, if I am growing sunflowers and you decide to build a garage that will block their access to the sunlight, I have no claim against you because 'all you have done is fail to use your land in a way that provides me with something I need' (*FF*, 78). A further gloss on this point: others 'have no right to a path across your land' (*FF*, 78). These cases are, I think, more difficult than Ripstein acknowledges. The case of the fan and the daffodils I give in the text makes the difficulty more transparent. Perhaps this is simply a case in which you block my access to the peaceful, undisturbed air on the other side of your property. But perhaps we should understand this as a case in which you force the wind that you have created on me. Or suppose you spray poison gas in the air; do you merely block my access to clean air or assault my land with poison? With these cases in mind, return to Ripstein's case of erecting the garage. Does the garage merely block my access to sunlight or force the darkness you have created on me? Similar reasoning can make the case of tearing down the garage problematic as well. Suppose you have built a dam that keeps water from reaching my land. You decide to tear it down, and doing so will cause my land to flood. Are you assaulting my land with water?

[9] In 'Deriving Morality from Politics' (n 5) I treated what I am calling here the problem of adjudication as an indeterminacy problem. Although these problems have much in common, it is useful to keep them separated because they have solutions in different branches of the government. I am indebted to Arthur Ripstein for helping me to appreciate this point. See Ripstein, *FF*, 173.

[10] In 'Deriving Morality from Politics' (n 5) I used the term 'enforcement problem' to refer to what I am here labeling the 'assurance problem'. As I discuss in the next section and as Ripstein

A unilateral right to settle the indeterminacy problems or to adjudicate disputes would give one person authority over all others. Hence such a right would be inconsistent with the equal freedom of all. The solution to these problems is the establishment of an impartial decision procedure for establishing laws and adjudicating disputes over rights. An institutional apparatus embodying such a decision procedure is able to resolve the indeterminacy and adjudication problems in a way that does not reflect any unilateral will. For this very reason, this institution is also able, and hence required, to solve the assurance problem. Since the institution has the right to determine the boundaries of individuals' rights, it has the right to compel individuals to respect that determination. The institution thereby has the right to enforce the rights of individuals. When it does so, people may be assured that their rights will be respected and this assurance does not reflect the unilateral will of any other person.

Now, we are in a position to appreciate the overall structure of Kant's political philosophy. Kant's argument is that the innate right to freedom requires that we have rights to our bodies and the possibility of acquiring property rights. But at least the latter are merely provisional in the state of nature. That is, although we can make claims on one another to abide by our respective rights, the definitive shape of these rights remains unsettled and the assurance that they will be respected is absent. Provisional rights can only be made conclusive through the establishment an institution that defines the scope of our rights and enforces those rights, in other words, the state.[11] Hence each of us has the right to have our interactions with others governed by a state.[12] Since, as Kant understands rights, having a right includes the authorisation to enforce that right, each of us may compel others to enter into a state.

II. BODIES AND THE STATE

Our rights to our own bodies seem to give rise to at least many of the same problems as our rights to property. Bodily rights clearly give rise to an

helpfully emphasizes, not all problems regarding enforcement are properly regarded as instances of the assurance problem, making this label more precise.

[11] Kant, *MM*, 6: 255–56.

[12] As it stands, this is an argument for a very minimal state, lacking many of the features and powers we typically attribute to states. I am indebted to Larry Temkin for reminding me of this limitation of the argument. Ripstein offers some arguments directed at showing how further elements of the state might be defended. See, eg, Ripstein's argument for public roads: *FF*, 182–231.

indeterminacy problem about what counts as interference. Consider an example of Ripstein's:

> If I shout loud enough to startle you when you stand on the edge of a cliff, but do not touch you, do I wrong you? This seems to be a question about our respective rights, which is not resolved by some factual consideration about the number of molecules that my shout displaced toward you.[13]

What we need is a rule about whether shouting in this context constitutes assault. That is something that neither of us is unilaterally entitled to impose on the other. Next, notice that even if we had such a rule, there might yet arise a question about whether what I do in a particular case constitutes shouting in the relevant sense. Hence, bodily rights are also subject to the problem of adjudication.

Before turning to the assurance problem, notice that there are some problems involving enforcement are that are not properly regarded as instances of the assurance problem. As Ripstein helpfully points out, two people may have potentially conflicting rights of self-defence in the state of nature. Each may identify the other as an aggressor and so attack the other. Neither person is required to defer to the other's judgement about who is aggressing against whom. But this is really a problem about indeterminacy or adjudication rather than a problem about assurance. The response to this problem consists in the establishment of a law or the issuing of a verdict that settles the boundaries of our respective bodily rights, thus settling who is aggressing against whom.

Let us turn, then, to the assurance problem. The assurance problem, as I have described it, seems to apply straightforwardly to our bodily rights. In the state of nature, my only assurance that you will respect my bodily rights depends on your unilateral choices. I am thus unable to rely on my rights in a way that leaves me truly independent of your will. Nonetheless, some aspects of Kant's view suggest that he does not recognise an assurance problem for bodily rights. In his interpretation of Kant, Ripstein explicitly denies that the assurance problem applies to bodily rights. I am going to spend some time examining Ripstein's argument for this conclusion because I think that the argument sheds considerable light on what is at stake in the assurance problem and illuminates an important difference between bodily rights and property rights. I will argue, however, that Ripstein's argument is ultimately unsuccessful.

Ripstein claims, and I agree, that the assurance problem would be a problem for property rights even if our property rights were determinate. So, imagine

[13] Ripstein, *FF*, 176–77.

that we have somehow managed to establish determinate rights to property in the state of nature. That is, it is clear what belongs to whom and what counts as interfering with the property of others. With this in mind, consider Ripstein's description of the assurance problem with respect to property rights:

> In this situation, without public enforcement, people lack the assurance that others will refrain from interfering with their property and, as a result, have no obligation to refrain from interfering with the property of others. The basic thought is that without such a system, nobody has the right to use force (or call on others to do so) to exclude others from his or her property, so nobody has an enforceable obligation to refrain from interfering with the property of others.[14]

Here Ripstein is claiming that, in the absence of assurance, no one could rightfully defend his or her property rights. This claim should strike us as rather mysterious. After all, Kant insists that the authorisation to defend one's rights is part of the very nature of having a right.[15] If we imagine that we have established determinate property rights, how could the absence of assurance that others will not interfere with our property rights render us unable legitimately to defend those rights?

The answer must lie in some way of articulating a sense in which *determinate* rights can still fail to be *conclusive* rights. Ripstein attempts to articulate such a sense by pointing to a purported tension in our rights to property in the absence of public assurance. On the one hand, you must refrain from taking what is mine. But on the other hand, '[i]f you refrain from taking what is mine, without assurance that I will refrain from taking what is yours, then you are permitting me to treat what is yours, and so an aspect of your capacity to set and pursue purposes, as subject to my purposes'.[16] The same problem arises for me. And so, 'if either of us refrains from taking what belongs to the other without assurance, we restrict our choice on the basis of the other's particular choice, rather than in accordance with a universal law'.[17]

I think this account still leaves the purported tension rather mysterious. How can respecting your rights in the absence of assurance permit you to violate mine? Respecting your rights under those circumstances seems as though it might be imprudent. But why should doing so affect the normative force of my rights? In particular, why should I conceive of myself as permitting you to ignore my rights?

[14] Ripstein, *FF*, 159.
[15] Kant, *MM*, 6: 231.
[16] Ripstein, *FF*, 162.
[17] Ripstein, *FF*, 162.

Ripstein's language suggests that in trying to respect your rights in the absence of assurance I somehow manage to undermine my own rights. But I suggest that it is not the attempt to respect your rights that generates the problem. Our rights in the absence of assurance are incomplete no matter how we try to respond to them. And this creates a problem for the possibility of rightful enforcement. To see the problem, let us first take a look at why Kant holds that having a right necessarily involves the authorisation to defend it. Kant claims that using force to defend a right is just 'hindering a hindrance to freedom'. So, if I try to take your pen, I am an interfering with your right and so with your freedom. When you stop me, you simply prevent me from doing something I had no right to do. Thus, you preserve your freedom without interfering with mine.

Now recall that we are imagining a situation in which you have determinate property rights but do not have the assurance that they will be respected. As I argued earlier, in the absence of assurance, the rights cannot yet do the job of allowing us to be independent of the constraint of others' choices. So, in this situation, our rights do not yet enable us to be free. Hence any force used in their defence is still just mere force—it does not hinder a hindrance to freedom. For this reason, I cannot use force to defend even a determinate property right and hence you cannot have an enforceable obligation to leave my property alone, which, from the point of view of right, just amounts to your having no obligation to refrain from interfering.

Ripstein argues that this conclusion does not follow for bodily rights—one may rightfully enforce one's bodily rights in the state of nature. By way of explanation, Ripstein argues, 'Anyone who touches you without your authorization hinders your freedom; to repel the trespasser is to hinder his hindrance.'[18] Why does touching you necessarily hinder your freedom? Ripstein answers that 'your person can never be physically separate from you'.[19] As I will argue in the next section, I do not think this is quite right. But something in the neighbourhood is correct. Your body is what places you in the world, making you a potential participant in interactions. For this reason, some kind of control over your body is, as I put it earlier, a precondition for your freedom. This extra role of bodily rights marks a difference between how our bodily rights and our property rights are related to our freedom. So, suppose that you have determinate bodily rights but do not have assurance. In one way, the link between your bodily rights and your freedom is broken here just as it is in the case of property rights. But in another way your bodily rights continue to

[18] Ripstein, *FF*, 177.
[19] Ripstein, *FF*, 177.

play a role in enabling you to be free, namely by satisfying the precondition on your freedom. Interfering with your body thus hinders your freedom. Hence defending yourself hinders a hindrance to freedom and is therefore a rightful use of force.

Ripstein is thus correct to insist that bodily rights do not raise exactly the same kind of problem as property rights. If bodily rights were determinate in the state of nature, they could be rightfully defended. In contrast, if property rights were determinate in the state of nature, they could not be rightfully defended. Ripstein's argument goes wrong at the final step. The difference in the possibility of rightful enforcement indicates that the implications of the assurance problem differ for bodily rights and property rights. It does not indicate that there is no assurance problem for bodily rights.

The assurance problem is simply that, in the state of nature, one must rely on the unilateral choices of others for the security of one's rights. This problem remains even if I am permitted to defend myself. One might object that if I am permitted to defend myself, the security of my rights does not depend on the unilateral choices of others but instead on my own defensive choices. This objection misses the mark in two respects.

First, as Ripstein helpfully points out, the right to enforce one's bodily rights in the state of nature is incomplete. Since conclusive property rights are impossible in the state of nature 'you can have no remedial right if someone commits a wrong against your person. … Thus your right to defend yourself is genuine, but if you fail to hinder a hindrance to your own freedom, it cannot be hindered after the fact.'[20] This suggests an interesting and powerful connection between bodily rights and property rights: even if we did not have an independent argument for the necessity of establishing property rights, the need to secure our bodily rights could provide such an argument. We need to be able to have property in order to be able to claim reparations for violations of bodily rights.

There is, however, a second and deeper reply to the argument that the permission to enforce one's bodily rights dissolves the assurance problem for those rights. Even if I may defend myself, my freedom is still constrained by your unilateral choices. If I must abandon my leisurely morning walk to run away from you or to stop and hurl rocks at you, I do not enjoy the discretionary space that my right entitles me to. In this way, even if I am able to thwart or deter any attempted aggression, I am still not able to rely on my rights. Instead, I rely on my power as measured against your unilateral choices.

[20] Ripstein, *FF*, 180.

In order to be able to rely on my rights, they must somehow be enforced apart from the choices that either of us makes. This is precisely the condition that the state secures. The state's enforcement of rights makes rights exert physical force in the world apart from anyone's unilateral will. So, Ripstein is right to insist that, if one's bodily rights were determinate in the state of nature, one could rightfully defend one's bodily rights. But this feature of bodily rights does not yet overcome the assurance problem.

It is important to distinguish the version of the assurance problem that I am advocating from another that is closely related. One might think that one lacks independence just insofar as one's rights are not secure. There is something right about this, but this is not the most fundamental problem. Instead, I have suggested that one lacks independence when the security of one's rights depends on others' unilateral choices. This version of the assurance problem makes it evident why Kant thinks that the state solves the assurance problem: the state solves this problem by establishing an impartial enforcement mechanism so that the security of one's rights has a source beyond anyone's unilateral will. This impartial enforcement mechanism may be better or worse, depending on the state. An ideal state would have a perfect enforcement mechanism and so, in addition to changing the character of the security of our rights, such a state would make our rights completely secure. So, although this interpretation focuses on the source of our security as the basic problem, it provides a natural way of situating the problem posed by the extent of our security. In the state of nature, we face a problem about the source of our security. The state solves this problem and its solution may be judged better or worse in terms of the extent of the security it provides.[21]

I have now shown how bodily rights face three of the problems that property rights face in the state of nature. Bodily rights raise an indeterminacy problem regarding what counts as interference, a problem of adjudication and a problem of assurance. This leaves only one problem that bodily rights do not seem to face: an indeterminacy problem about acquisition. In the next section, I will argue that bodily rights do actually face an analogue of this problem. But even without that analogue, the problems that bodily rights face would be sufficient to justify the establishment of the state. To appreciate this, notice that the solution to each of the three problems I have focused on with respect to bodily rights lies in a different branch of government. A public legislative authority solves the indeterminacy problem about interference. A public judiciary solves the problem of adjudication. And a public executive solves the

[21] I am indebted to Arudra Burra and Anil Gupta for prompting me to think through these issues further.

problem of assurance. The need to solve these three problems can thus justify each aspect of the state's authority. I suggest, then, that careful consideration of the normative demands to which our bodily rights give rise can justify the establishment of the state.

There is a line of argument in Ripstein's discussion that might be thought to push against this conclusion. I have cast acquisition as raising only an indeterminacy problem that is exactly parallel to the indeterminacy problem regarding what counts as interference. For this reason, the fact that property rights must be acquired does no unique work in the argument for the establishment of the state. Ripstein, however, seems to suggest that acquisition raises a unique problem. What Ripstein calls the problem of unilateral choice focuses on how one person could choose to put others under obligation by acquiring property. Ripstein here correctly identifies a difference in the way my bodily rights and my acquired rights affect your obligations. As Ripstein puts it: '[I]f I move from one place to another, I occupy space which is not available for your occupation while I am there. This change does not place you under a new obligation, but simply applies it to a different circumstance.'[22] In contrast, acquiring property does not simply pick a place for an existing obligation but rather brings a new obligation into existence.

Why should this difference raise a unique problem for acquired rights? Ripstein claims:

> [A] 'permissive law' that entitles me to acquire things makes a merely permissible unilateral act have rightful consequences for others. However, it could only have this status provided that it is authorized by everyone, so that my unilateral act is also the exercise of a publicly conferred power. If the public authority is entitled to confer the power on me in the name of everyone, then my specific exercise of the power is also in everyone's name.[23]

I cannot confer on myself the authority to change your obligations unilaterally. To the extent that that is all this passage is meant to indicate, the thought expressed is correct. But Ripstein seems to take it to mean something more. Not only can I not confer this power on myself, the only way this power could be conferred on me is via a public authority, where this means the established authority of the state. But notice that there is another option. If the permissive law to which Ripstein refers were itself justified by the requirements of freedom, the requirements of freedom would confer this authority on me. And as I argued in Section I, Kant does indeed regard equal freedom as requiring

[22] Ripstein, *FF*, 151.
[23] Ripstein, *FF*, 154.

the possibility of property ownership. So, I do not need to stand on my own authority when I try to acquire property rights in the state of nature; I can instead stand on the authority of the requirements of freedom. The problem for my attempt to acquire property rights emerges only in light of the inability of the requirements of freedom alone to settle a determinate procedure for property acquisition.

Ripstein seems to explicate the problem of unilateral choice as if it were prior to and independent of problems associated with the indeterminacy of the rules surrounding the acquisition of property. But if there were determinate rules for property acquisition supplied by the requirements of freedom alone, my choice to acquire property would not interfere with your independence. The need for a public lawgiving authority is not generated by the need to confer authority on us to acquire property but rather by the need to confer authority on the procedures that specify how property acquisition is to take place. I conclude, then, that property acquisition does not generate a unique problem that the state must solve. Property acquisition generates an indeterminacy problem. Bodily rights do that as well. Thus bodily rights can do the same work in justifying the establishment of the state.[24]

III. THE BOUNDARIES OF THE BODY

So far, I have argued that bodily rights share three of the problems faced by property rights in the state of nature. I have also argued that the existence of these three problems for bodily rights is sufficient to justify the establishment of the state. Thus, my main argument is secure even if only property rights suffer from an indeterminacy problem regarding acquisition. Nonetheless, I think that there is an analogue of this indeterminacy problem for bodily rights and that recognising this analogue is important for understanding the nature of bodily rights.

The problem I have in mind is about how we should understand the boundaries of our bodies. As I mentioned above, Ripstein maintains that 'your person can never be physically separate from you' and that 'your person is your

[24] Ripstein's understanding of bodily rights has implications for other aspects of his view. Ripstein interprets Kant as understanding a state's relationship to its territory on the model of a person's relationship to her body rather than to her property. Since bodies do not raise all of the relevant problems, this explains why Kant does not endorse the establishment of a global state (Ripstein, *FF*, 225–30). I agree with Ripstein's assessment of how Kant views the state's relationship to its territory. But since I hold that bodily rights can justify the establishment of the state, I maintain that Kant's rejection of the need for a global state was a mistake.

body'. This seems to suggest that you can never be physically separate from your body. These claims make sense on a certain picture of the body, one that Ripstein is correct to attribute to Kant. I am going to suggest, however, that this view is problematic.

Recall the brief account of the grounds of bodily rights that I sketched above. Kant's political philosophy is occupied with identifying the domain within which one is entitled to be independent, ie one's own master. Kant holds that the innate Right to freedom necessarily involves the right to one's own body because some kind of control over one's body is a precondition for independence. In other words, one needs some kind of foothold in the world as an agent in order for the question of independence from other agents even to arise. It is not mysterious why Kant identifies this foothold with our bodies. Moreover, at least at first glance, Kant adopts a very intuitive understanding of bodies. Kant claims that our bodies involve an 'essential unity',[25] and he makes it clear that he understands this unity in terms of our animal nature.[26] It seems then that identifying the boundaries of our bodies need involve nothing more than identifying the boundaries of the human animals that we are. And this, it seems, should simply require us to identify the physical material that is unified in the relevant way.

There are, however, cases in which this view runs into difficulty. Suppose that a falling tree branch hits you and slices off one of your fingers. That finger is now separate from the matter that is unified as an animal. This suggests a conclusion that is, in one way, very intuitive: the finger is no longer part of your body. The trouble, however, emerges when we consider whether the finger is still *yours*. Many people would be, I think, inclined to say that it is and that that explains why you have a right to reattach it if you can. Perhaps the thought here is that, although your finger is no longer part of your body, it is your property. I think, however, that a story on which that is true is rather difficult to tell on the Kantian view.

If the finger is your property, either it was your property before it was severed or only became your property after it was severed. The former possibility is difficult to maintain on the Kantian view for two related reasons. First, property rights are acquired rights. Some affirmative act is required to acquire property. So, if it were possible to acquire a property right in your body, you would need to do something to accomplish that. If you happen to sever your finger before you have done this, it seems that you have no recourse. Second,

[25] Kant, *MM*, 6: 278.
[26] Kant, *MM*, 6: 241.

notice that, if it is possible for you to acquire a property right in your body, it must in principle be possible for someone else to do so as well. Otherwise, your right to acquire a property right in your body could not be consistent with the equal freedom of others. But another person's property right in your body would be inconsistent with the bodily rights you have via the innate right to freedom. So, as long as you have the bodily rights that the innate right to freedom grounds, no one can have a property right in your body. Hence you cannot have a property right to your finger while it is still attached.

Could you acquire a property right to your finger once it is severed? If we accept the view that the finger is no longer part of your body, your bodily rights no longer stand in the way of acquiring a property right to the finger. But as we saw above it must be possible in principle for someone else to acquire that property right. If so, then even if you desperately want the finger back so as to have a chance of reattaching it, you would have no unique claim to it. While you lie on the ground reeling from your encounter with the tree branch, I may come along and grab the finger. You would have no more complaint against me than if I had grabbed an apple that you had been holding but dropped. Of course, if I want more than mere possession of the finger—if I want a property right to it—I must enter into a state with you, just as would be the case with the apple. But on this view, the finger raises no special problem simply in virtue of having once been a part of your body.

So, there are resources in the Kantian view to support the claim that it is possible to acquire a property right in your finger once it is severed. But this possibility does not vindicate the thought that you had a right to the finger all along. Perhaps that thought was misguided from the start—a confusion about the source of our rights analogous to the Lockean error of thinking that labouring on an object generates a property right. If so, then we must simply accept that the severed finger is now an unowned object in the world, one that potentially anyone could claim as property.

It is worth, however, considering what motivates the intuition that you still have some kind of claim to the finger even after it has been severed. We constantly lose hair and skin cells, but we are not generally concerned to defend our rights to them. The mere fact that an object was once a part of our bodies does not, then, seem to be the motivating factor. The prospect of reattachment in this case seems to matter. That is not simply because reattachment involves the repair of damage. Suppose we both lose our fingers to wayward tree branches. If my finger is too damaged to reattach, I might be able to use yours to repair my hand. But while you seem to have a claim to the severed finger that was once a part of your body, I seem to lack that claim. Here the sense that you have a claim to your severed finger seems to reflect the thought that, although the unity of your body has been disrupted, that disruption is not insurmountable.

This is not the only kind of case in which many people regard themselves as having a claim to a body part even after it has been detached. Consider the case of Henrietta Lacks, an African-American woman who died of cervical cancer in 1951.[27] Without the knowledge or consent of Lacks or her relatives, her doctors gave samples of her tumour to a researcher who was trying to find cells that would live indefinitely in culture. Lacks's tumour cells fitted the bill. They multiplied and never died, allowing researchers to use them as a staple in their experiments. Among their many contributions, the cells were used to develop the first polio vaccine. While the initial researcher did not profit from the cells, they were eventually commodified and now generate a considerable profit.

There are two issues here: the fact that the cells are still multiplying and being used and the fact that they are being treated as a commodity. Certainly, the latter consideration does some work in explaining the thought that Lacks was cheated, deprived of something to which she had a right. This is a complicated issue, and one that I will consider in the next section. Here, however, I want to suggest that even if the cells had never been commodified, there would still be some sense that Lacks's rights were bypassed. This sense is certainly not tracking the possibility of reunifying her with the cells. Instead, I suggest this sense reflects a way in which her bodily powers are still being put to work even in her absence. I take it that this sense might also reflect part of what would be objectionable if one's detached cells were used to clone one or to procreate without one's consent. In these cases, one's detached parts are still functioning, in some sense, in the way that bodies do even though they are detached. And this is what makes it seem that one can have a claim to those parts.

I want to note in passing one further interesting feature of the Lacks case. The cells in question were cancer cells. So, they were not playing a role in maintaining the unity of Lacks's body; rather, they were impairing that unity. This may be an important consideration for some kinds of ethical questions. Kant, for example, holds that removing diseased parts of one's body is consistent with one's duties of virtue to oneself, whereas removing healthy parts may raise problems.[28] But the distinction between healthy and diseased in Lacks's case does not seem to bear much weight in our sense that she had a claim to the cells. Reflection on this might, I think, reveal a further sense in which we need a more expansive conception of the role of bodily unity in determining the boundaries of our bodily rights. One continues to have a claim even to the perverted expression of one's bodily powers.

[27] D Grady, 'A Lasting Gift to Medicine that Wasn't Really a Gift', *New York Times*, 2 February 2010, D5.

[28] Kant, *MM*, 6: 423.

To return to my main suggestion, there are many reasons for denying that we automatically lose our rights to body parts when they become detached. Property rights cannot, on the Kantian view, do justice to this thought. That leaves only the possibility of recognising our bodily rights as potentially extending to objects that are physically separate. If so, then we need some way of determining when a detached body part is subject to these rights and when it is not. That is, we need determinate rules governing the boundaries of our bodies. These are rules that none of us can unilaterally impose. But it does seem as though these rules will authorise us, in effect, to choose to alienate parts of our bodies. Perhaps, for example, if I leave my severed finger in the forest, I will count as abandoning it and so lose my bodily right to it. Bodies thus pose the reverse of the problem posed by property. We need rules for property acquisition, which involve acquiring a right and hence imposing obligations on others, and we need rules for bodily alienation, which involve renouncing a right and hence relieving others of obligations.

In fact, once we recognise the possibility of bodily rights to physically separate objects, we can identify an even closer analogue to the problem posed by property acquisition. Consider the status of artificial body parts. Even on the original Kantian view, some artificial body parts seem appropriately included under the scope of one's bodily rights. An artificial heart, for example, plays the kind of role in the unity of one's body that might make it seem appropriate to think of it as a part of one's body rather than simply property that happens to be in constant physical contact with one's body. But what should we say about a prosthetic leg that one removes at the end of the day? The answer to this question is, I think, not obvious. Moreover, the answer has important legal ramifications in at least two areas. First, while it might seem natural to think that that someone who takes your reading glasses has engaged in theft, there is at least something to be said for the thought that someone who takes your prosthetic leg has engaged in assault. In this way, the proper classification of certain crimes depends on settling the nature of the rights in question. Second, notice that certain considerations bearing on the design of public spaces depend in part on how we conceive of the boundaries of people's bodily rights. Accommodating a wheelchair is not on a par with accommodating a mode of transportation, like a bicycle, but instead has the character of accommodating the person herself. One way of making sense of this involves taking a person's rights to her wheelchair to be bodily rights rather than property rights.

To be clear, I am not defending a particular view on how we should regard rights to prosthetic limbs and wheelchairs. Here I am only suggesting that there are meaningful questions to be asked in this area and we need authoritative answers to those questions. Just as we need to settle when we retain bodily rights to body parts that are now physically separate, we need to settle when we gain bodily rights to objects that were once not a part of our bodies.

That is, just as we need rules for bodily alienation, we need rules for bodily incorporation.

This brings us very close to the problem of acquisition posed by property rights. Acquiring a property right places others under a new obligation and, likewise, so does incorporating a body part. I argued in Section II that, even if the indeterminacy problem regarding acquisition does not apply to bodily rights, our bodily rights are defective in a way that justifies the establishment of the state. The conclusion of this section is that bodily rights are in fact subject to an analogue of the indeterminacy problem regarding acquisition, namely an indeterminacy problem posed by the possibility of bodily alienation and incorporation. Thus the extent of the parallel between bodily rights and property rights is even stronger than it might have initially seemed.

Although I have argued for important similarities between bodily rights and property rights, as I noted at the outset significant differences between these two kinds of rights remain. I am going to examine one such difference in the next section. But before turning to that discussion, I want to pause here to consider a potential objection. I have argued that bodily unity plays a more nuanced role in determining the boundaries of bodily rights than may at first be apparent. But one might start to wonder why bodily unity should be significant at all. As I noted above, the right to some kind of control over one's own body is a precondition for engaging in independent action. But why should that control extend to *all* of what we intuitively think of as our bodies?[29] Why, for example, do we automatically have a right to both of our kidneys? In the same way that recognising the indeterminacy problem regarding the boundaries of our bodies opens the door to more extensive bodily rights, it also seems to open the door to less extensive bodily rights.

To respond to this objection, let me first say a bit more about the sense in which having the right to some kind of control over one's body is a precondition for independence. I want to contrast two ways in which having a right to control over one's body might be a precondition for independence. First, consider the 'body as means' interpretation. To the extent that one lacks control over one's body, one is unable to act at all. In this way, control over one's body is a necessary means for one's activity in the world and hence one's independence. While there is something intuitive about this picture, it does not capture our unique relationship with our bodies, for there are other means that are necessary in this sense. We need, for example, air to breathe, food to eat and water to drink in order to function as agents.[30] One might attempt to

[29] I am indebted to AJ Julius for helpful discussions on this point.

[30] I am indebted to Anja Jauernig for pressing me on this point. See also n 4 for a related point.

argue that the innate right to freedom grounds some kind of right to all these things insofar as they are needed for our agency. But I want to set that possibility aside here because I think there is a more direct and unique sense in which the right to some kind of control over our bodies is a precondition for independence.

Let us turn, then, to the second interpretation, the 'body as identity' interpretation. This interpretation is suggested by the comments of Ripstein that I noted earlier. On this interpretation, the sense in which some kind of control over one's body is a precondition for independence is cashed out in terms of the need to identify one as an agent with whom interaction is possible. As I put it earlier, you need some kind of foothold in the world in order for the question of independence from other agents even to arise. Attributing to agents rights to their bodies addresses the need to identify agents as separate beings.

With the 'body as identity' interpretation in mind, let us return to the objection. The objection suggests that we could draw the boundaries of people's bodily rights more narrowly. In other words, we could identify agents with less than their whole bodies. We could, for example, identify agents with their brains (or better, perhaps, their heads, so as to ensure the possibility of interaction with others). Notice that no one would be tempted to identify you with your left foot. The objection gets its plausibility from the thought that agency is possible with much less than your whole body. But this involves slipping back into thinking of the body as a means. When we focus on identifying you with some part of your body, like your brain, things are a bit trickier. Your brain is only a brain, not a mere lump of squishy stuff, insofar as it is a part of a system. And no one is tempted to identify you with the mere lump of brain matter. If we tried to identify you with your brain, we would have in mind a living, active brain and that involves smuggling in the system in which that brain is operating. So, the answer to the question of identification cannot really be less than one's whole body. For this reason, I do not think that ignoring bodily unity altogether is a viable strategy. So, although I believe our bodily rights are indeterminate in the ways I have described, this indeterminacy is not as radical as the above objection suggests.

This means that we need not worry that the state's authority to resolve the indeterminacy problem for our bodily rights could result in the legitimate imposition of a system of compulsory kidney donation while we are living. As long as our kidneys remain physically united with us, the indeterminacy problem regarding bodily alienation and incorporation does not arise. It is worth noticing, though, that this issue becomes more nuanced once we are dead. On the view that I am advocating, it is entirely appropriate for the state to determine when we count as abandoning our body parts and death raises this very question. So, for example, the state might legitimately choose between an opt-in and an opt-out system for posthumous organ donation. My view thus provides a helpful framework for understanding the proper scope of the state's involvement in determining our bodily rights.

IV. TRANSFERRING BODY PARTS

As I indicated, I want to close by considering an important difference between property rights and bodily rights. Your bodily rights have their justification in the innate right to freedom. Although we need rules determining the boundaries of our bodies, it remains the case that bodily rights are not acquired but instead rights that we have simply in virtue of our status as free beings. For this reason, bodily rights are not transferable. This means that you have no direct right to sell your body parts. You may be able to make some parts of your body cease to be parts of your body, thus alienating those parts. But as we saw in the previous section, once you cease to have bodily rights to that part, no property right automatically emerges in its place. So, you may not be the owner of the part you want to sell.

Perhaps more surprisingly, the fact that bodily rights are not transferable also means it is impossible to directly donate your body parts to others.[31] This is, I think, a rather counterintuitive result. To take a commonplace example, if I want to donate my blood or my hair, surely I should be able to.

There are ways to get around this prohibition that allow something that looks very much like sale or donation. First, perhaps I may alienate part of my body in a way that makes me very likely to be able to claim the part as my property. Suppose, for example, that I cut off my own hair, while holding it in my hand the whole time. Although in principle anyone could now acquire a property right to the hair, since I maintain control over the hair, I never give anyone else an opportunity to claim it as property. Now I may sell or donate the hair as I see fit.

Second, perhaps I may alienate the part in a way that makes you very likely to be able to claim the part as property. Suppose, for example, that I allow you to cut off my hair and you hold it as you do that. Since you have control over the hair at the moment that I alienate it, you never give anyone else an

[31] Notice that this marks a difference between the problem I am focusing on and the more standard objection to commodifying an object. That objection focuses on distinguishing objects that may be properly bought and sold from those that should be given only as gifts. See, eg, E Anderson, 'The Ethical Limitations of the Market' (1990) 6 *Economics and Philosophy*, 179–205. I am arguing against the possibility of any kind of direct transfer of bodily rights, including gift giving. But since I argue that it is possible to indirectly transfer bodily rights, the question of whether there is an ethical objection to selling rather than giving those rights can be resituated, and here I leave open the answer to that question.

opportunity to claim it as property. I may agree to let you touch my hair in this way only on the condition that you pay me. So, although I cannot sell you the right to my hair directly, I can sell you the right to do something that practically ensures that you will be able to acquire a right to the hair.

More complicated cases may involve more intermediary contracts, but have essentially the same form. If I want to give you my kidney, I may need to contract with the doctors and nurses to allow them to remove it only on the condition that they then place it in you. And I may need to give you the right to keep it until my bodily right ceases and yours begins.

Given that we can circuitously accomplish the sale or donation of our body parts, what is the point of making us jump through these hoops? Doesn't the seemingly needless complexity of the system tell against it? I do not think that it does when you recall the alternatives. The view on which rights to our bodies are property rights leaves it mysterious why we happen to own our bodies. This is not merely a worry that we might be able to sell our bodies and hence ourselves into slavery. That worry already presupposes an answer to the prior question of why we are the first owners of our bodies and so in a position to sell our bodies. Why, for example, do our parents not own our bodies? It seems clear, then, that our rights to our bodies must be innate rather than acquired. Once we observe that these two very different kinds of rights are possible, we should not be surprised by the complexity of their interaction. To put the same point differently, once we observe that our bodies cannot be mere objects in the world available for anyone's potential use, we should not be surprised that it is difficult to treat them as if they were. So, while the complexity of bodily rights may initially seem counterintuitive, this complexity is needed to capture the special status of bodily rights.

V. CONCLUSION

I hope to have shown that on a Kantian view our bodily rights are both more and less like property rights than it may first appear. Bodily rights are more like property rights in that they involve similar defects in the state of nature and can therefore do the same work in justifying the establishment of the state. They are less like property rights in that they cannot be transferred. These two conclusions suggest a unique conception of bodily rights, one on which our bodily rights are politically constructed and yet have a form that is determined by the requirements of our freedom.

3

A Regime of Equal Private Freedom? Individual Rights and Public Law in Ripstein's Force and Freedom

KATRIN FLIKSCHUH

I. FREEDOM AND THE STATE: TWO ALTERNATIVE INTERPRETATIONS

THERE ARE TWO alternative ways of interpreting the relation between external freedom and the state in Kant. One views the state as a means to securing external freedom rights, the other treats external freedom claims as a means to establishing the state. These are non-equivalent interpretations: although the relevant relata—'freedom' and 'the state'—are the same in both, the assumed direction of fit in the means–ends relation between them is both times the inverse of the other. On the first view, individual freedom rights rule supreme; on the second, establishing a civil condition is paramount. One might think the distinction one without a difference: one might think that to establish the Kantian civil condition *just is* to secure individual freedom claims.[1] Securement of freedom rights might then be thought to be indistinguishable, as end, from state establishment. Despite its apparent attractions, one should approach this third interpretive possibility with caution: it is liable to fudge the difference between individualistic and non-individualistic ends in Kant's morality of Right.

I myself favour the second of the two interpretations; it is more in keeping with Kant's non-individualistic conception of the ends of individual

[1] 'Just is' claims of this sort are not uncommon in Kant interpretation. A prominent line of interpretation in relation to Kant's ethics, for example, holds that morally good choice 'just is' perfectly rational choice. On this view, 'perfect' hypothetical reasoning is indistinguishable from moral reasoning. *cf* C Korsgaard, *The Sources of Normativity* (Cambridge, Cambridge University Press, 1992). For an excellent critique of this line of interpretation, see J Timmermann, 'Value without Regress. Kant's "Formula of Humanity" Revisited' (2006) 14 *European Journal of Philosophy* 69–93.

moral agency, including political agency.[2] On my preferred view, although I shall not thematise it here, even the establishment of a series of individual states is strictly speaking no more than one element of the establishment of a thoroughgoing system of Right—thoroughgoing in the sense of spanning the circumference of the entire earth. Rights-relations between individuals at state level must be supplemented by rights-relations between states and these by rights-relations between persons across states. Systematic rights-connectedness at all three levels of public Right, not securement of individual freedom rights, is on this interpretation the final end of Kant's morality of Right.

Nonetheless, versions of the first reading are currently on the ascendant, especially in recent normative Kantianism. Here, state establishment is seen as justified so long as it secures individual freedom rights. Some even regard securement of individual freedom rights as the only end of a Kantian state, arguing that Kant's entire philosophy of Right derives from the innate Right to freedom of each as sole foundational premise.[3] On this account, no state action is justified that is not ultimately traceable to respect for and protection of the innate Right to freedom of each.

How does Arthur Ripstein's *Force and Freedom* fit into this interpretive dispute? Some early readers of Ripstein's book decried his position as libertarian in spirit.[4] This is mistaken. Acknowledgement of entrance into the civil condition as a necessary condition of possible freedom rights is now widely recognised as basic to Kant's position in the *Doctrine of Right*.[5] Ripstein is at pains throughout his book to emphasise the conceptual and moral necessity of public lawmaking to securing individual freedom rights.[6] This emphasis on state establishment as necessary to securing individual freedom immediately

[2] I think of political agency as a species of moral agency, though distinct from ethics. *cf* K Flikschuh, 'Justice without Virtue', in L Denis (ed), *Kant's Metaphysics of Morals. A Critical Guide* (Cambridge, Cambridge University Press, 2010) 51–70.

[3] *cf* L-P Hodgson, 'Kant on the Right to Freedom: A Defense' (2010) 120 *Ethics* 791–819. Similarly, J Pallikkathayil, 'Deriving Morality from Politics: Rethinking the Formula of Humanity' (2010) 121 *Ethics* 116–47.

[4] This was a dominant complaint amongst members of a reading group on *Force and Freedom* held in the Philosophy Department of King's College London in 2009.

[5] This is not to deny that there is nonetheless considerable dispute concerning the details of Kant's argument to his effect.

[6] 'Securing freedom rights' can have either of two meanings in this context: either freedom rights that are already morally vindicated in the pre-civil condition are given juridical protection through entrance into the civil condition, or freedom claims in the pre-civil condition can be fully vindicated only through entrance into the civil condition. I use 'securement' in the second of these two senses—Ripstein seems to me to share this view. For a position closer to the first meaning of 'securement', see S Byrd and J Hruschka, *Kant's Doctrine of Right. A Commentary* (Cambridge, Cambridge University Press 2010).

distinguishes his account from anything approximating a libertarian position. But does Ripstein endorse the first or the second of the two mentioned conceptions of the ends of political morality? Much in the book speaks in favour of the first view. Indeed, his sympathetic critics, far from branding him a libertarian, read him (and Kant) as championing the cause of individual freedom within the framework of a broadly liberal democratic state. However, much in Ripstein's book also speaks against this—to many readers intuitively pleasing— contemporary reading of Kant. While Ripstein's normative explication of innate Right by appeal to the notion of 'purposiveness' supports the first interpretation, his underlying defence of what, paraphrasing Jeremy Waldron, one might call the 'dignity of public lawmaking'[7] pushes his position closer to the second view.

Perhaps Ripstein's is that elusive third reading that gives us the best of both worlds: a commitment to individual freedom *through* a commitment to public lawmaking? As indicated, this apparent reconciliation of the two positions easily fudges the distinction between individualistic and non-individualistic political ends. It is more likely that Ripstein is ambivalent between either the freedom-based view or the public-law-based position. In what follows, I shall argue that for all his apparent emphasis on securing a regime of equal private freedom, Ripstein can be read as offering an extended Kantian defence of the dignity of public lawmaking and of the possible achievement, by means of public lawmaking, of rights-connectedness rather than individual freedom rights. Over the next three sections, I shall examine the role of purposiveness in Ripstein's account of the innate right to freedom of each and how it affects his subsequent discussion of public lawmaking, before going on to offer an alternative reading of innate Right, implicit in much of *Force and Freedom*, but with rather different implications for the point and purpose of public lawmaking. It goes without saying that Ripstein's book is rich in interpretive detail and philosophical nuance; I will not be able to do the book justice here; my focus will be quite selective, with most of my direct attention devoted to chapters 2 and 8.

II. INNATE RIGHT, INDEPENDENCE AND PURPOSIVENESS

It is now widely agreed that the property argument in Part I of the *Doctrine of Right*, not Kant's statement of innate Right in the Introduction, generates the (enforceable) obligation to enter with all others into a civil condition as the only condition in which provisionally valid rights claims can be given the

[7] J Waldron, *The Dignity of Legislation* (Cambridge, Cambridge University Press, 1999).

peremptory status of 'strict Right'. Nonetheless, how precisely one interprets the function of the property argument in relation to state establishment is increasingly thought to depend on how one conceives the prior relation between innate and acquired Right. In the Introduction to the *Doctrine of Right* Kant offers the following specification of the innate right to freedom of each:

> Freedom (independence from being constrained by another's choice), insofar as it can coexist with the freedom of every other in accordance with a universal law, is the only original right belonging to every man by virtue of his humanity. (*MM* 6: 237)

Disconcertingly, after a few elaborative remarks on the 'authorisations' connected with innate Right, Kant informs his readers that he has 'thrown [innate Right] into the prolegomena': although it forms part of the 'highest division of rights' in general, it can form no part of the division of the *Doctrine of Right.* This for the seemingly spurious reason that in contrast to the threefold classification of acquired rights, 'there is only *one* innate right' (*MM* 6: 238). Given Kant's explicit if unexpected exclusion of innate Right from the 'divisions' of the *Doctrine of Right*, how is one to understand the relation between innate and acquired Right—ie that latter class within the general division of rights which *is* central to the *Doctrine of Right*?

The scholarly literature is largely silent on this difficult systematic issue.[8] Given the centrality of the property argument, most exegetical attention to date has focused on those portions of the text. Kant scholars are not unaware of the innate right to freedom of each—to the contrary, most are all too aware of Kant's peculiar banishment of it to the 'prolegomena': the silence is a mark of interpretive reticence. This reticence contrasts with often forthright assumptions about innate Right in the burgeoning normative literature, where it is frequently simply presumed to function as the (unargued) foundational premise to the ensuing property argument. Interpretive claims to the effect that Kant simply affirms a right to freedom of each as the basis of all further rights are increasingly common.[9]

We can distinguish between foundationalist and non-foundationalist approaches to the innate right of each.[10] Foundationalist approaches treat

[8] But see most recently B Ludwig, 'Die Einteilung der Metaphysik der Sitten im Allgemeinen und die der Metaphysischen Anfangsgruende der Tugendlehre im Besonderen' (forthcoming).

[9] *cf* Hodgson (n 3); Pallikkathayil (n 3); A Stilz, 'Nations, States, and Territory' (2011) 121 *Ethics* 572.

[10] This return to foundationalist reasoning in relation to Kant's philosophy of law is ironic given the literature's insistence upon Kantian constructivism in relation to other of his work in practical philosophy.

the innate right to freedom of each as the unarguable normative premise of everything else that is argued for in the *Doctrine of Right*. The right is treated as intuitively self-evident or as grounded in or based upon rights-creating features or attributes of persons that are in turn intuitively self-evident. The assumption is either that persons have a right to freedom merely in virtue of being persons, or that they have such a right in virtue of their capacity to set and pursue ends, or their capacity for rational agency. By contrast, the non-foundationalist approach to innate Right as I shall here understand it does not regard it as itself constituting or as responding to a morally essential feature or capacity of individual personhood. Instead, the innate right to freedom of each specifies a particular form of moral relation between persons. Persons have rights, on this view, not because of rights-creating attributes they possess but insofar as they relate to other persons, and other persons relate to them, in a particular kind of way. For example, a person has a right to property in things not because having such rights is necessary to a person's exercise of a capacity to choose his or her own ends but just in case others respond to the person's property claim in a relevantly appropriate way. Crucial to the non-foundationalist view is the thought that what matters morally, in relation to rights, is the rights relation itself.[11]

Ripstein tackles the innate right to freedom of each most fully in chapter 2 of *Force and Freedom*. Much of what he says can be read as foundationalist in spirit. He holds, for example, that

> [b]y making the innate right to freedom the basis of any further rights, Kant imposes an extreme demand for unity on his account of political justice. The rights that each person has against others must be derived from it, as must the fundamental constitutional rights that protect political freedoms and freedom of religion. The same right to independence also limits state action to genuinely public purposes and the means that the state may use in achieving them. In particular, state power may not be used to subject one private person to the choice of another.[12]

The attribution to Kant of an 'extreme demand for unity', and the view of all further rights as derivable from the innate right of each as their 'basis',

[11] In *Force and Freedom*, Ripstein's property rights account is predominantly relational, though as we shall see below, his inclusion of 'purposiveness' in relation to innate Right distorts his rights relationalism: A Ripstein, *Force and Freedom: Kant's Legal and Political Philosophy* (Cambridge, MA, Harvard University Press, 2009) (hereinafter *FF*). Other relational readings of Kant's practical philosophy include S Darwall, *The Second Person Standpoint. Morality, Respect and Accountability* (Cambridge, MA, Harvard University Press, 2006), and O O'Neill *Bounds of Justice* (Cambridge, Cambridge University Press, 2000). Although O'Neill refers to hers as a practical or constructivist approach to practical reasoning, I believe her emphasis on the quality of moral relations between persons to take the most purely relational of current Kant interpretations.

[12] Ripstein, *FF*, 31.

suggests a conception of innate Right as first or founding principle. Later on in the same chapter, Ripstein explicates the innate right of each with reference to persons' power to set and pursue whatever ends they see fit, seemingly grounding it in the rights-creating individual capacity for 'purposiveness'.[13] However, Ripstein is not unambivalently foundationalist about it. While the innate right to freedom, understood as each person's independence from another's arbitrary power of choice, is said to 'carry the justificatory burden of the entire argument',[14] Ripstein interprets the independence requirement itself relationally, not attributively. Kantian independence is not a good to be promoted, but a moral claim of a kind that 'constrains the conduct of others'. Persons have an innate right to freedom against one another, not absolutely. A right to independence is not responsive to features or capacities of persons considered individually. Your independence from my arbitrary power of choice over you (and vice versa) can only be explicated as specifying a moral relation of a particular kind between you and me:

> Kant's account of independence contrasts with more robust conceptions of autonomy, which sometimes represent it as a feature of a particular agent. On this conception, if there were only one person in the world, it would make sense to ask whether and to what extent that person was autonomous. Kantian independence is not a feature of the individual person considered in isolation, but of relations between persons.[15]

One might accept this relational specification of innate Right as a reciprocal independence claim each raises against everyone else. One might still ask: in virtue of what feature about them do agents reciprocally claim independence from one another? One possible answer is that the question misses the point of a relational rights specification: to enquire into the grounds of the rights relation is to overlook the normative significance of the relation itself. Alternatively, one might cast about for a likely ground. *Force and Freedom* can be read as answering the question as to the ground with reference to the capacity for 'purposiveness' understood as a person's 'freedom to decide how to use the powers [he] ha[s]'.[16] In that case, we reciprocally raise independence claims against one another because we each have a capacity for purposiveness.

This response to the demand for a ground of reciprocal independence claims yields an impure relational reading of innate Right. According to it, the independence claim is construed relationally while the ground of that claim is

13 ibid, 39.
14 ibid, 14.
15 ibid, 15.
16 ibid, 40.

specified with reference to an individually held attribute or capacity. Ripstein, however, contends that 'independence' and 'purposiveness' are to be understood as equivalent terms in the context of innate Right: '[T]he protection of independence and the prohibition of one person deciding what purposes another will pursue stand in a relation of equivalence rather than of means to an end.'[17] The thought is that to acknowledge a person as independent from others' arbitrary power of choice *just is* to acknowledge his capacity to set and pursue his own ends: '[T]o be your own master is to have no *other* master.'[18] Our acknowledgement of a person's independence is not to be thought of as *responsive* to an independently acknowledged capacity for purposiveness. Rather, acknowledgement of purposiveness—one's being one's own master—*is the same as* acknowledgement of independence. In that case, what matters morally is not that persons have a capacity for purposiveness but that others act towards them as beings who can choose and pursue their own ends. Individual purposiveness can be morally significant, on a relational reading, only under conditions of coexistence; it cannot be of intrinsic moral value.

I struggle with Ripstein's equivalence claim. It makes sense to me to construe the independence claim relationally: a claim to independence from others' arbitrary power of choice is unintelligible absent coexistence. But I am not persuaded that purposiveness is more intelligibly construed relationally than non-relationally: if someone's purposiveness matters morally, it would seem to matter whether or not coexistence obtains. If people can set their own ends, they can do so whether or not others are around, and if it matters morally that they set their own ends, it matters whether or not others are around. If purposiveness matters, this is not because we stand (or should stand) in some sort of 'purposiveness relation' to one another.

Nor am I sure that to acknowledge a person's independence from another's arbitrary power of choice *just is* to acknowledge her purposiveness: I can acknowledge that I have no business exercising my power of choice over another without in so doing acknowledging her capacity to set her own ends. I may lack that sort of authority over her despite her lacking the capacity to choose and pursue her own ends. I can see why Ripstein does not want to invoke a foundationalist notion of purposiveness that conceives it as a rights-grounding capacity of individual persons which *entails* the demand for independence. In that case, the innate right of each would be conceived foundationally, not relationally. But on a relational understanding of innate Right, why invoke the notion of purposiveness at all?

[17] ibid, 34/5.
[18] ibid, 36.

Kant does not mention purposiveness in relation to the innate right of each. He does not say that independence and purposiveness 'stand in a relation of equivalence'. He does, however, say that the innate right to freedom of each contains a number of 'authorizations' that are 'not really distinct' from the innate right (*MM* 6: 238). Among these he lists a person's 'quality of being his own master'. This sounds similar to Ripstein's equivalence claim: the claim to independence from others' arbitrary power of choice is 'not really distinct from' the claim to being treated by them as one who is his own master. In both cases, the basic idea appears to be that to claim a right to independence from others' power of choice *just is* to claim a right to being treated by them as in possession of relevant faculties of self-governance.

Still, being treated as one who is his own master is not quite the same, at least in the given context, as being treated as one with the power to set and pursue his own ends. In the juridical context, being one's own master—being in command of oneself—points to one's capacity for culpability, ie to one's capacity for having one's actions—as deeds (*Taten*)—attributed to one (cf *MM* 6: 227). Conversely, one cannot be held responsible for any deeds which one did not commit—a further 'authorization' of 'being beyond reproach originally' (*Unbescholtenheit*) (cf *MM* 6: 238) that attaches to the innate right of each as 'not really distinct from it'.

Kant's reference to one's being treated as being one's own master thus seems to have a narrower, specifically juridical function compared to Ripstein's wider and substantive notion of purposiveness. To Kant's notion of being in command of oneself attaches the idea of culpability for one's actions; associated with Ripstein's notion of purposiveness is the more general thought of one's being left to do as one sees fit. My intention here it not to contrast the narrow juridical notion of capacity for culpability with the wider moral capacity for purposiveness. The point of reverting to the text is simply to ask what support there may be for Ripstein's startling equivalence claim. There is clearly some such support in Kant's suggestion that the independence claim is closely connected with a notion of command over one's actions. Nevertheless, Kant does not say that the self-mastery claim is *equivalent* to the independence claim; the thought appears to be that a claim to independence implies or contains attributability of their actions to agents—legal responsibility for action is analytic, in Kant's sense, to the independence claim. This is not to say that the two are equivalent, for independence may contain conceptual marks and normative 'authorizations' in addition to that of responsibility for one's actions.

Even aside from the issue of textual support, the substantive thickness of purposiveness has the effect of shifting the focus from Ripstein's initial emphasis on the relational structure of innate right towards a decidedly more foundationalist reading. It is not surprising if the subsequent discussion centres increasingly around protections which the innate right is said to afford each person against unwanted intrusion by others. Particularly striking is Ripstein's frequent resort to the idea of a person's control over his/her own body, and to a person's own body as an innate resource. Ripstein speaks of the innate right of each as summing to

> a system of equal freedom … in which each person is free to use his or her powers, individually or cooperatively, to set his or her purposes, and no one is allowed to compel others to use their powers in a way designed to advance or accommodate any other person's purposes.[19]

A person's innate powers include their intellectual and physical capacities: '[A]t the level of innate right, your right to freedom protects your purposiveness—your capacity to choose the ends you will use your means to pursue—against the choices of others.'[20] Again, 'your freedom to choose your own purposes just is your freedom to decide how to use the powers you have'.[21] And 'your person—your body—is yours to use for your own purposes, and if I take it upon myself to touch you without your permission, I use it for a purpose you haven't authorised'.[22] From an initial relational specification of the innate right as the claim to independence from another's arbitrary power of choice we appear to have moved—via the notion of purposiveness—to something of an inventory of what it is that can be said to belong to each of us innately—ie through no commission of any act of yours—and what it would therefore be wrong of others to use without one's consent. These 'innate possessions' (inner mine) include each person's innate talents and capacities as well as his or her physical bodies and associated powers. A system of equal innate freedom thus has to be conceived as one in which each person refrains from interfering with everyone else's self-referential use of his or her innate powers of control or innate possessions.

III. A SYSTEM OF EQUAL PRIVATE FREEDOM

By the end of chapter 2 of *Force and Freedom*, a dominant impression has emerged of the innate right to freedom as affirming each person's innate domain of external freedom, including, in particular, each person's powers of control over her own body and associated physical and mental capacities and talents. With respect to this innate freedom domain each is sovereign,[23]

19 Ripstein, *FF*, 33.
20 ibid, 33–34.
21 ibid, 40.
22 ibid, 45.
23 ibid, 35.

such that others' non-consensual interference with another's body and powers constitutes a violation of her innate right. The ensuing analysis of property rights—acquired Right—now looks set to tackle the question of how persons might rightfully extend their innate albeit highly limited domains of external freedom to cover rights in things that are acquired, ie not possessed innately.[24] I shall not here consider Ripstein's account of property rights; I want merely to note that Ripstein's ambivalent approach to innate Right impacts on his analysis of acquired Right in a manner he may not intend: given the focus on unhindered use of innate powers in the discussion of innate Right, readers may easily be moved to interpret acquired Right as seeking to extend innate powers of control over the external world and not, as I think Ripstein intends, as illustrating the morally problematic effects of our choices on others.

Instead of continuing with Ripstein's analysis of Kantian property rights, I want now to turn to chapter 8 of *Force and Freedom*, which is entitled 'Roads of Freedom' and which deals with certain aspects of public law-making in the established Kantian state. Here Ripstein's striking characterisation of public policy-making as aimed at securing a 'regime of equal private freedom' mirrors the earlier gloss on the innate right to freedom of each as envisaging a 'system of equal freedom'. The general concern of chapter 8 is with 'the class of purely public powers traditionally grouped under police powers'.[25] The particular focus is on the public provision of a system of public roads as illustration of a more general point Ripstein wants to make, namely that:

> the fundamental rationale for the exercise of the police power is to create a regime of equal private freedom. In order to do so, the state must create and sustain the systematic preconditions both of the exercise of private freedom and of the conditions of its ability to provide them.[26]

This characterisation of their 'fundamental rationale' is especially striking once we consider that the mentioned 'police powers' are the etymological and functional predecessor to what is today referred to as public policy-making.[27]

[24] For a particularly powerful Lockean account along those lines, see S Wheeler, 'Natural Body Rights as Property Rights' (1980) XIV *Nous* 171–94. Indeed, those who do detect libertarian elements in *Force and Freedom* can point to passages in which Ripstein does come quite close to depicting rights in external possession as analogous to—and possibly even as an extension of—rights in one's body. For example, 'the normative basis of acquired rights depends on your right to your own person, but rights to external objects are not reducible to your right in your person' (*FF*, 57 though the qualification distances Ripstein from a Wheeler-like account); 'your rights to property parallel your right to your person' (*FF*, 80); 'your body is your person and it constrains others … your property rights constrains others' (*FF*, 91).

[25] Ripstein, *FF*, 232–33.

[26] ibid, 238.

[27] My thanks to Martin Lodge for pointing this out to me.

According to Ripstein, therefore, the Kantian state envisages a mode of public policy-making that is focused fundamentally on the creation and re-creation of a regime of equal *private* freedom. This is a highly disaggregative approach to public policy—one which may remind recent generations of British citizens of the Thatcherite slogan that there is 'no such thing as society'. I do not believe that Ripstein intends the latter connotation—in the next two sections I shall say more about what I believe he intends instead. The idea of public policies as justifiable only to the extent to which such policies create and maintain a regime of equal private freedom is nonetheless consistent with the drift towards the foundationalist reading of the innate right of each in chapter 2.[28]

Consider Ripstein's road example, which is meant to demonstrate the indispensability in general of public authority and provision to the enjoyment of private freedom of choice and action. By now, of course, we are beyond mere reliance on the innate right to freedom of each and have absorbed the property argument with its extension of individual powers of control over external objects of their choice. Ripstein asks his readers to imagine a situation in which each rightfully owns one of a number of adjoining plots of land. Just as each has undisputed sovereignty over her body and related innate powers, so each here is to be thought of as possessing undisputed sovereign control over his particular externally owned plot of land. He can do on it and with it as he pleases, subject to desisting from interfering with his neighbour's equally doing as she pleases on and with her own plot of land.[29] Neighbours can make mutually agreeable arrangements regarding their plots of land: they can trade

[28] It is hard not suspect that the growing insistence on individual freedom rights as sole foundation of the 'Kantian state' ends in a *reductio ad absurdum* when it comes to considering public policy-making in such a state. For all my sympathies with Ripstein's criticisms of Ronald Dworkin and Charles Taylor's instrumental freedom conceptions at the start of chapter 8, it is hard not to suspect that these criticisms do not in the end miss the mark somewhat, given Ripstein's subsequent discussion of the foundations of public policy-making. If these foundations really are to lie in individual freedom of choice and action, it is hard to see how the 'Kantian state' thus conceived can generate anything like the idea of a 'public domain'.

[29] Indeed, according to Ripstein, so long as neither interferes with the other's plot of land—strictly, with the other's property right in his or her own plot of land—the creation of certain externalities for one another is not, as such, non-rightful. Your garden shed may create a dank, shadowy corner on my adjoining plot of land, for example. I cannot rightfully insist that you take down your shed on the grounds that your having it deprives me of sun. Nor on the other hand, can you claim a share of the profits if I start a mushroom farm in the shadowy corner provided by your shed on my plot. This seems to me far too stringent as an aspect of any metaphysics of Right. Whether or not one can rightfully complain that certain structures in another's adjoining plot deprive one of sun surely depends on the particular positive legislation of one's country of residence. In England, for example, one certainly can, under certain circumstances, legally compel one's neighbour not to cut up certain structures, or to fell trees, when these unreasonably affect one's access to sunlight.

one another's produce; invite each other onto one another's plot of land, and so on and so forth. But neither may trespass on the other's plot without his or her consent: that would be equivalent to touching a person's body without her consent.

Imagine you wish to visit a friend on his non-adjoining plot of land: this requires you to cross the plot of a neighbour situated between your plot and that of your friend. It is in this neighbour's power to grant or withhold consent. Even if this neighbour routinely consents to your and your friend's crossing his plot for the purpose of mutual visits between the two of you, your actions are not independent of the arbitrary choice of your neighbour who could at any point change his mind. Despite each of you possessing plots of land—despite the extension of each your innate right to rights over external objects—you are still not independent of others' arbitrary powers of choice over you. Generalising, we can say that, in the absence of some omnilateral authority with the capacity to bind all equally, 'every person is systematically subject to the choice of others'.[30] In the particular case at hand, 'the solution to th[e] problem is obvious: roads, understood as a system of public rights of way, guaranteeing that there is a path from every piece of privately held land to every other'.[31] The function of public roads, then, is to enable private persons to go about their rightful business unhindered by others' arbitrary exercise of power of choice over them.

It is, of course, fanciful to imagine a number of adjoining privately owned plots of land in relation to which a system of public roads is *subsequently* introduced. But the intended point is a conceptual one: no freedom (as independence) without public coercive authority to regulate the equal freedom claims of everyone. Yet it is one thing to say that any system of external freedom presupposes a public authority, another to say that it is the end of any legitimate public authority to create and maintain a system of equal private freedom. The latter is a normative, not a conceptual point. One question that arises in relation to the normative aspect of Ripstein's road example concerns its generalisability. Is the public provision of schools, say, or of a functioning healthcare system, of unemployment benefits or state pension schemes, traffic regulations or rubbish collection, etc, best thought of as aiming at the creation and maintenance of a system of equal private freedom?

In general, some aspects of public policy-making in liberal societies will be more preoccupied with questions about individual freedom than others. The oversight of religious education in state schools may be an example where

[30] Ripstein, *FF*, 247.
[31] ibid, 248.

individual freedom concerns weigh relatively heavily (though by no means exclusively!). Other policy areas will try to get around what is in fact often the *public nuisance* of individual choice through introduction of subtle incentives schemes that do exert pressure for policy-confirming behaviour on non-consenting citizens: environmentally friendly rubbish collection springs to mind, with its perennial attempts to induce people into sorting their waste in a manner that allows for recycling. Public health schemes with their ever-rising costs and related hard social and medical choices are a further example: are we after a regime of equal private freedom here, or concerned with the maintenance of a reasonably healthy population overall, given the positive effects of public health on social matters of state more generally?

In the *Doctrine of Right* Kant mentions some police powers, though his remarks strike me as too underdeveloped to draw any firm conclusions, one way or the other, about his considered views on the ends of public policy-making. The sort of things he does say tend towards a view of the state as entitled to the public regulation of individual behaviour and as obliged to ensure provision of public benefits on the grounds that such regulation and duties of public care are necessary to ensure *its*—ie the state's—continued survival. Thus, having noted the 'supreme commander's' right to impose taxes in support of organisations providing for the poor, foundling homes and church organisations, Kant says that:

> The general will of the people has united itself into a society which is to maintain *itself* perpetually; and for this end it has submitted itself to the internal authority of the state in order to maintain those members of the society who are unable to maintain themselves. *For reasons of state* the government is therefore authorized to constrain the wealthy to provide the means of sustenance to those who are unable even to provide for their most necessary natural needs. The wealthy have acquired an *obligation to the commonwealth*, since they owe their existence to an act of submitting to its protection and care, which they need in order to live; *on this obligation the state now bases its right to contribute what is theirs to maintaining their fellow citizens*. (*MM* 6:326, emphases added)

The emphases in this passage are not on the creation and maintenance of a system of equal private freedom but on the 'commonwealth', and on the obligations which the wealthy owe the poor as fellow citizens, not as individual private persons each with their own particular ends to pursue.

IV. INNATE RIGHT WITHOUT PURPOSIVENESS

Over the last two sections I have provided textual evidence from chapters 2 and 8 of *Force and Freedom* as supporting an increasingly dominant reading of Kant's philosophy of Right according to which the basic justificatory rationale for the state's public coercive authority is its capacity to secure individual freedom rights. Its relational beginnings notwithstanding, Ripstein's account of the innate right to freedom is given a foundationalist direction through his subsequent elaboration of independence in terms of purposiveness. In contrast to the notion of independence itself, his attempted relational reading of the latter is unpersuasive. In chapter 8, Ripstein advances a model of public policy-making based on an ingenious road-building example that is meant to exemplify the idea of a public regime of equal private freedom. Again, its generalisability as a public policy model as well as its plausibility as a reading of Kant's position seem to me to be contestable.

Ripstein's view of the 'fundamental rationale' of police powers as lying in the creation of a regime of equal private freedom is in any case given considerable modification. In the concluding sections of chapter 8 Ripstein discusses 'mandatory participation', explaining that individual citizens can be expected and indeed compelled to do their 'fair share'. In justification of such compulsion, Ripstein speaks not of a regime of equal private freedom but of the obligation to 'sustain a rightful condition'. The shift occurs in the context of the rejection of a welfarist approach to public policy-making: 'Instead of analysing public health or national defense in terms of benefits and burdens, it is better to assimilate them to the example of roads. They are required to sustain a rightful condition.'[32] The shift is even more marked in Ripstein's subsequent remark that 'the state's mandate to protect public health follows from its mandate to seek *its own* preservation'.[33]

This last remark is in keeping with Kant's own comments on the state's legitimate concern to preserve *itself*. One may insist that ensuring the maintenance of a rightful condition 'just is' to secure a regime of equal private freedom. As we saw in relation to innate Right, however, such equivalence claims are often doubtful on reflection. In this section and the next I want to suggest that an alternative explanation is available for Ripstein's at times seemingly insistent focus on individuals' powers of control and the related view of the state's concern to create a regime of equal private freedom. In this section I sketch a purely relational reading of the innate right to freedom of each that construes it as a claim of each to juridical equality vis-à-vis all others; in the next section I then argue that it is possible to read Ripstein's emphasis on a clear demarcation of each person's substantive rights from those of everyone else in terms of the self-limiting character of public law-making.

[32] ibid., 259.
[33] ibid, 261, emphasis added.

Let me start from Kant's claim in the Introduction to the *Doctrine of Right* that a morality of Right must determine what belongs to each 'with mathematical exactitude'. Much of what Ripstein says about the need for a strict demarcation of individuals' rights is reminiscent of this particular comment of Kant's. Consider the relevant paragraph in the *Doctrine of Right* more fully. Kant has just affirmed an analytic connection between Right and coercion: '[T]here is connected with right by the principle of contradiction an authorization to coerce someone who infringes upon it' (*MM* 6: 231). The ensuing paragraph explicates the assertoric statement that 'a strict right can also be represented as the possibility of a fully reciprocal use of coercion that is consistent with everyone's freedom in accordance with universal laws'. Here, use of coercion is non-punitive: use of coercion can *also* be represented as freedom enabling. Kant then constructs a 'representation' of a system of Right, relying on the analogy with a 'mathematical construction':

> The law of a reciprocal coercion necessarily in accord with the freedom of everyone under the principle of universal freedom is, as it were, the construction of that concept, that is, the representation of it in pure intuition a priori, by analogy with presenting the possibility of bodies moving freely under the law of the equality of action and reaction. In pure mathematics we cannot derive the properties of its objects immediately from concepts but can discover them only by constructing concepts. Similarly, it is no so much the concept of right as rather a fully reciprocal and equal coercion brought under a universal law and consistent with it that makes the presentation of that concept possible. (*MM* 6: 233)

Much is obscure in this passage—most of it beyond analysis and interpretation in the present context. But the claim that a doctrine of Right assigns what belongs to each 'with mathematical exactitude' occurs in this context. I here want to consider a purely relational reading of innate Right from the perspective of the mentioned 'construction' of a system of Right. Let us say, summarily, that the 'construction' of a system of Right has as its constitutive elements the general concept of Right (set out earlier in the text at *MM* 6: 230), the analytically related concept of coercion (given at *MM* 6: 231), and the idea of law-governed freedom (as articulated in the universal principle of Right at *MM* 6: 230–31). The mentioned 'construction' represents each rights claimant as standing in a relation of reciprocal coercion to all other rights claimants under a relevant universal law conceived in analogy with the causal law of the 'equality of action and reaction'. The resulting representation 'in pure intuition a priori' of a 'system' of law-governed reciprocal coercion constitutes the general 'schema' of a rightful condition.[34] That schema represents each rights

[34] On schemas, see *Critique of Pure Reason*, A137–47/B176–87.

claimant as standing in an externally law-governed connection with all other rights claimants. Now my contention is that, under this schema, what belongs to each *innately* is simply a function of each person's position relative to that of everyone else in that schema. What belongs to each innately has nothing to do with purposiveness but concerns the juridical relation in which each stands, within the constructed schema, relative to everyone else. Each stands in a relation of juridical equality vis-à-vis everyone else: no one is subject to anyone's arbitrary will and each is capable, therefore, of having her own actions, and only her own actions, attributed to her.

On the interpretation just sketched, innate Right specifies a purely formal, purely juridical relation between persons as possible bearers of rights.[35] Material claims about innate powers and capacities, or about persons' unilateral use of them, are irrelevant to the innate right to freedom of each. The latter merely affirms the legitimate claim of each to being treated by all others as *juridically* equal to all others within a possible system of Right. Ripstein is thus mistaken to depict the innate Right of each as affirming a set of physical and mental powers and capacities which belong to each innately. Why, then, may it still be possible to read *Force and Freedom* as consistent with the interpretation of innate Right just sketched? As we shall see more fully in the next section, the answer has to do with the dignity of public law-making.

V. THE DIGNITY OF PUBLIC LAW-MAKING

In the preceding section I sketched a relational account of innate Right, which conceives of the innate Right to freedom of each person as the claim of each to juridical equality vis-à-vis all others in any possible system of Right. This account predicates no rights-grounding capacities or powers of claimants in virtue of which they can each be said to have such a right, relationally or otherwise construed. The claim to juridical equality is a moral claim raised against others to being treated by them in certain ways. The account is consistent with Ripstein's relational specification of innate Right's independence claim but rejects Ripstein's further specification of independence as equivalent to purposiveness—a substantive, attributive notion that contravenes the requirements of a purely relational account.

Innate Right as here understood is thus *purely* relational and hence formal: no substantive entitlements attach to it. This means that innate Right is empirically non-instantiable—it specifies a purely moral, hence intelligible, rights

[35] I develop this analysis more fully in 'Originally Mine? Innate and Acquired Right in Kant's Doctrine of Right' (unpublished manuscript).

relation between persons. But in that case, we confront a problem. The morality of Right is an external morality, i.e. one concerned with the public regulation of outward conduct of persons toward one another. Such an external morality is coercively enforceable: persons can be compelled by the relevant public authority to act towards one another in ways consistent with universal laws of external freedom. An external morality can compel only externally; a public law-giver cannot compel persons to adopt any particular maxims of action, for example. If, then, innate Right is to be claimable externally, and if it is itself incapable of empirical instantiation, it requires indirect empirical instantation to be capable of being the object of external legislation. My proposal is that property rights make possible the indirect public legislation of innate Right. It is by means of the regulation and enforcement of property rights that a public legislator affirms and protects the claim of each to juridical equality in relation to all others.

To appreciate the proposed connection between innate and acquired Right, consider the structure of pre-civil property disputes in the *Doctrine of Right*.[36] In the pre-civil condition, persons raise property claims against one another. Any person claiming a property right over a given external object of her choice affirms her authority to exclude all others from further use of that object. A property right claim is thus always a claim to the legitimate restriction of others' powers of choice in relation to the object in question.[37] A dispute over property rights arises where those against whom the claim is made refuse to acknowledge the claimant's authority to restrict their power of choice in this way. Property disputes are endemic where no one accepts anyone's authority to restrict others' power of choice in this manner. For Kant, the pre-civil condition is such a condition of endemic property disputes whose resolution requires the establishment of a public will with the coercive authority to bind everyone's will. In the present context, the interesting feature of property disputes as Kant's conceives them is that they presuppose disputants' (implicit) reciprocal claims to juridical equality. No one is prepared to acknowledge others' natural juridical authority over him or herself. This is precisely what the innate Right to freedom of each affirms: each has a claim to independence from another arbitrary power of choice over her. The claim to innate Right is no more than the claim to juridical equality in relation to all others. But that claim is also a necessary presupposition of pre-civil property disputes as conceived by Kant.

[36] For a more extensive analysis, see K Flikschuh, *Kant and Modern Political Philosophy* (Cambridge, Cambridge University Press, 2000) ch 5.

[37] Ripstein makes this point especially forcefully at *FF*, 45.

In sum, property disputes would not occur absent implicit reciprocal claims to juridical equality. By the same token, the settling of conflicting property claims by an omnilateral public will and coercive authority would not be possible absent implicit claims to innate Right. Innate Right is 'folded into' acquired Right, as it were. But why is the former so 'folded into' the latter? I suggest this is because, in contrast to innate Right, acquired Right does not specify a purely formal rights relations. Acquired Right has materiality attached to it in the form of external objects that serve a medium of the juridical relation between claimants. As such, acquired Right is capable of empirical instantiation and public regulation by an external lawgiving.

On this account, it is less mysterious why innate Right cannot form part of the 'divisions of a *doctrine* of Right' even though it does form part of the 'highest division of rights'. Innate Right specifies a purely formal (intelligible) juridical relation between persons that is incapable, as such, of empirical instantiation. But a *doctrine* of Right is concerned with the possibility of a public, ie external lawmaking.[38] A public law-making becomes practically possible where a material medium of juridical exchange is available that can serve as direct object of publicly legislated rights relations between persons. Innate Right is presuppositional to the *Doctrine of Right* even though it can form no direct part of it: only insofar as we raise (implicit) claims of juridical equality against one another can property disputes occur in the pre-civil condition, but where they do occur, establishment of a condition of public law-making is obligatory.

However, the proposed line of argument may also be taken to suggest that even though innate Right cannot form part of the divisions of a *Doctrine of Right*—ie it cannot be a direct object of public legislation—its affirmation and protection as purely intelligible relation between persons can nonetheless constitute the indirect end of a *Doctrine of Right.* Let us return to Kant's remark about the law's 'mathematical exactitude'. It is because of its essentially coercive nature that laws of Right can only regulate external behaviour between persons. Property rights in turn make possible such an external public coercive form of law-making. The direct public regulation of property rights between persons indirectly affirms and protects the innate right to freedom of each—ie each person's claim to juridical equality vis-à-vis all others. Now at the core of innate Right lies the idea of humanity: each has an innate Right to juridical equality 'in virtue of his humanity' (*MM* 6:231). A public law-making cannot

[38] *cf MM*, 6: 229: 'The sum of laws for which an external lawgiving is possible is called the *doctrine of Right (ius)*.'

ignore this core quality of innate Right.[39] However, public law-making can be guided by the idea of the innate right of each as the limiting condition of any legitimate public law-making. The inaccessibility of innate Right as a direct object of public law-making then has a moral point—the point of reminding public legislators not to transgress against the idea of the juridical equality of each in relation to everyone else.[40]

Kant's demand for 'mathematical exactitude' in matters concerning public law-making can be taken as the demand for a precise determination and assignment by the public legislator of what materially belongs to each. Alternatively, it can be taken as the law's demand against itself for highest possible standards of legal scrupulousness given its coercive character. The second of these readings strikes me as more consistent, overall, with Kant's abiding emphasis on the underlying intelligible or nominal, hence purely formal character of morality—be it in its ethical or its juridical manifestations. I am inclined to think that the second of these possible meaning has normative priority over the first. However, I do not think that these two interpretations are mutually exclusive. It would, I think, be mistaken to seek to reduce the intelligible or pure formal character of innate Right to its material expression in property rights, contending that to enforce the property rights of each 'just is' to respect and protect innate Right. Such a reduction or equivalence claim would imply that the moral significance of innate Right can be fully captured in terms of property rights claims and adjudication. This strikes me as implausible given the purely formal, intelligible character of innate Right. However, the regulation and adjudication of competing property rights claims may be thought of as an imperfect means for the law's expression of respect for the innate Right of each. A legal system's endeavour to specify 'with mathematical exactitude' what belongs to each materially may then be its way of ensuring the highest standards of legal scrupulousness, given legal respect for innate Right.

It is this thought, finally, which takes us back to *Force and Freedom*. For while it is possible, at one level, to interpret Ripstein's focus on personal 'sovereignty' and on related rights of external possession as an at times obsessive concern with individual freedom, it is equally possible to read that focus on the public securement of external possessions as a reflection of the law's self-limiting character, given its coercive authority over those subject to it.

[39] As reflected, for example, in the opening article of German Basic Law: 'Die Würde des Menschen ist unantastbar'. For excellent discussion and analysis of the genesis of Art 1, including its Kantian roots among others, see T Stein, *Himmlische Quellen und irdisches Recht* (Frankfurt, Campus Verlag, 2007).

[40] J Ebbinghaus, 'The Law of Humanity and the Limits of State Power' (1953) 3 *Philosophical Quarterly* 14–22.

Reading *Force and Freedom* in this alternative vein does require rejection of the role of purposiveness both in relation to innate Right and in relation to acquired Right. Of the former Ripstein says, as we saw, that purposiveness is functionally equivalent to independence in the juridical domain, such that 'you are sovereign as against others not because you get to decide about the things that matter to you most, but because *nobody else* gets to tell you what purposes to pursue'.[41] Of property rights he says:

> Your right to property is your right to limit the conduct of others in relation to particular things. It is an expression of your purposiveness in relation to the purposiveness of others, and so cannot be reduced either to your relation to the object you own or to the restriction on he conduct of others.[42]

But Ripstein also says, in relation to innate Right, that 'Kantian independence is not a feature of the individual person considered in isolation, but of relations between persons'.[43] Of acquired Right he says, among other things, that it raises a 'deeper problem'—deeper, presumably, than the issue of property itself. This deeper problem is that of 'how one person's act can place another person under a new obligation. How can an act entirely done by your initiative, to which others are not parties, have binding effects on them?'[44]

I submit that the notion of purposiveness both times intrudes upon and obfuscates the otherwise relational character of Ripstein's innate and acquired rights conceptions alike. I submit that the foundationalist connotations of purposiveness are out of keeping with the widely acknowledged nature of Kant's non-foundationalist philosophical thinking in general, and that the purely relational approach to thinking about rights which Kant's *Doctrine of Right* affords us is, though normatively unfamiliar, potentially more rewarding philosophically than well-rehearsed arguments about the rights-grounding features and capacities of individual persons. If one brackets purposiveness from Ripstein's accounts of innate and acquired Right, not much is lost from what I take to be Ripstein's principal philosophical intention behind probing the depth and originality of Kant's political and legal thought, which is to remind his readers of the essentially non-instrumental character of public law-making as aiming, at bottom, at nothing other than the securement of rights relations between persons and as guided in that purpose by the idea of the innate Right of each as a non-instantiable idea of legal rectitude which requires indirect instantiation by means of property rights but which no form of external law-making can transgress against without incurring loss of legitimacy.

[41] Ripstein, *FF*, 34.
[42] ibid, 93.
[43] ibid, 15.
[44] ibid, 145.

Part II

Formality

4

Rights and Interests in Ripstein's Kant[1]

ANDREA SANGIOVANNI

Arthur Ripstein's powerful and compelling reconstruction of Kant's legal and political philosophy defends six main claims:

1. *The basic aim of political philosophy is to determine standards for assessing systems of public and private legal entitlements.*
2. *Both legal and moral entitlements are claims to compel (by force if necessary); a legal or moral entitlement is a* **right** *when it is a genuine* **authorisation** *to compel (by force if necessary).*[2]
3. *We each have an innate (moral) right to freedom that serves as a basis for and constraint on all other rights (including private and public legal rights).*
4. *Freedom can only be restricted for the sake of freedom.* Any entitlement or set of entitlements that does not serve to protect or establish a system of equal freedom under universal law cannot rightfully be enforced.

[1] I wish to thank Ian Carter, Mathias Kumm, Pablo Gilabert, Oona Hathaway, George Pavlakos, Nicos Stavropolous, Annie Stilz, Laura Valentini, Leif Wenar, and especially Arthur Ripstein for very helpful comments on previous drafts of this paper.

[2] Although Ripstein does not distinguish 'entitlements' from 'rights' I believe it is useful to do so to avoid confusion. An 'entitlement' in the sense I am using the term purports to be a Kantian 'right' though it may fail in actually being such a right, ie in being justifiably enforceable. The distinction is analogous to the distinction between de facto and de jure authority. If we don't make the distinction, then we will be apt to overlook the difference between a legal entitlement that *succeeds* in providing an authorisation to coerce because it is part of a justified system of entitlements (in my terms, the entitlement would then be a [genuine] right) and one that does not succeed but that purports to do so (in my terms, the entitlement would not be a [genuine] right). For example, Ripstein writes, the 'fundamental feature of all [genuine] rights is that they are parts of a system of equal freedom under universal law' (A Ripstein, *Force and Freedom: Kant's Legal and Political Philosophy* (Cambridge, MA, Harvard University Press, 2009) 180, hereinafter *FF*). We must add the modifier 'genuine' here, otherwise any system of legal rights would be part of a system of equal freedom.

5. *Freedom is independence from, ie non-subjection to, the choices of others.* A system of equal freedom under universal law is a system in which each subjects' powers (including their body and means) are not usurped or destroyed by others.
6. *What counts as independence, and hence as non-subjection, can be determined without appeal to interests, or harm, or well-being.*

In this chapter, I will accept claims 1–5 but reject 6. Throughout I do not assess, at any point, whether Ripstein's argument is a faithful and illuminating interpretation of Kant (which I believe it is), or whether it is plausible to ground an entire political philosophy in the idea of freedom as independence alone (which I believe it is not).

I. THE IMPORTANCE OF INDEPENDENCE

The right to independence under universal law is the foundation on which Kantian legal and political philosophy stands.[3] As Ripstein observes, the 'idea of independence [under universal law] carries the justificatory burden of the entire argument, from the prohibition of personal injury, through the minutiae of property and contract law, on to the details of the constitutional separation of powers' (14).[4] A system of legal entitlements is justifiable, that is, if and only if it serves to protect or uphold every subject's right to freedom qua independence, consistent with every other subject's right to an equal freedom. There are three parts of this formulation (which restates the core of the Universal Principle of Right)[5] that need to be clarified before we can move on: (i) what is it for two or more people to have rights to *equal* freedom? (ii) What does it

[3] The fact that it is foundational should not be taken to mean that it cannot be derived from a further concept or idea, or that it is somehow 'self-evident'. The innate right to freedom, for example, could be given a transcendental justification as the necessary presupposition of any system of reciprocal legal coercion. All I mean by 'foundational' here is that the right serves as the most basic constraint on legitimate law-making, on which all other constraints must be grounded. I thank Katrin Flikschuh for discussion on this point.

[4] See also Ripstein, *FF*, 3, 180.

[5] The Universal Principle of Right (UPR) states that: '[A]n action is right if it can coexist with everyone's freedom in accordance with a universal law, or if on its maxim the freedom of choice of each can coexist with everyone's freedom in accordance with universal law.' The UPR gives rise to each person's innate right to '*Freedom* (independence from being constrained by another's choice), insofar as it can coexist with the freedom of every other in accordance with a universal law', which 'is the only original right belonging to every human being by virtue of his humanity'. See Immanuel Kant, *Practical Philosophy*, ed M Gregor (Cambridge, Cambridge University Press, 1999) 386–7, 93–4, *Metaphysics and Morals*, 6: 230; 6: 237–38 (hereinafter *MM*).

mean for a system of entitlements to be *consistent*, such that every subject's right to freedom is consistent with every other subject's right to the same freedom? (iii) What is it for one person to be *independent* from another (III)?

(i) The Kantian asserts that any pattern or distribution of freedom, to be rightful must be *equal*. Talk of equal freedom seems to presuppose that persons are free to different *degrees*, and that it is wrong if some are more free than others. Freedom would then need to be measurable (at least ordinally).[6] Yet, Ripstein denies this. Ripstein writes:

> [Freedom] is not a matter of people having equal amounts of some benefit, however it is to be measured, but of the respective independence of persons from each other. Such independence cannot be defined, let alone secured, if it depends on the particular purposes that different people happen to have. … Instead, a system of equal freedom is one in which each person is free to use his or her own powers, individually or cooperatively, to set his or her own purposes, and no one is allowed to compel others to use their powers in a way designed to advance or accommodate any other person's purposes.[7]

The thought seems to be this. Freedom does not depend on what people turn out (contingently) to want or desire or need. It only depends on whether people are able to use the means at their disposal to set their own purposes—*whatever* purposes those might be—unhindered by the attempts of others to compel them to choose otherwise. Like the relation 'to the left of' or 'uncle of', freedom is therefore *non-comparatively* relational: there is no 'degree' to which one be free independently of one's relations to others. Compare the relation 'heavier than', which is only *comparatively* relational: if I am heavier than you, then I possess a non-relational property (namely mass) to a greater degree than you. The relation is defined by a comparison between my mass and your mass. The relations 'being to the left of' or 'being the uncle of', on the other hand, do not consist in a comparison between one or more non-relational properties possessed by the relata. It is not as if one person possesses 'leftness' or 'uncleness' to some degree independently of their relation to the other person. The same, then, goes for freedom: if there is no 'quantum' of freedom that one can possess independently of one's relation to another, there can, therefore, be no sense in comparing the degree to which two people are free.

[6] Steiner, who begins with many (though not all) of the same premises as the political Kantians, sees the importance of this question, and grasps the nettle. See, eg, H Steiner, *An Essay on Rights* (Oxford, Blackwell, 1994) 44ff. For an excellent discussion of the measurement of freedom, see I Carter, *A Measure of Freedom* (New York, Oxford University Press, 1999).

[7] Ripstein, *FF*, 33.

I do not see how the conclusion follows. We can grant that freedom defines a non-comparative relation between persons—such that, for example, it makes little sense to talk about Robinson Crusoe's freedom—without conceding that it cannot be measured. Compare 'to the left of'. While there is no non-relational property of 'leftness' that a thing possesses, it surely can be said of A that it is further to the left of B than C. This is because, while the relation 'to the left of' cannot be *reduced* to non-relational facts about spatiotemporal location, it surely *supervenes* on them. So, once we fix a reference point, it becomes unproblematic to compare two things to see which one is farther to the left of something else. The same goes for freedom: once we have more than one person, we can begin to speak of degrees of freedom. Could one claim that freedom is more like 'uncle', which does not admit of degrees? The problem is that the property of 'being an uncle' is binary: either you are an uncle or you are not. But it would be implausible to argue that freedom as independence is binary in the same way. Otherwise, we would be forced to say that the person whose pen was stolen is just as unfree as the slave, since in both cases the means at their disposal have been subjected to another person's choices.

Perhaps the Kantian will grant that degrees of freedom (and hence degrees of subjection) can be measured.[8] And, in what follows, I will grant them this assumption. I flag the problem right at the beginning to show how important the concept of 'subjection' and its contrary 'independence' is within the Kantian system. It must not only be defined in such a way as to capture how both the slave and the person whose property has been stolen are 'unfree' in the relevant sense, but also explain why one is more unfree than the other. As we shall see below, the political Kantian cannot do this without an appeal to the interests upon which relations of independence supervene.

(ii) What does it mean for Kant for a set of rights to freedom to be *consistent*? Here we need to be careful. Kant cannot have in mind logical consistency (or compossibility) among *rights in a general sense*. For example, a system of Hobbesian natural *liberty* rights—in which each of us has the same permission to pursue the means we judge to be necessary to our self-preservation—is logically consistent but not consistent in the Kantian sense. It is logically consistent because my liberty right to kill you if I want your hut only means that I lack a duty not to kill you; it says nothing about your duties to me. My liberty right to kill *you* is therefore logically consistent with your same liberty right to

[8] Hodgson and Stilz, for example, appear to accept that freedom can be measurable (though they provide no metric for how to assess it). See L-P Hodgson, 'Kant on the Right to Freedom: A Defense' 120 *Ethics* 791, 816; A Stilz, *Liberal Loyalty* (Princeton, NJ, Princeton University Press, 2009) 51.

kill *me*.[9] I believe the best account of Kant holds that logical consistency is meant to apply only to a *special* case, namely consistency among what I will call *protected liberties*.[10] Protected liberties are liberty rights which correlate with third-party duties not to interfere with the exercise of that liberty. An example might be our protected liberty to determine what use to make of our body: we have a permission to do as we please with our body, and others have a duty not to interfere. Systems of protected liberties are consistent, then, when the exercise of one person's protected liberty does not make the exercise of others' protected liberties either impossible or impermissible. If we both had protected liberties to take whatever means we believed were necessary for our self-preservation, then our protected liberties would be inconsistent across a wide ranges of cases. They would be inconsistent, for example, in cases where I believe that killing you is necessary for my self-preservation, since that would entail that I have both a permission to kill you (derived from the drawing the implications of *my* protected liberty in this case) and a duty not to kill you (derived from the implications of *your* protected liberty in this case). This account fits with Kant's claim that acquired rights in the state of nature are only *provisional* rather than *conclusive*: they can only *purport* to generate genuine duties on others not to interfere.[11] Until there is an adjudicatory mechanism to resolve conflicts generated by the exercise of our (purported) protected liberties, we cannot know which side's claims win out. In the absence of such a mechanism, we therefore have a permission to do *not* whatever we like but 'what seems right and good to us', ie a permission to act in whatever way we sincerely believe would be permitted under a system of consistent rights qua protected liberties.

(iii) So far we know that freedom as independence is a non-comparative relation, that everyone ought to have the same rights to independence, and

[9] There are interesting questions here about what counts as a logically consistent set of rights in general (ie across all instances of rights). Would, for example, a set of rights in which one has both duties to *x* and duties to not-*x* be logically consistent? Some, like Hillel Steiner, say it wouldn't. Others, like Matt Kramer and Neil Simmonds, say it would. For Simmonds and Kramer, inconsistency requires much more than Steiner, eg it requires someone to both have a duty to *x* and lack a duty to *x*. The problem with Steiner's view, they believe, is that it precludes the possibility of conflicts of rights. See M Kramer et al (eds), *A Debate over Rights: Philosophical Enquiries* (Oxford, Clarendon Press, 1998) 185ff. I thank Ian Carter for alerting me to this distinction. I cannot pursue this here but I believe that Kant's view is closer to Steiner's, so I adopt this reading in what follows. It is worth mentioning that deciding the dispute in any case doesn't have any implications for the argument that follows.

[10] On protected liberties in this sense, see also AJ Simmons, *The Lockean Theory of Rights* (Princeton, NJ, Princeton University Press, 1992). *cf* Kant's discussion of the priority of duties to rights in Kant, *Practical Philosophy*, 394–95, *MM*, 6: 239.

[11] See, eg, Kant, *Practical Philosophy*, 409–11, *MM*, 6: 256–57.

that rights to independence ought to be construed as protected liberties whose implications are logically consistent. But what does it mean, exactly, for someone to be independent, ie not subject to others' choices? This is a crucial question for the political Kantian to answer because the right to independence (and its correct institutionalisation in an actual system of private and public rights) provides the sole basis and standard for the assessment of legal systems; as Ripstein himself notes, 'Kant imposes an extreme demand for unity on his account of political justice' (31).

It is striking that there is little sustained discussion of the concept of subjection in *Force and Freedom* (let alone the *Doctrine of Right*).[12] At the point where Ripstein introduces the right to freedom under universal law, he analyses the notion of subjection in terms of actions that either *usurp* or *destroy* your powers to set ends. Agents *usurp* your powers when they, for example, coerce you or physically force you to do something, and they *destroy* your ability when they, for example, kill or maim you. I take it that in both cases Ripstein means that an agent A usurps or destroys a person B's powers *in such a way as to subject their choices* only when they do so in a reasonably foreseeable and avoidable way (though not necessarily intentionally).[13] Otherwise, when I maim you by falling by accident from a building onto your arm, I have violated your right to freedom by subjecting your choices, which would make my act (absurdly) wrong.

The trouble is that 'usurp' is a moralised concept: to usurp means to *illegitimately* take over a power or jurisdiction, or, alternatively, to take over a power or jurisdiction that is *rightfully* someone else's. A moment's reflection should reveal that to moralise the notion of subjection in this way would spell disaster for the Kantian view. Consider:

> An action should be prohibited by a system of entitlements just when and because it subjects others' choices.

If we substitute, 'illegitimately take over another's power or take over a power that is rightfully another's' for 'subjection' (and hence leave aside for the

[12] I draw the following few paragraphs from A Sangiovanni, 'Can the Innate Right to Freedom Alone Ground a System of Public and Private Rights?' (2012) 20 *European Journal of Philosophy* 460. On this point, see also L Valentini, 'Kant, Ripstein and the Circle of Freedom: A Critical Note' (2012) 20 *European Journal of Philosophy* 450.

[13] Much more would be needed to clarify the notion of foreseeability and avoidability used here, since both foreseeability and avoidability come in degrees, where wrongness, for Kant, does not. How foreseeable and avoidable must an action that destroys or usurps your powers be before it counts as violating your right to freedom, and hence wrong? I leave these problems aside.

moment the other way in which we can subject others' powers, namely by destroying them), we get:

> An action should be prohibited by a system of entitlements when and because it illegitimately takes over another's powers or takes over a power that is rightfully another's.

This formulation says little more than: an action should be prohibited just when and because it should be prohibited (ie 'illegitimate'). But what we want to know is *when* 'taking control of another's powers' is illegitimate; what we want to know is *which* 'powers' or 'means' rightfully count as another's. Indeed, the same problem potentially affects the idea of *destroying* another's powers: if I foreseeably and avoidably kill you in self-defence, have I wronged you?[14] It is tempting to say that your freedom is only violated when I *illegitimately* destroy your powers, but then the account never really gets off the ground.

II. AN EXAMPLE

So we need to find a notion of subjection that *explains why* rather than *presupposes that* the actions it singles out are wrong. To bring out the importance of answering this question, it is useful to focus on a concrete case involving innate rights to the use of our body. Innate right abstracts from questions regarding the means (other than the body) that persons use to set and pursue ends. This restriction simplifies our task: because the arguments for the existence and limits of *acquired* right depend on the success of the argument for *innate* right, a problem in the latter will infect the former as well.

Consider the wrongness of rape. The Kantian seems, at first glance, to have a very powerful argument. Rape is prototypically an action in which someone's choices have been subjected to another, where someone has been used as a mere means,[15] where someone's control over their own body has been

[14] The case of destroying another's powers may be easier to deal with if we consider self-defence as an *excuse* rather than a *justification*. But there will be other cases, such as trolley cases, where this kind of option will be less easy to defend. On Kant and self-defence, see Ripstein, *FF*, 177.

[15] It should be noted that Ripstein (along with others such as Thomas Pogge, Marcus Willaschek and Allen Wood) believes that the UPR does not presuppose the moral theory of the second *Critique* or the *Groundwork*: while it may be derived or justified by reference to it, it need not be. I mention the idea of 'mere means' here to signal that the challenge would apply even to accounts that insist that the UPR cannot be justified without some appeal to the moral theory. Taking a view of this latter sort would allow the Kantian to appeal to the resources of the moral theory (eg the formula of humanity) to 'fill out' or otherwise clarify the implications of the UPR.

usurped. And, indeed, one might think that the Kantian view does very well with regards to a *special* case of rape, which competing harm- or interest-based views seem to have trouble with, namely what has been called the 'harmless rape'.[16] Imagine someone sneaks into your house at night, and has sex with you while you are sleeping; you never find out, no one else knows and the rapist is killed the moment he walks out of your front door. The rape is clearly wrong, yet there is no psychological or physical damage, and no other interests of yours seem to have been set back. Harm- and interest-based accounts of the wrongness of rape therefore seem to fail in cases like this, much like they fail in cases of harmless trespass.[17] The Kantian seems to do well on the other hand. As Ripstein writes:

> The person who uses your body or a part of it for a purpose you have not authorized makes you dependent on his or her choice; your person, in the form of your body, is used to accomplish somebody else's purpose, and so your independence is violated. This is true even if that person does not harm you, and indeed, even if he benefits you. (15)

But now consider a different case. Someone sitting across from you at the library is gazing intently at your hands, in order to sketch a portrait of them. You never notice and no one else ever sees the portrait; the drawing is then lost and the person dies soon after leaving the library. Notice that this case is, from the Kantian point of view, structurally *exactly the same* as the harmless rape. In both cases, someone 'uses your body or a part of it for a purpose you have not authorized' (15); and in both cases, there is no hurt or profit or other downstream effects of the act. *There is nothing in the account of usurpation or using as a means, I contend, that marks a significant difference between the cases.*

As we will see in a moment, I see no other way of plausibly drawing the desired distinction—a distinction any minimally plausible account of our

[16] The 'harmless rape' is discussed and used as an argument against harm-based views generally in J Gardner and S Shute, 'The Wrongness of Rape', in J Horder (ed), *Oxford Essays in Jurisprudence*, 4th series (Oxford, Oxford University Press, 2000) and A Ripstein 'Beyond the Harm Principle' (2006) 34 *Philosophy & Public Affairs* 215; see also *FF*, 92 fn 9. Gardner and Shute provide a distinctively Kantian account of the wrongness of rape, employing the idea of using someone as a mere means to make their point. Although Ripstein does not make use of the formula of humanity (he resists the idea that Kantian political and legal philosophy is just an 'application' of the Categorical Imperative), both accounts share a family resemblance. The arguments I adduce here against Ripstein can also be used to target Gardner and Shute.

[17] Compare the case which Ripstein uses to prosecute his case against harm- and interest-based views (such as John Stewart Mill's): 'If I touch you without your consent while you sleep, or use your property without your consent while you are absent, I draw you into my purposes and wrong you, even if, as it turns out, you never learn of my action, and your body or property suffers no identifiable harm' (*FF*, 22).

innate right in our own bodies should be able to draw—without appealing to interests (and hence appealing to harm and well-being). What makes the harmless rape wrong in a way the portrait case is not is that we have a deep and important interest in *sexual integrity* that is lacking in the portrait case. What explains this interest, in turn, is the central place that a free sexuality plays at the centre of any flourishing life, given the way we are as human beings.[18] There is no equivalent interest in control over who draws us in public places that compares. So the best analysis of the harmless rape will say, quite naturally, that this interest in sexual integrity is sufficiently strong to ground a duty on the part of others not to rape us. Because there is no similarly strong interest in controlling who can draw us in public, there is no enforceable right that protects that interest. Once we put things in this way, it also becomes possible to argue that, in fact, raping someone who is unconscious *does* harm them (contra Ripstein and Gardner and Shute). Raping someone who is unconscious sets back their interests in sexual integrity. If we accept that setting back someone's interests counts as harming them, then the idea that there is no harm in the 'harmless' rape is false.[19]

There is, of course, much more to say about whether welcoming interests into the picture forces us to reject the Kantian account of right in toto. And, if not, further questions about how interests could be integrated into the Kantian framework without diluting its force and simplicity. But this would take us far beyond the limits of this chapter. Instead, I will briefly consider six objections one might make to salvage Ripstein's account from our initial challenge. The objections each aim to show that Ripstein could respond to the challenge without a further appeal to interests.

The first objection contends that I have overlooked the importance of physical touch. On this view, you only illegitimately use or usurp someone's body if you physically touch them. Because there is no touch involved in the portrait case, there is no wrong. But why should the metaphysics of touch—independently of how touch is connected to central human interests—matter for an account of our innate rights? Say that someone takes photographs of you in your bedroom, and then posts them on the internet. This strikes us as wrong, a blatant violation of our right to independence, yet no touch has been involved. How is the portrait case any different? But of course it is, its

[18] A convincing account of the wrongness of rape, which makes appeal to exactly such an interest in sexual integrity, is D Archard, 'The Wrong of Rape' (2007) 57 *Philosophical Quarterly* 374.

[19] On the idea of harm as a setback to interests, see J Feinberg, *The Moral Limits of the Criminal Law*, vol 1: *Harm to Others* (New York, Oxford University Press, 1987). See also Archard (n 18).

difference marked by the importance of *privacy* for a flourishing life. I return to privacy, and its connection to independence, below.

A second objection points to the role of hypothetical consent. Surely, the objector argues, you would have consented to have a portrait of your hand drawn and, similarly, you would not have consented to being raped. That is what marks the difference: we can count your hypothetical consent in the portrait case as if it had been actual consent. This is implausible. Suppose you would not in fact have consented to the portrait: should that matter? Or suppose that you would have consented, but did not in fact consent, to someone having sex with you: should that matter? The answer, in both cases, is no. The permissibility of each action does not rely on knowing or estimating the truth of a counterfactual. Indeed, reflection on cases where hypothetical consent *does* seem, at first glance, to make a difference reinforce the point being made here. Consider, for example, cases of emergency medical intervention in which consent cannot be obtained. In these cases, it is tempting to say that medical intervention is justified because one *would have* consented. But this is a mistake. Suppose, to continue the example, that I, the paramedic, know that you would have asked not to be treated had you been conscious (you told me your views on these things in no uncertain terms just the other day). In the absence of proof of *actual* consent (eg a living will or non-resuscitation order) no paramedic should act on that special information. The reason is precisely that *hypothetical* consent is not *actual* consent. A better explanation of the paramedics' permission (or even duty) to intervene when someone is not conscious and alert makes no use of the idea of hypothetical consent. Rather, the explanation appeals to our strong *interest* in receiving medical intervention when incapacitated, which grounds a permission (and sometimes a duty on others, eg paramedics) to intervene. Hypothetical consent doesn't come into the explanation at any point.[20] Compare the harmless rape: we do not say that people have a right not to be raped while unconscious because they never would have consented to being raped in this way. Rather, we say that people have a strong interest in not being raped when unconscious, which grounds the duty not to do so. Whether they would have consented is irrelevant. Of course, we also believe that people in medical emergencies who are conscious and aware have a permission either to *waive*, by actual consent, the claim-right to treatment (or *block* the permission to intervene). But to conclude that the role of *actual* consent in such cases establishes that we ought to act on the

[20] Or, at most, the appeal to hypothetical consent just summarises or restates the guiding idea, that people have, in normal circumstances, a strong interest in treatment.

basis of whether they *would have* consented is a non-sequitur.[21] Again, it is the appeal to interests (rather than to consent) that marks the relevant distinctions between our rights in the medical intervention, rape and hand portrait cases. Actual consent only becomes relevant once those rights have been defined and delineated in terms of the interests at stake.

The third objection refers to *tacit* rather than *hypothetical* consent.[22] The objector claims that when you go out in public you *tacitly* consent to a series of actions that would be prohibited were you to remain at home (eg to have my picture taken, to be drawn, accosted, etc). If you had not wanted to be accosted, drawn, etc, you could have just stayed home. This is a much better objection than the previous one because, unlike hypothetical consent, tacit consent is widely considered a species of *actual* and so genuinely binding consent.[23] There are two problems. First, tacit consent is only genuine if the costs of expressing dissent are not too high. If I have little option but to appear in public, for example, then the idea that 'if you didn't want to be photographed, accosted, looked at, drawn, and so on, you could have just stayed home' rings hollow. So let us suppose, for the sake of argument, that the costs of staying home are not too high. The second and more serious problem is that the objector has not specified how we ought to determine which actions to include on the list of actions to which I tacitly consent when appearing in public. Compare: 'When you go out in public (or into a bar), you tacitly consent to being (harmlessly) raped if you happen to become unconscious. After all', some would say, 'it wouldn't have been too costly to stay home (or avoid drinking so much).' In response, we would say that the claim overlooks the fact that being raped is very different in character than having our hands drawn. It would, *for this reason*, be unreasonable to put 'rape' alongside 'hand-drawing' on the list of things to which we consent when appearing in public (or going into a bar or drinking). What helps us to determine what gets on the list? The answer, I am suggesting, will invariably point to the weight and importance of our interests, to sexual integrity in one case and to not being drawn in the other. It is those interests that explain what can reasonably be put on the 'list' of actions to which you can be rightly said to tacitly consent to by appearing in public (or going into a bar or drinking).

[21] Similarly with rape: that we believe that people have a permission to waive their right not to be 'raped' should they genuinely and actively consent to an elaborate role-play does not establish that we ought to act *as if* they had consented when they did not in fact consent, even were we to know that they would have consented.

[22] I owe this objection to Oona Hathaway.

[23] The classic account is AJ Simmons, *Moral Principles and Political Obligations* (Princeton, NJ, Princeton University Press, 1979).

The fourth objection makes use of Ripstein's distinction between *affecting the context in which you act* and *subjecting your choices*. If I 'open a competing business that lures away your customers, or use my property so that you no longer have the pleasant view you once did' (21–22), Ripstein says that I have merely changed the context in which you act rather than made you dependent on me. Using this distinction, we might then say that when someone draws your hand they merely affect the context in which you act; when someone rapes you, on the other hand, they subject your choices. This response begs the question. We want to know *why* drawing a hand portrait doesn't subject your choices in the relevant sense but raping you does. The objection just assumes we already have the standard we are looking for.

The fifth objection has two variants. According to the first variant, the objector complains that Kant does not believe that examples in concrete cases can be used, on their own, to impugn a theory. As Ripstein notes, 'Kant's mode of argumentation reflects his attitude toward examples. He develops many examples in the course of his argument, but rejects the idea that examples can replace arguments, or that philosophy is charged primarily with accounting for examples' (6). A defence of Ripstein that appeals to this idea misses the point of the examples. The examples of the harmless rape, hand portrait, pictures, etc, are meant to illustrate a broader point about the role of interests in grounding rights. They are not meant somehow to stand on their own.[24] In any case, I take it as obvious that any minimally plausible view about the rights we have must be able to account for the distinction between rape and drawing someone's hand. Rape, after all, is not just a borderline case. As Ripstein goes on to say, 'But to say that Kant does not regard examples as dispositive is not to say that his arguments lead to conclusions that cannot survive reflection' (7). The force of the examples here is meant to suggest that the account, as given, cannot survive reflection.

According to the second variant of this objection, Kant's legal and political philosophy does not aim to offer determinate guidance in particular cases such

[24] Indeed, one can produce any number of further examples to make the same point. Take, for example, the idea that it would be wrong of me to run my fingers through your hair without your authorisation. But now say that your hair is on fire, and my hands happen to be wet. I don't have time to ask for your permission, and so I just douse the fire by running my fingers through your hair. Is that wrong? I submit, once again, that to account for the difference between these two cases we must appeal to a balance of interests and to considerations directly stemming from well-being. See also the examples adduced to make a similar point in V Tadros, 'Independence without Interests?' (2011) 31 *Oxford Journal of Legal Studies* 193; Sangiovanni (n 12).

as the ones mentioned above. Its indeterminacy in these respects, the objector continues, is one of its *strengths*. As Ripstein writes:

> Kant's argument as a whole not only concedes indeterminacy, but, the indeterminacy of the application of basic concepts of right is a cornerstone of his argument for the need for a state. Abstract concepts do not classify particulars on their own, and people might, in good faith, disagree about their application, as Kant puts it 'no matter how good and right loving they might be'.[25]

Adapting this claim, the thought would be that it would be up to the state (via legislation) to determine whether people can legitimately be raped in their homes without their authorisation, as it would be up to the state to determine whether people can have their hands drawn in public. As long as people have the same rights, it would be legitimate to enforce a system of entitlements allowing rape as it would be to enforce one that doesn't.[26] Once again, any minimally plausible account of freedom as independence ought to have the resources to draw a distinction here. While there are many areas of the law in which a theory at this level of abstraction could legitimately remain silent (or, perhaps better, indifferent), this is surely not one of them.[27] As Ripstein goes on to say, 'concepts of right provide conceptual resources for thinking

[25] A Ripstein, 'Form and Matter in Kantian Political Philosophy: A Reply' (2012) 20 *European Journal of Philosophy* 487, 489.

[26] *cf* what Ripstein says in response to an article of mine (n 12) in which I pursued a similar argument: 'Sangiovanni overlooks the explicit structure of the universal principle of right. It does not look to the effect of one person's action on another. Instead, it focuses on whether every member of plurality of interacting beings *could* enjoy such rights under universal law. As I sought to explain in *Force and Freedom*, you can have a right to decide what purposes you will pursue with your own body or property, because everyone *could* have that right, but, by contrast, you *could not* have a right that others use their bodies and property in ways that best serve your preferred ends' (n 25, 490, emphasis added). I don't understand this response: in what sense is it true that a system of entitlements in which harmless rapes are permitted 'could not' be realised under universal law? If we take the constraint of universal law in a thinner sense, such that a system of entitlements is consistent with the idea of equal freedom as long as each person's rights are consistent with everyone else having the same rights, then the system of entitlements that permits harmless rapes *is* compatible with universal law, since it gives everyone an *equal* right to rape others. If, on the other hand, the constraint of 'universal law' is understood in the more substantive sense I suggested in (ii) and (iii) above, then the response begs the question. What is at stake is whether the idea of subjection implicit in the UPR has the resources to outlaw harmless rape but not hand portraits. Ripstein's reply has this form: 'The UPR does have the resources to outlaw harmless rape but not hand portraits, because everyone *could not* have the right to engage in harmless rapes without subjecting others, whereas they *could* have the right to draw hand portraits without subjecting others.' This leaves entirely unanswered the question: '*Why* does a system of entitlements permitting harmless rapes count as a system of subjection, but not a system of entitlements permitting hand portraits?'

[27] Notice that the argument does not depend on the claim that a theory that couldn't classify particulars in a determinate way must be faulty (*cf* H Sidgwick, *The Methods of Ethics* (Indianapolis, Hackett Publishing, 1907) 421).

through particulars, especially the distinction between interfering with a person's means and changing the context in which those means are used'.[28]

The sixth objection claims that I must reject the essentially Kantian idea that a system of entitlements grounded in independence is *non-comparatively* relational. Take the relation 'to the left of': there is no way to define what the relation consists in by referring solely to facts about the non-relational properties of the relata. The relation 'taller than', on the other hand, is only *comparatively* relational: the relation 'taller than' consists in one thing having a non-relational property, namely height, to a greater degree than another thing. There is no comparable degree of 'leftness' that a thing possesses independently of its relation to other things. Ripstein claims the relations of subjection are analogous: there is no way to define what subjection consists in by referring to some freedom-independent property of each of the relata. This is why Ripstein often says that freedom, as a relation, is *irreducible*—and, most importantly for our purposes, why he often says that freedom is irreducible to *interests*. Do I need to deny this?

I don't, and this is key to understanding the force of the argument. Return to the relation 'to the left of'. While it is true that the relation cannot be *reduced* to non-relational facts about spatiotemporal location, the relation surely is *a function of* non-relational facts about spatiotemporal location. The relation, that is, depends, or more precisely, *supervenes on* non-relational facts about spatiotemporal location (while not being reducible to them). And that is exactly what I am claiming with respect to interests: while I accept that relations of freedom are not *reducible* to relations of interests, relations of freedom must be a *function of* relations of underlying interests. To determine whether two people stand in relations of freedom with respect to one another, we first need to know what interests are involved in their relation, just as we did in the harmless rape and portrait cases. Because interest-based theories of independence are not forced to deny that freedom is non-comparatively relational, the objection fails.[29]

I conclude that on Ripstein's Kantian view what counts as independence cannot be determined without appeal to interests, or harm, or well-being. While this does not refute Ripstein's Kantian political philosophy in toto, it does show that, until an account of such interests is provided and shown to be consistent with our moral status as free and equal beings, the argument remains incomplete.

[28] A Ripstein, 'Form and Matter in Kantian Political Philosophy: A Reply' (2012) 20 *European Journal of Philosophy* 487, 489.

[29] Indeed, this is also true for most accounts of negative freedom which affirm that freedom is absence of interference *from other agents*; on such views, you are only free to the extent that others are not interfering with you. See, eg, Carter (n 6) 25–27. Carter also defends the idea that freedom *also* has a *comparatively* relational aspect; hence the title of his book.

5

Independent People

AJ JULIUS

I

IN AN APPENDIX to *Force and Freedom* Arthur Ripstein says that Kantian right is concerned with the practical upshot of spatial incompatibilities in the action of separately embodied persons. The bodies of human persons are 'impenetrable solids in space'. Because their bodies 'occupy space, the only way their activity can be rendered consistent under universal law is if they neither occupy nor interfere with the space occupied by others'. The fact of spatial incompatibility 'is incorporated into the law of freedom that no person may invade the space occupied by another' (373).[1]

Let's take a little more time over this problem of space.

'Any action is *right*' by Kant's universal principle of right 'if it can coexist with everyone's freedom in accordance with a universal law.'[2] If some action of yours can coexist with everyone's freedom in accordance with a universal law, Kant adds, an action of mine that hinders this one of yours *wrongs* you.

I am going to assume that rightness is primarily a property of kinds of action and derivatively a property of their instances. An action is right if it belongs to a rightful kind. A kind is right if its every instance can coexist with everyone's freedom under a universal law.

Coexistence needs explaining. But we might guess that the clearest-cut coexistence failures occur where an action kind's instances hinder other actions of their own kind.

Think of the kind *occupying a space*. I'll define this so that, for any small space and span of time, a person's filling the space with her body during that span is

[1] All Ripstein quotations are from A Ripstein, *Force and Freedom: Kant's Legal and Political Philosophy* (Cambridge, MA, Harvard University Press, 2009).

[2] All Kant quotations are from the *Metaphysics of Morals* in Immanuel Kant, *Practical Philosophy*, ed and trans MJ Gregor (New York, Cambridge University Press, 1996).

an instance. By occupying a space I hinder your entering it, or I hinder your staying there. My occupation hinders yours. This kind of action can't be right, then, and the wrongness of your invading a space that I occupy is not to be explained by the fact that your invasion hinders my occupation of it.

But now consider the action whose instances each consist, for some small space *S* and times *t* and *u*, in a person's [filling *S* throughout (*t*, *u*] if no part of another person's body is in *S* at *t*.] Call this *occupying an otherwise unoccupied space.* My entering some empty region and remaining there can hinder your own entrance into or tenure of the spot. But your occupation of the space would not constitute your occupying an otherwise unoccupied space. I was there first. If I don't hinder a conditionally described action just by making false the antecedent of the description—if my hindering your [doing *x* if *p*] instead requires that I hinder your *x*ing and that *p* be *true*—then my occupying an otherwise unoccupied space does not hinder other action of its own kind. It's left open that this kind is right and so that your invasion of a space that was empty when I entered it wrongs me.

II

That an object is mine, says Kant, is that other persons wrong me if they use it without my consent.

> It is possible for me to have any external object of my choice as mine, that is, a maxim by which, if it were to become a law, an object of choice would *in itself* (objectively) have to *belong to no one (res nullius)* is contrary to rights. (6: 251)

This 'postulate', although it is 'incapable of further proof', is followed in the text by a sort of defence or motivation:

> For an object of my choice is something that I have the physical power to use. If it were nonetheless not within my *rightful* power to make use of it, that is, if the use of it could not coexist with the freedom of everyone in accordance with a universal law (would be wrong), then freedom would be depriving itself of the use of its choice with regard to an object of choice, by putting usable objects beyond any possibility of being *used*; in other words, it would annihilate them in a practical respect and make them into *res nullius*, even though in the use of things choice was formally consistent with everyone's freedom in accordance with universal laws. (6: 250)

I wonder about this. Does a rightful use of external objects require that persons hold property in them?

Think of the action kind whose instances each consist, for some object distinct from the bodies of persons, in a person's using that object during some stretch of time. Most such uses of an object by a person hinder some other person's using the same thing at the same time. Instances of the action hinder action of their kind. If this were the only object-using action kind, no such kind would be right.

But here again we could get creative. Let an instance of *using an otherwise unused object* consist, for some object *O* and times *t* and *u*, in a person's [using *O* throughout (*t*, *u*) if no other person is using it at *t*]. When I do this I make it false that your using the object during that span would constitute your using an otherwise unused object. So my use of the unused does not hinder any other use of the unused, and it is eligible to be right.

This law of freedom stands in obvious analogy to the law of occupying-the-unoccupied. Each forces the externally incompatible actions of embodied persons into a definitionally secured interpersonal consistency. It does that by carving out a kind of action such that by 'getting there first' and doing her thing of that kind a person makes it the case that all other actions externally incompatible with hers are *not* of this kind.

Suppose, then, that the laws of freedom recognise, as a rightful action kind, the using of an otherwise unused object. Then one kind of object-using action—a person's using a thing that was idle when she took it up—is right. Usufruct, the law of using the unused, seems to deliver that possibility of a rightful use of external things for which Kant's postulate plumps.

III

Ripstein persuades me that this is not enough. His argument draws on a conception of purposive action that he ascribes to Kant and to Aristotle. He expresses the basic idea when he writes that 'you can only *do* something if you set out to do it, and you can only set out to do what you take yourself to have the power to do' (40).

The following passage might stand for several in which Ripstein develops the consequences for right:

> As a matter of fact you may be able to set yourself the end of making a mushroom omelet without having rights to objects that are not in your physical possession, but you could not have an entitlement against others to set yourself the end of making one. If there were no such rights, someone else would be entitled to take the eggs you had gathered while you were sauteeing the mushrooms, and you would not be entitled to do anything to stop her. Your entitlement to set and pursue purposes would thus depend on the particular choices made by another. (91–92)

This argument takes issue with the proposal that my use of external objects is protected only by the bodily right that you violate when you interfere with my physical possession of them. But an easy adaptation will bring out the inadequacy of usufruct. Against usufruct, and in parallel with the second quoted sentence, Ripstein would presumably observe that my use-grounded right against others using any omelette ingredients that I'm already using doesn't prohibit their using them before I've begun to cook. I imagine that he would conclude, in parallel with the first quoted sentence, that under this law I lack an entitlement against others to set for myself the end of cooking the omelette.

Spelled out a bit the inference could be this.

> I can now set myself the end of a mushroom omelette only if I can now take it that others will not hinder my cooking some mushrooms.
>
> For any end *E* and action *x*, if I have a right against others to set the end *E*, and if I can now set myself the end *E* only if I can take it that others will later not do *x*, then I now have a right against others that they later not do *x*.
>
> I now have no right against others that they later not hinder my cooking some mushrooms.
>
> so I now have no right against others to now set myself the end of a mushroom omelette.

The Aristotle–Kant view of purposive action sponsors the first premise, about setting ends. But the argument also relies, at its second premise, on a principle about rights to set ends. Your right to set an end requires a right that others not do what, if you're to set the end, you must take it they won't do. I am happy to take that principle up and indeed to accept the entire argument.

In usufruct it will sometimes happen that I set the end of making a mushroom omelette. I can do this when mushrooms abound so that others are sure to leave me some. Once I've adopted the omelette purpose and started in to cook, I come into a right against others that they not interfere with my cooking by making off with the particular ingredients I'm using. Now I meet the necessary condition for a right to set the end that is laid down by the argument's second premise.

But the right has come too late. I set the end before I won the right to set it.

I think there's probably a purposive practical stance, *affirming* and pursuing a purpose, that I can take toward a purpose whether or not I've already set it. By starting to use the ingredients I incur under usufruct a right against others hindering my further use of them. Because I now have a right against their doing what would stop me from making an omelette, it seems open that I now have a right to *affirm* and pursue the end of an omelette.

This is not good enough, I think. I can't accept that a person's entitlement to affirm and pursue a purpose emerges only after and thanks to her original adoption and pursuit of it. And I can't accept that I depend for my entitlement to affirm and pursue the purpose on the happenstance that others forbear from impeding the initial stages of my project even as they were authorised to scuttle it. This is the sort of thing that Ripstein has in mind, I would guess, when he objects, at the third quoted sentence, that under the law of physical possession my entitlement to pursue my purposes 'depends on the particular choices made by another'.

In usufruct a person arrives at her right to hold and pursue an external-means-requiring purpose only after she's adopted it and begun to pursue it by using those means and only if the others chance not to exercise their own entitlements to frustrate her opening moves. That's not right.

IV

This argument from independence, whatever its force against usufruct, is no reason to settle for property. Property draws the same objection.

Suppose that I can come to own a thing by claiming or receiving a title to it that I enjoy independently of any actual or planned use of the thing. Suppose that I don't in this way own any mushrooms and that I can't grow mushrooms using only what's mine.

It may be that I can now take up the purpose of making a mushroom omelette. I can do this if I see the task as falling in my power. The task is in my power if I have some way of inducing the inputs' current owners to hand them over to me. Or if I can grab the ingredients and cook them up before anyone grabs them back.

But of course I lack any right against others that they fall in with this plan. No one wrongs me, under property, by declining to pass me the mushrooms she owns. A mushroom owner is in her rights to hide or lock her stuff away, to drive me off when I try to use it, to recover it by force if I succeed briefly in taking it over. She is entitled to do what hinders my use of the mushrooms. But I can set the omelette as an end only if she won't hinder my use of the mushrooms. So I who own no mushrooms lack an entitlement against others that I set for myself the end of a mushroom omelette.

In the supermarket aisles of our actual property society you will presumably encounter persons who have set particular suppers as their ends although they do not yet own the ingredients. 'Why you are putting those mushrooms in that cart?' 'I'm making a mushroom omelette tonight.' A shopper like this has managed to set out after her gastronomic end because she could see it as falling within her power. She was thinking that an offer of cash for the ingredients would move the grocer to give them up.

When a shopper purchases the ingredients, the onetime owners relinquish their rights to interfere with her cooking. She finally enjoys against them a right that they not withhold the means to her purpose. She has the makings not only of an omelette but of the right to set herself the omelette-making end.

But again that right has come too late. If the means were bought for the sake of the end, the end was set before she had a right against others to set it.

Perhaps the new owner of the ingredients enjoys a right to *affirm* the end she's already pursuing and to carry on with it. But if this is true it's true thanks to the accommodating particular choices of farmers and merchants. She owes her achievement of her right to do what she was already doing to the forbearance of persons who, after she'd set the end but before she'd bought the means, were entitled to act in ways that would have shut her project down.

A typical putative end-affirming right in the property society bears a strong resemblance to the would-be end-affirming right that's characteristic of usufruct. The right takes hold only once I've bought the things my purposes demand, and so it typically follows and depends on rather than preceding or protecting my initial pursuit of the purpose. And I only ever achieve the right if and because others choose to part with their goods despite their entitlements to hold on to them. If like me and perhaps like Ripstein you think that a right to set ends has got to come first and that it's necessarily invulnerable to other persons' particular choices, then like me you should worry that property puts such independence out of reach. Independence will have you worried about property.

V

And not only about property. The argument also calls into question the law of occupying otherwise unoccupied spaces with which I pretended to solve the space problem.

Suppose that some purpose I might take up requires that I stand *right over there*. Often enough I can form that purpose, as when I'm sure of reaching the spot first because I'm the only person who's interested or close. But my right to affirm the purpose and to act for its sake comes on line only after and because I've taken the position. Until I reach the spot others are entitled to go there ahead of me and so to act in ways that would put the purpose out of my power while contracepting my right to pursue it. Under the law of occupying the unoccupied my right to set a typical geographically specific end postdates my decision to make it my own, and I depend for the right's establishment on the fact that persons have stood aside who were also authorised to get in my way.

This criticism overlooks another possibility of redescription. If our actions can be defined into consistency, our ends can be conceived so that everyone has an independent right to set them.

I'll have a nice picnic only if it doesn't rain. I can't stop the rain from falling. It seems to follow, according to the Kant–Aristotle view, that I can't set out to have a nice picnic. To have a nice one is not something that I can *do* in the way that I can do such things as I can set out to do.

This truth does not put nice picnics beyond the reach of purposive action, beyond choice. A closely related purpose is available for adoption: I can set out to [have a nice picnic if it doesn't rain].

A defender of the law of occupying the unoccupied might seize on the phenomenon of settable-because-conditional ends. To vary the tale of a picnic, imagine that it's already raining but that my picnic will be nice enough if I lay my spread under the park's one tree. A nice picnic requires that I occupy that dry place. Because I can claim no right against your settling there first, I don't enjoy a right of adopting a nice picnic as my purpose. But that leaves open my right to set out to [have a nice picnic if no one assumes the dry location before I get there]. *This* right would precede my embrace of the end it protects, and it would not depend for its force on others' choices.

Usufructarians could go on to make a similar point about usufruct. Independently of anyone's choice I enjoy under that law a right to set the purpose of [building a house if no one walks off with the lumber] or the end of [cooking an omelette if no one else puts the mushrooms in her quiche].

It seems cheap, a reply perfectly insensitive to the concerns that move the objection. But why? This end-redescribing proposal purports to show that the law of occupying the unoccupied or the law of using the unused induces for every person a zone of independent purposiveness. Laws of this kind see to it that, for an entire class of space-requiring ends, a person enjoys against everyone else a right to set any of those ends and does not depend for that right on others accommodating particular choices.

If we're resisting this answer to the demand for independence, that's probably for the following reason.

We have it in mind that, if a picnic-minded person takes [having a nice picnic if no one gets to the dry spot first] as something that's *worth doing*, this is because she takes [having a nice picnic] as worthwhile. And we are thinking that, if someone sets as her end, not this unconditional picnic, but the merely conditional [having a nice picnic if no one gets there first], that's because she can't, under the space law, dismiss the prospect that others will reach the spot first and so hinder her picnic. In the teeth of others' capacity and permission to frustrate her unconditional picnic plans, she settles for the conditional picnic. Of the ends she's able to set, this one brings her action closest to the purpose she sees as worthwhile, the picnic itself.

Against certain lucky backgrounds, as when she's the only picnic person for miles around, she'll manage also to set the unconditional end. But the law of occupying the unoccupied falls short by leaving this to chance. We want it ruled out as a matter of the law's own content that a person would *ever* settle for *E*-conditional-on-others'-accommodating-choices just because that's the end, closest to *E* itself, that is settable given the undismissed prospect of hindrance by others' choices.

To put this in what Ripstein rightly regards as the crucial perspective, notice that a *servant* might set herself the end [having a nice picnic if her master doesn't order her to work on Saturday afternoon]. If she goes for that conditional end, in place of an unconditional picnic, it's because her master might force her to do chores then. Because he might hinder a Saturday picnic she can't set out after the unconditional picnic that's the object of her justificatorily basic endorsement.

For all its stupidity this stupid solution to the problem of independent purposiveness is pointing the way toward a smarter one. To bring this out I'd like to turn to the topic of my favorite chapter of *Force and Freedom*. I'd like to talk about traffic law.

VI

The glory of traffic law is that it allows a traveller to concern herself only with the law and never with *traffic*.

I am headed south, you're going west. If each keeps on as she's going, we'll collide. I decide not to cross the intersection just now. Why not?

Maybe I expect you to barrel ahead. Maybe I can't rule out that you will continue. Then I might take the fact that you will or might keep going as a reason to stand still. If you keep going you will hinder my own progress by knocking me off course or by disabling my body or vehicle. To move forward I've got to stay put. And so I yield.

I hate it when that happens. I hate that your going presents itself as a reason for me to stay. You are not a rolling stone or a runaway trolley. You are a person whose movement into the intersection answers to my own freedom.

The law arranges for me to arrive at this decision from a different motivation. I could decide to yield at this junction because I'm required under the law to yield there. A two-way stop sign is posted, and you have the protected direction; or it's a four-way, and you got to it first; or the traffic light is giving you green. If I'm stopping because it's the law, I'm not stopping because you're going to go. I yield, not to your body, your momentum, or your car, but to your right of way.

What are the things that a person might set out to do because she regards them as worth doing? She might act for picnics, omelettes or houses. She might head west or south. But she also might set out after freedom. Something that's worth doing for its own sake—and so something that need not be done as a concession to the external constraints thrown up by others' actual or incipient choices—is to act consistently with the freedom of other persons.

If the traffic law permits you to move ahead now, then under this law I have no right to set the end of [going south as soon as is physically possible]. For you are permitted to do what would hinder this. But this law might reserve for me the right to set as my end [going south as soon as that's consistent with your freedom]. Because you have the right of way, only my yielding is consistent with your freedom. So I act on my end by waiting for you to pass, and your going ahead does not hinder my pursuit of it.

This right to a conditional end avoids my earlier complaints about a right to set the end of doing-*E*-if-others-don't-hinder-my-doing-*E*. If I set out to [go south if that's consistent with your freedom], the reason won't be that you might hinder me from doing what I take as basically valuable. Instead I'll be doing this because I care about your freedom: I value my trip's consistency with your freedom independently of anything you might do to hinder my trip.

This solution has been hiding in plain sight. Returning to Kant's statement of the universal principle of right, we find that it protects as rightful that action which can coexist not with the things that others do but with their freedom. There's a frank circularity to this formula. Kant is identifying the freedom he's talking about with persons enjoying the right to set out to do anything that's consistent with others' enjoyment of that freedom.

VII

I think that *property* owes its appeal to the possibility of understanding the ends it protects in this circular way.

Maybe there's no such ordinarily described end as [cooking an omelette] such that a person's right to set the end will precede her typical setting of it and will take hold independently of others' choices to act in the ways that permit it. But in the property society I enjoy the right to set myself the end of [making an omelette if I come to own the means of omelette making] whether or not anyone sells me eggs, mushrooms, pots and pans, or a stove. My various rights, for various ends *E*, to set myself the end of doing-*E*-if-I-buy-the-means-to-*E* come together in my general entitlement to [use as I see fit any means that I acquire]. That entitlement, which is often invoked by Ripstein as the basic tenet of property, is presumably my right, for any *E*, to set out to [do *E* if I come to own the external means to *E*]. If I have this right at all, I have it independently of your particular choices.

It's easy enough to dismiss this as another trick. What I judge basically worth working toward, you might suspect, is not *E*-if-I-come-to-own-the-means-to-*E* but *E* period. I care about owning the means to *E* because they're the *means to E*. If I set the merely conditional purpose, that's because it's the one I can set given that others might hinder my pursuit of an unconditional omelette by withholding the ingredients.

This is not the only way to see the matter. To give property its best shot we should suppose for a moment that the law of freedom encompasses a right of property in external objects. On that hypothesis my using only what I own is a using of external objects that's consistent with others' freedom. If I care about freedom—if I set out, among my other purposes, to uphold others' freedom—then I might well set out, not to make an omelette period, but [to make an omelette if I come to own the means to omelette making]. I might do this not because the coercive enforcement of property makes of this end a 'second best' to an unconditional omelette but because, independently of anyone's coercion of me, it's the version of an omelette that's worth going for.

But this resolution of the independence problem is not proprietary to property. If usufruct were instead put forward as the content of the law of freedom with respect to the use of external objects, then we could also understand the end of building-a-house-if-others-don't-grab-the-hammer-first on the pattern just explained. House-building coexists with others' freedom as that's understood by usufruct only if others are not already using the lumber and tools. So a right to set out to [build a house if others don't use the tools first] is a right to set out to [build a house consistently with others' freedom]. It's a right to set out after what I might well judge to be basically worth doing independently of what others will or might do that impedes it.

If this is the way to independence, then it's seeming that we could reach it through a law of any otherwise eligible content. But the problem of independence imposes more structure on its solution than has been noticed so far. To explain this I need to return to the streets.

VIII

Suppose now that our intersection is neither lawless nor governed by a public traffic law. Instead the law of occupying the unoccupied holds sway. If you are going to stop for a moment, in a spot that I'm on course to enter before you'll have left it, then my moving ahead will hinder your occupation of an otherwise unoccupied space. If you are going to do this I might stop because you're going to stop and so as not to hinder that.

This decision to yield poses as a kind of mixed case. It resembles the lawless decision I described insofar as it amounts to my stopping because of what you are going to do. It resembles the decision to obey a traffic law insofar as it's not my stopping because your action would *hinder* my going. The second resemblance suggests that this decision might sort with obedience of a traffic law, on the side of independent purposiveness; the law of occupying-the-unoccupied ensures that I need never take your projected hindrance of my possible action as a reason to stop since I can, at the relevant intersections, find that reason in *my* possible hindrance of *your* projected action. But I am thinking that this is not good enough—that when I stop so as not to hinder your stopping I am subjected to your choice.

Imagine as before that I had set out [to go south as soon as is consistent with others' freedom]. Because you are going to linger in my path I've got to narrow this purpose, adopting as my specific plan that I [delay my southward progress for a moment so that I won't invade a space that you're going to occupy]. This narrowing of my purpose is compelled by the fact of your own particular action in advance of your road-occupying end. It's your projected tenure of the middle of the road that makes it true of me that I must set that narrower end if I'm to act on the broader one. The fact of your setting out to do what would be hindered by one version of my acting on my broader end compels me to boil my intention down to the version that doesn't hinder what you're going to do.

The traffic law refuses this adaptation of one person's end to the other's choice. It saves for everyone the right to set as her end [moving in a direction, or standing still, if that's consistent with others' freedom]. And for each action that might advance such an end, it determines that action's consistency with the others' freedom independently of any facts as to whether others are taking particular action that's externally inconsistent with it. If my going is contrary to your freedom, that's not because my going will hinder what you're going to do. It's because you have the right of way, a right you owe to the green light and not to your own tendency of forward motion. I can carry out my aim of moving consistently with your freedom even as I don't make it my purpose to act consistently with any particular action of yours.

IX

Your right of way saves me from having to take your westward motion as my reason to yield. But in deciding whether to leave the house I'll often take the fact that thousands of others are moving west, east, south and north as a reason to stay home. In this way I seem to yield to the choices of other persons and not to just to their rights. My earlier remark that traffic law frees a traveller's deliberation from constraint by traffic probably struck you as wildly mistaken. A typical subject of traffic law, if she's lucky enough to live in a crowded place, is *obsessed* with traffic. Great stretches of her practical thinking are given over to the question of how to get where she's going given the trips that others are taking.

I will shortly argue that this appearance is not to be trusted. But if it were correct I would take it to show, not that I've misconstrued the ground of traffic law, but that the existing positive traffic law is not living up to the demand for independence that grounds it. We should make a better law.

I am tempted to say that we should make *trains*. We should build a bunch of trains and run them on a public schedule so that in deciding whether to set out on any particular journey I can ignore the traffic reports in favour of a timetable. This would have the pleasant result that people reach particular worthy destinations after trips of predictable durations. But it would perhaps also serve freedom. It would tend to free our movements from subjection to the travel choices of all the others.

But on second thought it is clear that no technology will suffice for that freedom. Even in the smartest of mass transit systems I can get where I'm going only if I can find a seat on some train. When the 3:13 is full other persons' particular choices will have compelled me to pursue my original end of [going south as soon as is consistent with others' freedom] in some straitened form like [delaying my departure to 3:52].

Maybe an ideal traffic law requires a bigger timetable. It could first find out from all persons which particular destinations they're trying to reach by which times consistently with others' freedom. It would then transmit to their smartphones a schedule of legally permitted individual departures and routes computed independently of persons' actual motions or dispositions to leave.

This is another nightmare. Scheduled in this way we would lose the right to walk or ride around. I hope that the right to move includes the right to wander or to mosey: setting out with no particular place to go, taking a turn down any weird alley that catches my interest. A timetable that licenses only particular scheduled trips from points A to points B denies me the independent right to set ends of motion that depend constitutively on the motion's spontaneous or exploratory character.

We might just forfeit the right to wander if the timetable were securing the independence of our rights to set any of a general class of other ends. But the timetable cannot do that either. A timetable that governs only my daily travel decisions leaves my pursuit of longer-run purposes subject to others' choices. When I'm deciding whether to sleep and eat at a greater or shorter distance from the site of some ongoing project I'll seem to have predicted the commuting plans of others so as to predict the timetable's permissions of my own commutes. I might decide against a long commute, not because the timetable forbids *that decision*, but because the commutes it allows me will be slow and infrequent given that other people are going to jam the intermediate spaces.

This might inspire a bigger timetable, a schedule of rights of way not just for particular trips but for all longer-run pursuits of space-occupying purposes. But that's not too attractive either. Not only would the grand timetable banish all improvisation. It calls for the impossible: a single planning moment that precedes all persons' particular pursuits of lifelong plans of action

We can do better, I think. One final clarification of the nature of traffic law will show that this law emancipates even spontaneously decided and directed trips from constraint by others' decisions to make such trips of their own.

X

Let our paths cross one last time. I am going downtown, you are headed across town, and our possible collision lies over a patch of sidewalk that's not governed by any sign or light. One of us will have to yield. An independently purposive decision to yield can't be a decision to [stand still because moving would hinder or be hindered by the given motion of the other person]. But it's not obvious what else this decision can be. How can one person yield to the other's right of way if neither person comes into the encounter as the ordained bearer of that right?

But suppose that you've set out to [cross town if that's consistent with my freedom]. I've set out to [go downtown if that's consistent with your freedom]. I submit that these two ends together call for you and me to do either one of (you go, I stop) or (I go, you stop). We might each take those purposes as lending equal support to each pattern and then *pick* one of the two. For example I might wave you across, proposing that I yield, and you might accept the proposal with a nod or a glance. I think that each pedestrian can do her part of (you go first, I go second) while taking my end of a freedom-consistent motion and your end of a freedom-consistent motion as supporting that pair of actions.

It might seem that when I decide to yield as part of your going ahead and my yielding, I am narrowing my end—from [continuing downtown if that's freedom-consistent] to [waiting a second until you've passed]. It might seem that I am doing that so as not to hinder a thing you're already doing, namely [heading across town consistently with my freedom]. This comes across as another asymmetrical adaptation of one person's purpose-pursuing to the other person's choice.

I think that another understanding is in reach, however. If you had set out to [go west now], then, true enough, your pursuit of that purpose would constitute the fact of your moving in a particular direction at a particular time such that I'm doomed to hinder that motion or to suffer its hindrance if I persist in my original trajectory. It would give me a reason to turn away from any trajectory that's incompatible with this thing you're doing. In acting for that reason I would be adopting a narrower version of my end so as to fall in with your particular choice.

But your intention to [go west if that's consistent with my freedom] is not one that, in deciding when to move ahead, I may take as your given tendency *to go west now* or at any other particular time. What your end of freedom-consistent westward travel is bringing you to do, in the way of particular dated westward steps, is not determined independently of this deliberation that includes my own thinking about when to move. It is still to be decided within our currently unfolding decisions of how to act for our ends of freedom-consistent motion. Before you and I work that out, your freedom-consistent trip *bears no determinate incompatibility relation to my own possible bodily motions.* And so my decision to yield is not my choosing against some motion because it's incompatible with the accomplished fact of what you're doing.

Another objection. If I'm yielding because a pattern of your continuing and my yielding is made rationally appropriate both by your end of [crossing town if that's freedom consistent] and by my end of [going downtown if that's freedom consistent], then it might seem that I'm acting *for your end.* The implication that I can't act for my end without acting for yours seems to give the lie to independent purposiveness.

Our encounter suggests to me that there's more than one way in which a person's end can rationalise a particular action. Your end can sponsor your action in virtue of the fact that the action directly serves the end as when it causally contributes to or helps to constitute your end's attainment. But your end can also help to make it true of some action of mine that, by leaving you free to pursue your end of freedom-consistent motion, the action advances my own end of acting consistently with your freedom. Here I can take it that your end rationalizes my action although I don't see my action as something to be done because it contributes to your end's *achievement.*

XI

Even the nod and the glance are probably dispensable. A loose convention to some such effect as that participants in the sparser flow of foot traffic yield to participants in the denser one can serve as your and my cue to opt for (I stop, you go) as a profile that's supported by our ends of freedom-consistent motion. Of course I'd better not be thinking that I should stop because that convention disposes you to go independently of my own decision. But the convention might instead work just to make the one pattern salient so that each can decide to adopt her part, not as a response to what the other's going to do, but as an unconstrainedly recommended way of travelling consistently with the other's freedom.

Some conventionally orchestrated cooperations for street freedom have an especially misleading surface. The New Yorker who steps in front of an oncoming taxi appears to present its driver with a particular determinate motion—HEY, I'M *WALKING* HERE—to which the driver must yield if she's not to run him over. Locals know better than to take this literally. Each party's studiously pretended obliviousness to the other person's progress lends an exciting suspense to the age-old ceremony through which they settle, seemingly at the last non-fatal moment, on one particular pattern for acting on their ends of freedom-consistent motion. 'I'm walking here' really means 'I'm walking here consistently with your freedom, as you are driving consistently with mine, and this is me reminding you that we need to converge, soon, on a particular pair of freedom-consistent motions.' It's a characteristically ironic performance, a rather beautiful thing.

A freedom-grounded law of traffic isn't bound to take the form of an antecedent assignment of rights of way to every point of possible external incompatibility between our actions. We can obey the law, when we reach those points, by spontaneously cooperating for freedom there. Faced with an intersection we can decide for a particular interpersonal pattern of externally compatible movements through it. We can take this up as a way in which each will do what she's already set out to do—travel consistently with the other's freedom.

I believe that this street-level cooperation for freedom is not after all an *alternative* to the mode I discussed earlier, the recognition of antecedently legislated rights of way. Even where I yield to you in obedience of a stop sign, we are there and then cooperating for freedom. We are each taking my end of travelling consistently with your freedom and your end of travelling consistently with mine as calling us for to organise our walking and yielding into the particular profile that the stop sign mandates. We're doing this so that each will have decided how to advance her end independently of what the other was going to do.

When I postpone my drive beyond the rush hour this need not be because too many others are leaving now. If we've all set ends of travelling in particular directions consistently with others' freedom, I can regard my later departure as part of a pattern that's supported by those ends. For example it might happen that, as a matter of convention, subjectively urgent trips take precedence over subjectively casual ones. This can sound like another nightmare of heteronomy: puffed up with the importance of your particular purpose you are going to go, and I stay home because you're going to go. But the urgency of trips can function instead as a factor of salience, a cue for picking one pattern from the many others through which we might act on our ends of travelling consistently with freedom. We could work the same focal magic by deferring urgent trips in favour of trivial ones, or by flipping coins. If every other person is deciding to make her particular trip in this way—as one of many trips sponsored by all our ends of freedom-consistent travel and picked out purely by the convention—then I am not deferring to anyone's disposition to make her particular trip let alone to her judgement of its urgency.

I concede that this is hard to recognise as a description of actual traffic. I live in Los Angeles. If it's not what we're doing now, we should give it a try.

In the end this ideal of free movement is probably easier to appreciate on foot. As I walk through the city I claim no right against other walkers that they yield to my particular motion. Often I stop short or change direction in a way that's partly explained by my concern to act consistently with their freedom. But the explanation is not that my original trajectory was inconsistent with what the others were already doing. The others had also set out to walk consistently with my freedom and are now yielding or advancing as part of a profile of everyone's motion supported by that purpose. As my own reason to stop or turn aside, then, I may take the fact that my action forms part of a pattern of walking rationalised by our ends of walking consistently with the others' freedom. Walking by myself is something that I do with other people if I do it freely.

XII

I see no reason to confine this conception of the law of free motion to any particular subspace of inhabitable space. Nor can I understand the point of confining it to *space*. I am thinking that independence requires that all the space we might ever occupy as we act for our purposes, and all the external resources we might devote to them, fall under a single law of social traffic. This law is to determine the freedom-consistency of potentially mutually hindering actions independently of the facts as to which of these actions are being or will be done.

A law of this generality can't be a timetable. It can't be an antecedent assignment of rights of way and rights of access to objects, determined before we ever interact. We will have to set its particular terms as we go along. But our improvisation will obey a general law that has force independently of our activity and that was there before we started: the law of freedom requiring that we pursue our particular space-occupying and means-using ends consistently with others' freedom.

I also doubt that this law incorporates a general right of private property in spaces or objects. If there's a compelling rationale for property, it's that property frees our pursuit of object-requiring ends from constraint by others' choices. I've just claimed that this ideal of independent purposiveness is to be had by our all following laws that share out our access to resources on terms set independently of persons' dispositions to grab or use those goods. When it comes to deciding which particular laws to follow in this spirit, the imperative of independence does not favour private property over any other detailed scheme of access to external means.

Suppose that this last claim of mine is false. We *don't* secure independent end-setting rights by subjecting our potentially incompatible actions to joint decisions guided by everyone's aim of upholding others' freedom. Your pursuit of your purposes is *not* independent of my choice when it's bound by a requirement to resolve the potential incompatibilities of our action through deliberation that includes my own decision. Independence reserves for each person a right to pursue means-using purposes in a way that owes *no* fealty to any other person's decision.

If there's a trademarked virtue of property, it's that under property my deciding that you won't use an object I own settles the question of that use's consistency with my freedom independently of any decision that you might make about how it's to be used. To embrace this case for property is to restore a troubling resemblance between property and usufruct.

You own some land. I have none. I set out to [feed myself while doing as little work as is consistent with others' freedom]. You set out to [feed yourself while doing as little work as is consistent with others' freedom]. In advance of your aim you intend to [bring it about that I'll grow a crop for you]. You move to do this by granting me entry to your land if and only if I'll grow a crop there for you.

If property is to secure the right of strictly unilateral disposition over owned resources that is now on offer as its distinctive rationale, then your policy of refusing entry unless I work for you must constitute a determinate intention as to what will happen on this land that I've got to take as given in deciding myself whether to go and what to do there. Because you are bent on keeping me off the land unless I work it for you I can advance my own purpose if and only if I now resolve to grow your crop. Your settled action compels me to take up what had been, before I faced this choice of yours, an alien purpose.

XIII

Right is concerned with external incompatibilities between the possible actions of embodied persons. What concern is that? Which practical problem do these incompatibilities raise? What is the point of a moral mechanics?

The problem can't be that we're in danger of doing physically, spatially incompatible things. It's not going to happen. Nor does Kant seem worried only that we will fumble worthy particular projects when each person's pursuit collides with the efforts of others. The first is not a problem, the second does not cry out for freedom as its solution.

A great accomplishment of *Force and Freedom* is to have isolated a genuine problem raised by the potential collision of bodily actions that only rights to freedom seem poised to solve. This is the problem of extending to every person a right to set ends that holds independently of others' choices even as every person depends for the power to accomplish her ends on others omitting to choose what's incompatible with the action through which she pursues them.

I've argued that this independence is real where everyone, whatever her particular ends, sets out to [work for those ends consistently with others' freedom]. It requires that we dispose of the space and the objects our purposes demand through decisions to occupy and use them in profiles that these freedom-minded ends make rationally appropriate. When we all interact on this basis, no one is compelled to go along with what the others are already doing.

Having taken on Ripstein's conception of the point of right I find that it leads me to two sharp disagreements about right's content and status. One is already in the open. I doubt that independent purposiveness offers a good justification for a general right of private property in external objects.

A second disagreement is about the nature of the practical guidance that right supplies. On my picture it will not suffice for independence that persons forbear from specific externally individuated kinds of action—kinds individuated independently of the motives for which they're done. It's not enough that I omit to bum-rush your space or that I keep my hands off your stuff. If in acting for my ends I am bent on occupying a particular empty location or on making off with a particular idle tool, then you are compelled to defer to these actions by doing only what's externally compatible with them. But when I make it my purpose to [pursue my other ends consistently with your freedom], *this* practical stance does not constitute a tendency of action standing in determinate incompatibility relations with the things you might do. Instead of confining your action to what's externally compatible with itself, my freedom-minded intention joins yours in throwing rational support to one or another pattern of your and my compatible actions.

Kant says up front that the domain of right is the domain of coercively enforceable external obligations. He is thinking that right is upheld if people do what's consistent with others' freedom, and that they can do that whether or not they are acting for the sake of others' freedom. Against this proposal I've just argued that right obligates me to act for freedom: consistency with your freedom itself requires that I make that consistency my maxim. It would seem to follow, by the letter of Kant's announcement, that others may force me to do that. But no one may force me to act for a particular motive. I deny that right's freedom-grounded obligations are satisfied independently of motive, and so I deny that they're all coercively enforceable.

This marks a pretty drastic revision, I know. But I am thinking that we should go ahead and make it. It's true that Kant has set out in *The Doctrine of Right* to characterise the universe of external and enforceable obligation. But he's also trying to say when and why it's okay for one person to hinder another's action.

The second project calls for some account of the problem raised by external incompatibility. Ripstein convinces me that, if this is a problem, that's because only certain patterns of mutual hindrance can coexist with every person's enjoyment of a right to set ends independently of others' choices. But I've just argued that no profile of externally compatible, externally individuated action *suffices* for that independence. You are not independent unless I am acting for the sake of your independence. If this is right we'll have to choose between Kant's two descriptions of his topic: between the study of external obligations and the reconciliation of mutual hindrance with independent purposiveness. For now I've chosen the project whose point I hope I'm finally coming to see.

XIV

The novel *Independent People* by Halldór Laxness tells the story of an Icelandic sheep farmer who values two things above all others: his independence and his sheep. When we first meet Bjartur he's managed to put together a herd, some acres of grassland and a farmhouse. 'Size isn't everything', he says to his dog, acknowledging that the house is not big.

> Take my word for it, freedom is of more account than the height of a roof beam. I ought to know; mine cost eighteen years of slavery. The man who lives on his own land is an independent man. He is his own master. If I can keep my sheep alive through the winter and can pay what has been stipulated from year to year—then I pay what has been stipulated; and I have kept my sheep alive. No, it is freedom that we are all after, Titla. He who pays his way is a king. He who keeps his sheep alive through the winter lives in a palace.[3]

Things don't turn out very well for Bjartur, and he makes several big mistakes. To keep his sheep alive through the winter he starves his family. To build a taller house he borrows against the high price commanded by Icelandic wool during the First World War. When peace breaks out and the price comes down, he loses his empty house along with the rest of his stake.

I take it that many of my fellow left-wing readers come away from this book confirmed in their view that independence is a joke. Even a man who tends sheep in the Icelandic interior finds his life course set not only by the weather—although, *yes*, by the weather—but also by his unchosen subjection to a matrix of social relations. By the price of wool in terms of coffee. Rather than a free life the most he can hope for is a happy one, a high price instead of a low.

I disagree. Bjartur's folly is not that he aspires to independence in society but that he confuses that independence with private property. An owner of

[3] H Laxness, *Independent People*, trans JA Thomson (New York, Vintage, 2008).

sheep has the right to set sheep-related ends but in the property society is more or less sharply confined to doing what can be done with sheep. If he wants to do something else, he will have to find someone who's willing take his wool for cash with which he can buy the means to his other ends. In this way he depends for his entitlement to set non-sheep ends on merchants, bailiffs, manufacturers, bankers and Danes.

(Unfortunately Bjartur compounds his fetishism of ownership by also making a fetish of *sheep*. Refusing to sell even one ewe for a cow that would give more milk for his children, he appears truly to have set for himself the ownership of sheep as a final end.)

For all his errors Bjartur gets one thing right. He is for freedom—and he is sometimes even free as when, with no master to order him back to the house, he walks over the heath reciting his poems to his dog.

It might yet turn out that people living together can be free people, independent people. That will not happen when everyone has managed to exclude all the others from her portion of external means. For a better example of how to do it I propose the law of the street. To escape constraint by others' choices we should share out the space for and means to our independently adopted ends through a law that binds us independently of those choices. This is a law that everyone will uphold, not because she must limit her activity to what can be sustained on her lot, but because, like Bjartur, she is after freedom and so is trying to do what leaves the others free. The law will set us free by giving us this chance to act for freedom's sake.[4]

[4] I am grateful to Arthur Ripstein for his corrections of a badly mistaken predecessor to this chapter. For conversations about freedom and property I thank Matt Boyle, Lee-Ann Chae, Louis-Philippe Hodgson, Robert Hughes, Japa Pallikkathayil and Stephen White.

Part III

Public Right

6

Why Is Willing Irrelevant to the Grounding of (Any) Obligation? Remarks on Arthur Ripstein's Conception of Omnilateral Willing

GEORGE PAVLAKOS*

I. PRELIMINARIES

WHETHER KANT'S DOCTRINE of Right takes legal obligation to be a different kind of obligation than moral obligation is a contested matter. Crucially, legal obligation would be an *aliud* to moral obligation if its grounds were of a different kind than those of moral obligation. Such difference is claimed by the adherents of legal positivism, who maintain that the grounds of legal obligation are social facts as opposed to invariable action-guiding standards, which are usually considered by non-positivists to ground moral obligation. Over the years the doctrine of right has been read both as a defence (or proof) of legal positivism and as offering a powerful case for non-positivism. Arthur Ripstein's recent reconstruction rightly seeks to place the doctrine of right beyond such crude dichotomies in suggesting that legal obligation be accounted for in terms of omnilateral willing, or the form of willing that pertains to coercive public institutions that are invested with moral authority. Thus, while residing in social institutions, omnilateral willing realises a genuinely moral demand, namely the demand to secure equal freedom for autonomous agents in their mutual interaction.

* I am grateful to Barbara Herman and Stanley Paulson for valuable comments and discussion, which led to considerable improvement of the argument herein. Any errors that remain, in particular with respect to the interpretation of Kant's philosophy, are my own. Further I am grateful to Sari Kisilevsky for inviting me to contribute to the volume and Arthur Ripstein for his continuing interest in what I have to say. I would also like to acknowledge the financial support of the Grant Agency of the Czech Academy of Sciences through a project on 'The Role of the Principle of Proportionality in the Decision-Making Process of Courts' (grant ID: 15- 23955S).

In what follows, I wish to probe the ability of omnilateral authorisation to overcome the dichotomy between positivism and non-positivism. I wish to suggest that qua determinant of the grounds of legal obligation, omnilateral willing disguises what legal and moral obligation have in common and conveys the impression that we, as agents, can be obligated in two distinct ways that are disconnected from one another. I will locate the reason for the misrepresentation in what appears to be a standard interpretation of the role of agent motivation in legal and moral obligation. Ripstein's account appears to be presupposing the same picture, even as he tries to move beyond it. In the end I will be arguing that Ripstein is right in his diagnosis that individual willing falls short of grounding legal obligation. His mistake is to think that some other form of willing can deliver the grounding question, because none can.

The first part will take on board what I hope are some uncontroversial remarks about what it takes for a social fact to contribute to the content of an obligation. Taking these remarks as a point of departure, I shall, first, outline what I take to be the standard story about the role of motivation in legal and moral obligation and then move on to demonstrate how this story infects Ripstein's idea of omnilateral authorisation. Then I argue that, given the standard view, an undesirable proliferation of conceptions of normativity arises, which is incompatible with Kant's fundamental account about what obligates agents. Finally I move, painting here with a broad brush, to a more unified account of obligation which I believe lies more within the spirit of Kant's practical philosophy.

I am fully aware that, in formulating my contribution in those terms I am, somewhat surreptitiously, dragging Professor Ripstein into a discussion of law and ethics that, in his own words, he never intended to address in detail in *Force and Freedom*.[1] Yet I hope that he will agree with me that this remains a pressing matter, which will continue to cast its shadow over every analysis of Kant's concept of law.

Finally, a disclaimer: I should warn the reader that, under no circumstances, am I raising a claim to exegetical accuracy with regard to Kant's writings. Rather I am offering an argument which is premised on key ideas of Kant's philosophy. However, I do wish that what I say remains compatible with the spirit of Kant, if not pointing in the direction of a more coherent interpretation of his ideas.

II. RATIONAL DETERMINATION AND AN OPEN QUESTION

Let me begin with a puzzle: suppose the law states that I ought to do X. It seems to me a legitimate question—at least within Kant's practical

[1] A Ripstein, 'Reply to Flikschuh and Pavlakos' (2010) 1 *Jurisprudence* 317, 323.

philosophy—to ask whether I am actually obligated to do X, and this for at least two interrelated reasons: first, because the addressees of all normative prescriptions are persons (there is, as it were, no simpler unit of agency in the Kantian universe); second, to the extent to which normative prescriptions are directed at persons, it seems natural to suppose that for anything to count as an obligation it has to be something that we can square with the story Kant tells us about how agents are obligated *simpliciter*. This is the story of the moral law: nothing (incentives, brute facts or social institutions) that purports to obligate can do so unless it figures as a normative reason before the deliberating agent.[2] Moreover, to figure as such a reason, it will need to be reflectively endorsed as 'a maxim through which the agent can at the same time will that it should become a universal law'.[3] Assuming the correctness of this picture, we can state our initial puzzle as follows: it is conceivable that for any social fact[4] that purports to obligate an agent A, it will remain an *open question* whether it also succeeds in grounding an obligation for A.[5] In other words, each time the agent is addressed by normative utterance <NU>: 'You ought to do X!', there is nothing in that fact alone to rule out the question: 'Am I obligated to do X?' For, under the Kantian conception of agency, the question about the obligatory force of <NU> is antecedent to any facts of pedigree outside the reflective test of agency. Let us label this 'the open question of obligation'.

As for open questions, the main problem is one of determination (or the lack of it). Until we can lock on to something that can generate a determinate answer, the question will hang over us and so will its troubling effects. The problem ramifies, for it presents itself not just in connection with the Kantian account but also with any other account that takes agency itself to be validating of whatever may count as a reason for action (obligations being the most central cases of that class of reasons).[6] In contemporary legal theory, Mark

[2] This is different from saying that only whatever each agent takes to be binding on them has normative force. The test of endorsement 'kicks in' with particular agents, yet its content refers to an ideal dimension: it is 'agency simpliciter' which endorses, not a particular physico-psychological unit. This will turn out to be most important when we explore the role of motivation in legal and moral obligation, Section IV below.

[3] Immanuel Kant, *Groundwork of the Metaphysics of Morals* (various editions).

[4] I assume it to be rather uncontroversial that legal obligations invest in social facts (mostly, doings and sayings of state officials).

[5] I do not mean to suggest that all normative reasons amount to obligations. There are of course plenty of normative reasons that are not obligatory. However, I take it to be obvious why obligations should be central in the context of the present inquiry.

[6] Or, for that matter, any account that considers normative properties or facts to be irreducible. See the *locus classicus* GE Moore, *Principia Ethica*, 2nd edn (Cambridge, Cambridge University Press, 1993). However, I do not mean to suggest that all such accounts will be compatible with the Kantian account of obligation. For a succinct criticism of moral realism from the point of view of Kant's practical philosophy, see C Korsgaard, *The Sources of Normativity* (Cambridge, Cambridge University Press, 1996).

Greenberg has proposed to tackle the indeterminacy implied by the open question through the rational determination condition (RDC).[7]

According to the RDC, in order for any social facts to determine the content of the relevant legal norms, more than a relation of supervenience is required—all that supervenience can deliver is metaphysical determination, or the condition that the facts of a particular legal practice (LP) determine *factually* a legal norm (LN) across possible worlds. More is required, however, in order to establish the *normative* relevance of social facts to the content of any legal norm. Rational determination captures this requirement in pointing to normative entities (for simplicity: *reasons*) that make the social facts of the practice relevant to the content of legal norms. More specifically, Greenberg proposes a two-stage model for cashing out rational determination: in the first stage what determines the truth of legal propositions are models, or sets of rules, that make (rational and non-opaque) connections between the factual components of the practice and the content of legal norms. In a second step, models must be validated by reasons. On pain of failing to provide for rational determination, reasons must be conceived of as being external to either the facts of the practice or the legal norms they purport to connect. Finally, Greenberg proposes to understand reasons not merely as rational but also as evaluative standards—value facts; value facts are, in his words, 'all-things-considered truth(s) about the applicable considerations—the Truth, for short'.[8] The particulars of Greenberg's proposal aside, the crucial point he makes is that the connection between the factual components of legal practice and the content of legal norms must be such that makes *normative* sense to the rational reasoner, along the lines of the RDC.

Greenberg's account is particularly apt for capturing what is essential in the Kantian account, even as it sets a threshold that is lower than the Kantian test of the Moral Law.[9] For the RDC redeems successfully the Kantian concern of introducing a *normative constraint* on the connection between institutional facts and the content of an obligation: that connection must make normative sense if legal facts are to contribute to law's being normative from the point of view of agency. What renders it less stringent than the Kantian condition

[7] M Greenberg, 'How Facts Make Law' (2004) 10 *Legal Theory* 157, reprinted in S Hershovitz (ed), *Exploring Law's Empire: The Jurisprudence of Ronald Dworkin* (Oxford, Oxford University Press, 2006) 225–64.

[8] ibid, 189. Dworkin's rejoinder is interesting. He argues that Greenberg connects values only indirectly with legal propositions for, actually, in his theory values are only standards for the evaluation of theories (models), not legal propositions themselves. See Dworkin's 'Response' in Hershovitz (n 7) 291, 310–11.

[9] Thus Greenberg's account would meet with the consent of anyone adopting a non-reductive normative theory provided their account would seek to illustrate a connection with the agent's reasoning.

of the moral law is the fact that it does not yet preclude the precise content of rational determination. To that degree it can serve as a starting point for assessing the role of omnilateral willing in the grounding of legal obligation without prejudicing the outcome of the assessment. I will later suggest, in Section V, that omnilateral willing fails to determine the open question of obligation, because it drives a wedge between the sources of legal and moral obligation.

III. MOTIVES, GROUNDS AND OBLIGATIONS

The RDC provides a good analytical tool for assessing accounts of obligation: in remaining neutral as to what can appropriately determine obligation—with an eye to bringing the *open question of obligation* to closure—it merely indicates the form of determination, leaving its substance open. Take the case we are concerned with, legal obligation. Why not assume that legal obligation is subject to its own special version of rational determination? Indeed, rational determination rests on different or at least differentiated grounds from those determining moral obligation. Should something along these lines be plausible, then omnilateral willing might be the right thing for pulling off the trick in the case of law, in which case we may worry later about the precise relation of legal to moral obligation (as well as the further relation between their respective grounds). Were one to take on board this picture, it would be natural to argue that different grounds for determining what contributes to the content of obligation amount to different (or differentiated) kinds of obligation: legal, moral, etc, perhaps ad infinitum, save for imposing some loose constraint from family resemblance, which would hold together the diverse kinds of obligation. However, one may be quick to object that while a pluralism-in-obligation may be possible on many other occasions, it is inaccurate in Kant's case: Kant, our objector would continue, is pretty clear about what rationally contributes to the determination of obligation: it is the test of the moral law. Or is it?

The objection strikes me as natural. It seems to stumble, however, on a standard picture about moral psychology of obligations (legal and moral) that is attributed to Kant and which, in my view, informs the background of Ripstein's concept of omnilateral willing. I am not claiming that Ripstein approves of the standard picture, using it to support his own account. Rather, as I will be arguing shortly, Ripstein in attempting to move beyond the crude claims of the standard story never challenges its deep premises, which in the end infiltrate his own project. Here is the structure of the remainder of the discussion: I shall first outline briefly the standard picture and then argue that Ripstein's conception of omnilateral willing remains within the premises of the standard picture. Next, I will spell out the paradox to which both accounts lead. Finally,

I will attempt to offer an alternative reconstruction which presents a unified story of moral and legal obligation, at least at the level of moral psychology.

IV. MORAL PSYCHOLOGY

Let us grapple first with the view that what determines the *open question of obligation* has different candidates in morality and in law. This is a crucial issue for, as we have seen, rational determination is the key to individuating obligations, hence different grounds of rational determination will lead to distinct types of obligation. How is it that law and morality can generate different grounds for the rational determination of the respective obligations they impose? The answer requires a brief excursion into Kantian moral psychology. To support the claim, its proponents adduce a fact about the manner in which either domain engages the motivation of the agent: while morality requires that the content of the obligation be simultaneously the content of the incentive of the agent, legal obligation is premised on totally different grounds. Here the incentive of the agent is irrelevant to the existence of obligation, for legal obligation concerns the external behavior of agents, not their motivational reasons. In addition to the above claim, it is argued, in connection with Kant, that the content of legal obligation analytically entails an authorisation to coerce one who infringes upon it.[10] Consequently, the determinants of legal obligation display two key differences from those of morality: they do not involve the motivation of the agent; and they do involve external imposition of behaviour.

This reconstruction has led to the claim that Kant is a positivist when it comes to legal obligation: in other words, he endorses some form of the separation thesis, or the claim that there exists no necessary connection between legal and moral obligation.[11] What is more, under a more stringent version of the claim, legal obligations are grounded on coercive social institutions, whereas moral obligations are grounded on a pure test of reason.

Ripstein rightly would like to reject the dichotomy lurking in this picture.[12] One need not think—in Ripstein's view—that rational determination[13] in respect of legal obligation should be conceived of in a manner that is radically disconnected from rational determination in the case of moral obligation.

[10] Immanuel Kant, *The Doctrine of Right* (various editions) 6: 231 (pagination follows the Edition of the Prussian Academy).

[11] See instead of others, M Willaschek, 'Which Imperatives for Right? On the Non-Prescriptive Character of Juridical Laws in Kant's *Metaphysics of Morals*', in M Timmons (ed), *Kant's Metaphysics of Morals. Interpretive Essays* (Oxford, Oxford University Press, 2002) 65–87.

[12] Ripstein (n 1) 321.

[13] Ripstein never uses the term rational determination, hence it would be more accurate to say: the function performed by rational determination. For economy, I shall use 'rational determination' throughout.

When Kant invokes institutions with an eye to legal obligation—Ripstein maintains—he invests them with a very clear moral content: 'Kant's strategy is to show, first, that a certain form of human interaction is *morally* required, and that, further, that form of interaction is morally impossible in the absence of institutions.'[14] In other words, in creating the space for a class of actions that are morally required, institutions 'inherit' (some portion of) their morality. It is the same morality that underpins the omnilateral willing that public institutions bring to expression. Now, given that omnilateral willing is what determines rationally the contribution of institutional facts to legal obligations, one would expect there to exist a continuity of grounds for moral and legal obligation. Not so, for here comes a further statement:

> Omni-lateral willing does not purport to provide citizens with an internal motive for conformity with the requirements of right. … Like all requirements of right, its focus is on what people do, not on why they do it; the only incentive it provides is external … the omni-lateral will is not a pooling of individual practical authority. Neither its form nor its content is reducible to individual wills, but its normative basis is that it secures the rights of its members. (323)

Thus, omnilateral willing and the institutions that substantiate it are given a distinct status as grounds of obligation. Of course, omnilateral willing is not found on the same level as socio-institutional facts. For, as we said, social facts are indeterminate when it comes to their contribution to the content of legal obligation. Facts need to be rationally determined with a view to eliminating the open question of obligation: in other words, eliminating the possibility of being addressed by an authoritative utterance U and yet make room for the question: 'Am I really obligated to do as U says?' Omnilateral willing, rather, undertakes the task of rationally determining the contribution of social facts to the content of legal obligation. This clarification notwithstanding, the question stands: why open up a gap between that which the omnilateral will wills and what the moral law commands? Why not keep the two together, considering that omnilateral will is about the realisation of a domain of interaction that is anyway morally required?

The question appears all the more pressing because the RDC—notwithstanding its minimal requirements on content—is still pushing in the direction of a unified account of obligation. Recall the point of the RDC: it was to account for the need to determine the grounds of obligation qua obligation *for the agent*. Even though this does not readily eliminate the possibility of having a pluralistic account of grounds, it does seem to place a special onus on the pluralist to argue for such a position. For, in linking obligation to agency, the RDC entails that any pluralism of grounds would lead to a pluralism of

[14] Ripstein (n 1) 321 (emphasis added).

agency. Yet, the latter type of pluralism—pluralism of agency—could easily deteriorate into fragmentation. Here we are, changing our identity as agents each time we adopt another set of criteria for what counts as obligatory. This 'pull' or gravitational force of the RDC toward unity is not meant to offer a conclusive argument; it does, however, put some pressure on Ripstein's conception of omnilateral willing. Why then insist on it?

I suspect that the key reason why Ripstein takes such great pains to keep omnilateral willing as a distinct source of obligation is the deeply entrenched view (which I earlier attributed to the standard picture) that obligation is determined in relation to willing. Complete involvement of individual willing will lead to fully fledged moral obligation, whereas its absence will leave room for a different kind of obligation that is premised on external imposition. Hence, any variation in the involvement of willing will give rise to a difference in the kind of obligation generated.[15]

Here is how the argument might run in full: moral obligation, on the one hand, requires that the agent make the Moral Law (or, which is more accurate, the maxims that pass the reflective endorsement test of the Moral Law) the content of her motivation. Conversely, in law individual willing plays no role at all; the agent need not endorse what counts as obligatory, for legal obligations concern entirely and purely the external behavior of agents. Law does not care for the motivation of the agents it addresses, nor does it try to elicit the appropriate states of the will, appropriate in that they aim to match the relevant legal obligations. Instead, it uses coercive means to bring the behaviour of agents into line with the conduct it prescribes.[16]

And here is how the standard picture of moral obligation might impose its form of thinking on Ripstein's account: in morality, where the motivation of the agent is relevant, the one who wills is the agent. In law, where only the external behavior of agents is of any relevance, a different type of willing would be required. This expansion, by analogy, of the role of willing to the case of moral obligation would have an important consideration going for it. Coercive imposition, on its own, could with difficulty meet the main requirement of the rational determination condition, one that we took to apply minimally to any obligation. Recall the rational determination condition: its key requirement for the existence of an obligation is that it appear before the

[15] In questioning the standard view, I may appear to be rejecting the role of willing in accounts of obligation. The appearance would be false. It is, of course, only in one sense that willing is irrelevant to the determination of obligation, ie when it is conceived of as consisting in psychological states of particular individuals. Conversely, willing in the sense of what would be willed by an ideal agent is perfectly compatible with accounts of obligation. In fact, willing in the latter sense is an integral part of the Kantian account of obligation (see Section V, below). I thank Barbara Herman for helping me bring this point into focus.

[16] *cf* with Ripstein's recent reconstruction in his 'Reply' (n 1).

agent qua obligation. When it comes to legal obligation, the standard picture purports to meet that condition through coercive imposition. However, this might seem too weak for meeting the constraint of rational determination.

It is precisely this demand—ie to explain the normative pull of legal obligation—which Ripstein's idea of omnilateral willing purports to meet. According to Ripstein, if the external imposition of behaviour were to originate from any individual agent unilaterally, it would fail to impose any obligation, for it would then constitute a distinct instance of interference with the agency of those whom it addressed. Conversely, for it to amount to genuine (legal) obligation, external imposition would need to be grounded in a type of willing capable of rendering coercive deeds or sayings of others as the sources of valid obligation, even though they displayed prima facie the structure of interference with the free choice of the agent.[17] This additional condition is supposed to provide a normative argument as to why individual willing is insufficient to deliver legal obligation. It also aspires to moving beyond the standard picture by pointing to a distinct type of willing, rather than doing away with willing in the case of law.[18]

Responding to that need, Ripstein introduces the idea of omnilateral willing as the specific type of willing that corresponds to the 'needs' or 'requirements' of legal obligation, one that remains an instance of willing all the same. Omnilateral willing is called upon to generate the authorisation of legal reasons by the collective in a manner that preserves the equal freedom of each of its members under conditions of mutual interaction.[19] Even though it remains an instance of willing itself, it is not to be thought of as an aggregate or some other function of the individual wills of the members of the collective, but rather as a separate instance of willing, one that is, as it were, unanalysable in its role as the ground of legal obligation.[20]

[17] On the standard picture the key difference between moral and legal obligation is that in the first case I bind myself (legislate the Moral Law to myself), whereas in the second case I put others under an obligation by my actions. My contention of this picture is that the two stages are closely intertwined: the operation of binding myself is not a solipsistic or subjectivist undertaking, but rests on grounds that any rational agent ought to endorse (norms). Relatedly, the normative impact of my deeds on others' agency does not rest on some *sui generis* normative basis, but on norms that are normatively binding on any rational agent. To that extent the grounds of moral and legal obligation are, to say the least, co-original. I am indebted to Katrin Flikschuh for prompting me with her comments to drive home this point.

[18] An obvious advantage of this move is that it generates coherence between the two domains of obligation: morality and law.

[19] Yet, even on this construction some considerable overlap between the two kinds of reasons, moral and legal, must be retained, given the prominence Kant attributed to the idea of individual autonomy in his practical philosophy. In particular omnilateral authorisation cannot lead to laws that autonomous agents could never have chosen themselves.

[20] Ripstein (n 1) 323.

But does omnilateral willing (and the institutions in which it invests) bestow a special authority upon the deeds of others that is independent of what grounds our obligations anyway? I think it would if two conditions obtained: first, if obligations in general were, in the first place, indeed determined by states of the will; and second, if omnilateral willing were to function as filling the gap stemming from the absence of individual willing. Neither, in my view, obtains, for willing as a psychological state of whomever is irrelevant to the grounding of any obligation, be it legal or moral. To that extent Ripstein is right in identifying the grave insufficiency of individual willing for grounding legal obligations. His mistake is to think that some other form of willing can deliver the grounding question.

Before proceeding to argue these points, I would like to suggest a way of illustrating graphically the consequences of extending the class of grounds of obligation, by adding omnilateral willing to it. If a new class of grounds were to be imported, it would have an impact on the content of the Moral Law. As we know, the Moral Law sets the requirements for something to count as an obligation *simpliciter* for the acting agent.[21] To that extent anything that purported to ground obligations *for* rational agents would have to feature in the description of what counts as obligation under the Moral Law. For the Moral Law, has, amongst its tasks, that of explaining the normativity of whatever counts as an obligation for any rational agent.

Thus, an expansion of the class of grounds of obligation, say, by evoking omnilateral willing, would require that one perform 'surgery' on the Moral Law, which might then read something like this:

> You ought to act on [a maxim through which you can at the same time will that it should become a universal law] *plus* [that which is authorised by omnilateral willing].

The incongruence of this formulation does not require special argument. It is at odds with Kant's key ideas of autonomy and self-determination and would require, were we going to attribute it to him, an extensive rewriting of his practical philosophy. If Kant is not determinately clear about the relation between legal and moral obligation (or the moral law and the universal principle of right), allowing thus for a large margin for interpretation, he is resolutely clear about the seat, form and structure of practical normativity. In that respect, the formulation of the moral law seems to me exclusive.

[21] 'Obligation simpliciter' purports to capture the class of obligations that apply to everyone and is conceptually contrasted to obligations that are perspectival (obligation for A, obligation for B, etc).

V. RECONSTRUCTION

Before I continue, let me take stock. It would appear that what is at work in Ripstein's choice, introducing a separate ground for rational determination in the form of omnilateral willing, is the same thing that informs the standard picture of moral obligation, as discussed earlier. Here, as before, what is at work are two argumentative paths that purport to work *in tandem*: the first one claims that the grounds of legal and moral obligation are distinct owing to the difference pertaining, on each occasion, to the motivation of the agent. The second adds that all legal obligation contains something that is not found in moral obligation at all: external imposition (or coercion) through social institutions; hence, one must account for a specific difference in the grounds of legal obligation. In this context, onmilateral willing consolidates the separation between the grounds of moral and legal obligation in claiming to meet the normative constraint imposed by something like the rational determination condition.

It follows that in order to question this reading one must level a twofold attack: first, to take on the thesis that motivation matters at all to the grounding of (legal and moral) obligation; second, to argue that coercion (and omnilateral willing) does not concern the grounds of legal obligation, but merely something akin to an enabler for legal obligation. In the remainder of this chapter I shall attempt primarily to deliver the first prong of the attack, while offering some implicit suggestions for delivering the second. I argue in favour of a distinction between grounds and motives that can easily be accommodated by Kantian meta-ethics. This distinction takes one a considerable distance along the way toward the conclusion that motivational reasons qua psychological states are irrelevant to the grounds of both moral and legal obligation. Conversely, it is reasons qua normative facts which in both cases can ground an obligation. Resting on this finding, I proceed to argue that coercive institutions—those that Ripstein takes to be bearers of a separate ground for legal obligation (ie omnilateral willing)—are merely enablers of legal obligations.

For a start, questions of motivation ought to be kept distinct from questions of the grounds of obligation, not just in law but first and foremost in morality. I think that one of the great virtues of Kant's meta-ethical account of duties, and one that is mainly responsible for its groundbreaking character within the history of ideas, is the contention that those duties are grounded not on the motivational states of agents but on a universal test of reflective endorsement. Thus, the motivational states of agents, regarded not only in isolation but also in the aggregate, when those agents act in concert, are irrelevant to the grounding of obligation. To that extent, when it comes to the grounding of obligations, moral reasons and reasons from right might share more than is commonly assumed.

On a plausible interpretation, Kant's key meta-ethical contention is that motivation is irrelevant to the grounding of practical obligation[22] if motivation is conceived of as an operation that is in addition to or is distinct from the universal test of reflective endorsement, which is prescribed by the Moral Law.[23] To put it in more instructive vocabulary: what makes it the case that I ought, say, to repay my debts is not my *desire* to repay my debts but the (normative) *fact* that I ought to repay my debts.[24] My desire to repay my debts is not antecedent to that fact but consequent to it, at least to the extent that I do not suffer any additional pathology in my moral psychology. Along these lines the Kantian idea of moral obligation entails that I am acting morally when I make the (normative) fact that I ought to pay my debts the content of my motivating state. This is significantly different, however, from saying that the one or the other motivating state grounds the truth of the fact that I ought to repay my debts. Even though the operation of reflective endorsement involves as its starting point subjective states of the will, which eventually are scrutinised in the light of the requirements of the moral law, the final stage of the reflective endorsement test is a state of the will only in name, for it coincides with that which would have been willed by an ideal agent. The content of such idealised or counterfactual states of the will is given by propositions that are truth-evaluable, as opposed to actual states of the will, which do not admit of truth-values. To speak with Michael Smith, such idealised or counterfactual states are no longer psychological states but (normative) facts.[25]

With this conclusion in place, the issue of coercion can be given a new twist: while in morality one must start from subjective psychological states and work one's way, through a test of reason, to non-subjective normative facts, in the case of law the process is the reverse: here the Kantian philosopher is not

[22] My interpretation seems to be in line with a growing body of literature in Kantian ethical theory, which argues for a distinction between moral obligation/permissibility and moral praiseworthiness. The argument, to the extent to which I can distil it in a generic form, is that moral obligation, as a property pertaining to acts, ought to be individuated independently of praiseworthiness, as a property pertaining to acts with respect to agents' motivation. While obligation is determined on the grounds of what constitutes a right reason, praiseworthiness requires us to look into the psychology of agents. Some authors (Markovits) go as far as to claim that praiseworthiness too needs to be worked out in accordance with what is deemed obligatory. For the relevant literature, see T Scanlon, *Moral Dimensions* (Cambridge, MA, Harvard University Press, 2008); J Markovits 'Acting for the Right Reasons' (2010) 119 *Philosophical Review* 201; U Heuer 'Intentions, Permissibility, and the Reasons for Which We Act' in G Pavlakos and V Rodriguez-Blanco (eds), *Reasons and Intentions in Law and Practical Agency* (Cambridge, Cambridge University Press, 2015), 11–30.

[23] Admittedly, this requirement concerns primarily moral reasons. However, to the extent at least, that the Moral Law is placed at the foundation of practical reason in its entirety, as I believe Ripstein would agree with, the way moral reasons work is decisive for all other kinds of reasons.

[24] Talk of facts is perfectly compatible with the Kantian philosophy to the extent that we take facts to be constituted through the test of the Moral Law.

[25] M Smith, 'Internal Reasons' (1995) 55 *Philosophy and Phenomenological Research* 109, 122–23.

interested in the question 'how does one elevate subjective motivational states to objective reasons?' but, instead in the question 'how does one put objective reasons—those arrived at by way of sound moral reasoning—into the business of guiding the behaviour of actual agents?' Coming as an answer to the latter question, coercion (or enforcement) assumes simply the role of an enabler for an obligation that pre-exists it. In this sense, coercion in law is the flip-side of the test of reason in morality: as, in the case of morality, the subjective motives of agents cannot be relied upon to *ground* sound obligations, so, in the case of law, the subjective motives of agents cannot be relied upon to *pursue* sound obligations. Whereas in morality a test of 'pure reason' undertook the role of 'purifying' subjective motives, coercion in law undertakes the role of aligning subjective motives together with a view to acting on sound reasons (obligations). In either case what grounds obligations are normative truths (facts). However, these facts need to be linked to agents' capacity for action: internally in morality (by considering the raw psychological set of agents); externally in law, by eliciting a uniform response of actual agents to right reasons through coercion (enforcement).[26]

To assume, with Ripstein, that institutions undertake a symmetric function to individual states of the will in a process of collective authorisation is not satisfactory. To begin with, for the reasons rehearsed above, what determines the grounds of moral obligation are not psychological states of the will at all. Second, since the Kantian account of the grounds of moral obligation does not involve any psychological states, there is no need to look for a symmetric structure in the realm of right. Rushing through some of the more obvious steps of the argument, it would follow that omnilateral willing cannot generate distinct grounds for obligation.[27] Conversely, if my analysis is correct, and grounds ought to be kept distinct from motives, there emerges an altogether different understanding of what might constitute omnilateral willing. Omnilateral willing would rather refer to the requirement of taking into account

[26] A note of caution is called for: on the reconstruction I propose, the 'normative work' is not done by coercion but by the reasons which can be legitimately enforced. It is not the case that the state can enforce whatever it can coerce upon its citizens but, conversely, it may use coercion to enforce obligations that count as genuine from the point of view of practical agency.

[27] Interestingly Ripstein seems to assume something like the interpretation I am proposing when he argues that the point of coercive enforcement is not to impose *sui generis* obligations but merely to set things right *simpliciter* (A Ripstein, *Force and Freedom: Kant's Legal and Political Philosophy* (Cambridge, MA, Harvard University Press, 2009) 87). I think it is consistent here to suggest that that which determines what is right is not introspection about anyone's actual incentives but instead those normative facts (norms) which, from the point of view of morality, are capable of grounding an obligation. With respect to those norms agents have an obligation of virtue to make them the content of their motives (e.g. incentives), as Ripstein himself contends (ibid, 358). For a similar view attaining to the continuity between moral and legal obligation, *cf* P Guyer, 'Kant's Deductions of the Principles of Right', in M Timmons, *Kant's 'Metaphysics of Morals'. Interpretive Essays* (Oxford, Oxford University Press, 2002) 23–64, 26.

others as persons whenever agents (individually or collectively) engage in the reflective enterprise of establishing the reasons they have.[28]

Where, then, to look for the role of institutional arrangements? Painting with a broad brush, institutions seem to play the role of bridging the gap between obligations that are valid *simpliciter* and their instantiations in particular contexts of interaction between agents.[29] A principal effect of this interplay between the universal and the particular is the fact that the same obligation may admit of distinct instantiations in different institutional contexts. However, and this is key in my opinion, difference or diversity in content does not necessarily entail difference in the grounds of obligation. As a consequence, the same obligation may find different institutional expressions without any need to suppose that its grounds change too. To that extent, institutions may be regarded as *enablers* rather than *grounds* of obligations.

Enablers behave toward grounds in a different manner than motivating states. Different enablers may correspond to the same ground even if they lead to obligations that are distinguishable in their content. The ground remains the same because the function of the ground does not compete with that of the enabler on the same level: the ground continues to determine the normative or practical force of the obligation even though its 'direction' might take a different turn depending on the enabler that is in play. However, and this is crucial, it is the ground that still has the last word even on the question of which enablers are relevant (and to which extent) on each occasion.[30]

[28] To that extent I would be tempted to argue in a Kantian spirit, albeit not in the spirit of Kantian exegesis, that practical reasoning about moral and legal obligations is unified on the grounds that it includes an omnipersonal dimension. Such a contention would bestow a 'cosmopolitan bias' to our understanding of the normative impact of globalisation on legal and political institutions in recent years. It should be noted that this theme has seen a recent revival in legal and political philosophy: see AJ Julius, 'Nagel's Atlas' (2006) 34 *Philosophy and Public Affairs* 176–92; N Stavropoulos, 'The Relevance of Coercion: Some Preliminaries' (2009) 22 *Ratio Juris* 339–58. Also, for a more narrow application of the significance of coercion for legal obligation in international law, see Pavlakos and Pauwelyn, 'Principled Monism and the Normative Conception of Coercion under International Law', in M Evans and P Koutrakos (eds), *Beyond the Established Legal Orders: Substantive Interconnections Between the EU and the Rest of the World* (Oxford, Hart Publishing, 2011) 317.

[29] For a more thoroughgoing discussion of the distinction between *reasons simpliciter* and *reasons in a domain*, see G Pavlakos, 'Practice, Reasons and the Agent's Point of View' (2009) 22 *Ratio Juris* 74–94.

[30] Things are different when we move to motivating states. If psychological states of the will are assumed to play a distinct role in the grounding of obligations, then they compete with anything else that purports to be a ground—in fact they carry the grounding role. Now, if a case could be made successfully that there exist collective states of the will, or states of the will that exist over and above their individual constituents, then a genuine difference in terms of grounds could be introduced between moral and legal obligation. If, however, no such case is likely to succeed, as I think Ripstein would also agree, then all states of the will can do is to function anew as enablers.

But if the function of the enabler is all that the alleged difference between moral and legal obligation boils down to, then Kant's account of obligations of right is seen to be only a special case of his general account of moral obligation. For want for a more thoroughgoing argumentation, which would demonstrate that institutional authorisation is capable of generating distinct grounds for obligation, it is safe to say that there exist obligations *simpliciter* which in spite of, or rather because of, their interaction with the various enablers that come their way determine the grounds of every other obligation that arises within the various domains of what we do together.

Understandably my analysis will have left a lot of questions unanswered, especially with regard to the role and function of coercive institutions in respect of legal obligation. However, its scope and claim should be given a more modest tone: in the first place what it tries to do is to displace the received view that the different foci of law and morality (external behaviour in the first case, internal incentive in the second) entail a difference in kind between obligations of law and obligations of morality. If this step has been completed successfully, then the standard view on the role of coercion will come under considerable pressure—and with it, Ripstein's suggestion that omnilateral willing deserves the status of a special ground for legal obligation.

7

Ripstein on Kant on Revolution

DANIEL WEINSTOCK

ARTHUR RIPSTEIN'S *FORCE and Freedom* undoubtedly now stands as the most important and compelling commentary on Kant's legal and political philosophy. Its importance is due to at least two noteworthy features. First, it takes the systematic, critical pretensions of Kant's legal philosophy, and most notably the doctrine expounded in the *Rechtslehre*, quite seriously indeed, and succeeds in overcoming the uncertain reputation that work has had within the critical corpus. And second, Ripstein's intention is not merely exegetical and interpretive. He wants to take Kant's legal and political philosophy seriously as a philosophical framework for thinking about questions that still occupy political and legal philosophers to this day, questions concerning, for example, the grounds of political obligation.

Ripstein does not shy away from defending both the coherence and the plausibility of even those Kantian doctrines that have been viewed most negatively by commentators. The doctrine that I will be focusing on in this chapter has to do with the right to revolution.

Kant famously—I should perhaps say notoriously—thought that revolution, even revolution that sought to overthrow a tyrannical regime, was absolutely forbidden. That doctrine has been seen as both morally implausible and as philosophically incoherent.[1] It has been seen as morally implausible because it seems to condemn the victims of tyrannical regimes to putting up with even the worst excesses. Their only hope on the Kantian view is internal reform, reform that may perhaps be spurred on through the exercise of a political right that Kant did insist upon, namely the right to freedom of speech and of criticism.

[1] Among Kantians who have seen Kant's views on the issue of the right to revolution as internally inconsistent, see T Hill, 'A Kantian Perspective on Political Violence', in *Respect, Pluralism, and Justice* (Oxford, Oxford University Press, 2000), and C Korsgaard, 'Taking the Law into Our Own Hands: Kant on the Right to Revolution', in A Reath, B Herman, and C Korsgaard (eds), *Reclaiming the History of Ethics: Essays for John Rawls* (Cambridge, Cambridge University Press, 1997).

It has been seen as incoherent because Kant's 'systematic' view, as expounded in the *Rechtslehre*, that revolution should be legally prohibited, stands in tension with the enthusiasm he expressed in *The Contest of Faculties* for the moral promise latent in the French Revolution, an enthusiasm that for Kant clearly betokened moral progress.[2] These two apparently contradictory positions give rise to the question that has plagued Kant scholarship for generations: how can one see a moral sentiment as betokening moral progress when it is elicited by something that ought to be legally prohibited?

In the chapter on revolution in *Force and Freedom*, Ripstein does a lot to restitute the moral and philosophical plausibility of Kant's view. He does not, however, address the issue of how Kant could have held both that revolution should be legally prohibited and that the enthusiasm that it gave rise to was a sign of a moral disposition. In this chapter I want (after giving a thumbnail sketch of Ripstein's reconstruction of Kant's anti-revolution argument) to do two things. I want first to suggest that there is some unfinished business in Ripstein's reconstruction of the Kantian position before it can be completely philosophically satisfactory on its own terms, ie before the purported incompatibility with the view expressed in *The Contests of Faculties* is taken into account. I will then make some much more speculative remarks about how to reconcile the two apparently opposed views.

I

Kant's views on revolution are best understood in contrast to the very different view that was developed by Locke.[3] For Locke, the state becomes empirically necessary because of the difficulty that people experience in the state of nature once their rights-claims come into conflict. The state of nature presents 'inconveniences' that it is reasonable for people to want to escape, having to do with the lack of an impartial arbiter of conflicts.

[2] The passage in which Kant expresses approval of the attitude elicited by the French Revolution on the part of disinterested onlookers is well known: 'The revolution which we have seen taking place in our own times in a nation of gifted people may succeed, or it may fail. It may be so filled with misery and atrocities that no right-thinking man would ever decide to make the same experiment again at such a price, even if he could hope to carry it out successfully at the second attempt. But I maintain that this revolution has aroused in the hearts and desires of all spectators who are not themselves caught up in it a sympathy which borders almost on enthusiasm, although the very utterance of this sympathy was fraught with danger. It cannot therefore have been caused by anything other than a moral disposition within the human race.' Immanuel Kant, 'The Conflict of Faculties', in *Kant's Political Writings* (2nd edn), ed H Reiss (Cambridge, Cambridge University Press, 1991) 182.

[3] See K Flikschuh, 'Reason, Right, and Revolution: Kant and Locke' (2008) 36 *Philosophy and Public Affairs* 375.

Kant's view is, first, that there are no full-blown rights in the state of nature, only provisional rights which are incomplete because they lack mechanisms of enforcement and adjudication. Rights require a civil state which institutes an 'omnilateral' perspective (as opposed to a uni- or multilateral one) on the basis of which adjudication and enforcement can occur that is compatible with the innate right to freedom of all—that freedom that, as Ripstein shows, is the fundamental building block of the entire Kantian political and legal edifice. The setting up of a public power is for Kant a logical precondition of agents being insulated against the unfreedom that results from being subject to the unilateral plans and purposes of others.

In Kant's view, an important premise of the right to revolution as it is developed in Locke, and in those of his followers who have interpreted him as having developed a robust right to revolution, is mistaken. There are for Kant no full-blown rights in the state of nature. There are only rights *claims*. Thus, agents in the state of nature are not possessed of the kinds of rights that can be delegated to a political authority as in the Lockean version of the social contract story. Rights are only possible in a civil state. As Ripstein puts it, 'rights are only conclusive if disputes about them are resolved in accordance with law'.[4] To the extent that the Lockean justification of revolution depends upon citizens merely 'taking back' the rights that they had entrusted to a political authority in order to allow them to avoid the 'inconveniences' of the state of nature, Kant's account, if successful, shows Locke's to be conceptually confused. If Kant is right, there is nothing for putative revolutionaries to 'take back', as rights only emerge when a public authority is put in place. Revolution thus results not in the transfer of rights back to their original owners; rather it gives rise to the elimination of rights.

A second mistaken premise has to do with peoplehood. As is well known, Locke's contractualist argument is to the effect that individuals constitute themselves as a people before they exercise their sovereignty through the setting up of government institutions. For Kant, political and legal peoplehood is constituted in the first instance by the setting up of political institutions that can actually express the will of the people, not the will of this or that person, or the will of some—conceivably very large—proportion of the population, but of the *people*. As Ripstein puts it, according to Kant, 'a people differs from a mob only in being united under laws' (*FF*, 336).

A third mistaken idea on Kant's reading of Locke's view that is emphasised by Ripstein is that entering a civil state is not a discretionary act of will on the part of the people. That is, whereas Locke thought that the people *could* constitute a sovereign political authority to emerge from the inconveniences of

[4] A Ripstein, *Force and Freedom. Kant's Legal and Political Philosophy* (Cambridge, MA, Harvard University Press, 2009) 331 (hereinafter *FF*).

the state of nature (which implies that they could also choose not to, were the balance of inconveniences to tilt against the setting up of a state being the prudentially best option), Kant thought that entering a civil state is non-optional. It is only through the constitution of such an authority that we can ensure that the conditions are in place that make it the case that we will not be subject to the arbitrary will of another, and thus that we will be able to enjoy our innate right to freedom. Joining such a civil state is morally required. I can even, on Kant's view, coerce a recalcitrant individual to join the civil state, since his standing outside of it poses an obstacle to my being able to enjoy the condition of not being subjected to the will of another or of others (and this is the case regardless of how the recalcitrant individual actually acts toward me—it is his mere standing outside the civil state that constitutes the obstacle, rather than any tangible threat that his actions might actually pose for me).

Put all this together, and you can see why Kant would hold that there could be no right to revolution, and why that position is actually possessed of considerable prima facie philosophical plausibility. If a civil state is a requirement of my freedom, where freedom is understood as my being able fully to enjoy rights at all (with what that implies in terms of adjudication and enforcement), then he who would disrupt or destroy the civil state that I am presently in does me an injustice. Yet this is precisely what revolutionaries do. For revolutionaries act as private, rather than as public agents, and their actions, if successful, therefore return us to a pre-civil state. They thus eliminate the very bases upon which the freedom of the asocial social beings that we are is possible. So it is not just that revolutionaries do something that is constitutionally prohibited (it is indeed difficult to imagine a constitution allowing for revolution, as opposed, say, to amendment). They act in ways that are morally unjustifiable as well, by destroying legal arrangements that are logically required in order for the realisation of the innate right to freedom of human agents to be possible.

So far, so plausible. The problem arises when one considers that there are some pretty rotten governments out there, and that Kant does not seem to give people who are subjected to them much of a way out. They enjoy the 'freedom of the pen', to be sure, and can use it to remonstrate against unjust rulers. And there is an obligation that Kant imposed upon rulers that they should strive to improve the way in which they govern. But, it could and has been argued, that is cold comfort indeed to those who live in despotic regimes, in the absence of any legal mechanism that would require governments to live up to this moral requirement, and in the absence of any guarantee that the argument made by citizens making use of their freedom will be listened to, let alone accepted.

To put the point somewhat more formally: if the state is logically required as a condition of agents being able to hold rights, then there seems something paradoxical, verging on the contradictory, in denying agents the right to depose governments that violate these very rights, or at least a significant proportion thereof. There would seem to be at least some plausibility to the claim that agents should have the right to get rid of regimes that fail utterly to realise the potential for rights-creation that their coming-into-being gives rise to.

It is here that Ripstein makes a move that would appear to lessen the sting of Kant's apparently uncompromising position. Making use of a set of distinctions introduced by Kant in the *Anthropology*, he argues that though people have to 'put up' with despotic regimes, ie regimes where there is force and law but no freedom, they need not put up with 'barbaric' regimes in which there is force without law or freedom—presumably where thugs exercise their will over the population without the pretence of the nicety of law or of mediating institutions. They are permitted, on Kant's analysis as reconstructed by Ripstein, to take steps to oppose barbarisms. Indeed, they are duty bound to do so, because in the absence of the institutional mechanisms that might allow an observer to be satisfied that an authority instantiating an omnilateral will is in place, they find themselves with respect to this authority and with respect to one another in a state of nature.

Barbarisms just involve the unmediated exercise of the discretionary will of a ruler. It thus fails to instantiate the minimal condition for a social state to be a civil state. There is, to employ Ripstein's terms, no institution embodying an 'omnilateral' perspective. To the extent that barbarisms are states of nature, there is not only a right but also an obligation to take steps to escape from it, even if this requires coercive methods.

Ripstein's reconstruction of the Kantian argument removes the air of paradox that surrounds it: people are not being asked to accept that they must as a matter of justice countenance all manner of injustice. When the situation is bad enough, they can, indeed they must, act.

On the other hand, despotisms, ie unjust regimes that nonetheless have some of the institutional trappings of republics, must be put up with. As Ripstein puts it, 'despotism could be a form of the general will, because the arrangements made for the members of a despotic state are legal, and secure them in what is theirs' (*FF*, 339). To the extent that they possess these properties, Kant's view as reconstructed by Ripstein is that they ought not to be opposed by revolutionary means. Even when the laws that they enact are oppressive, even when they are enacted in the pursuit of private rather than public ends, and even where there is no realistic hope that the public authorities in a despotism will be attentive or responsive to the pleas made by citizens through their use of the 'freedom of the pen', citizens must abstain from revolutionary action.

Does this reconstruction make Kant's position more plausible than it might have seemed at first blush? I want to argue that it does not, because the distinction between (presumably reformable) despotisms and barbarisms cannot bear the weight that Ripstein places upon it.

II

The plausibility of Kant's position as reconstructed by Ripstein depends upon investing the attributes that despotisms possess with enough moral weight to justify making the claim that when people rebel against despotic regimes, they themselves do something even more unjust, no matter how unjust the despotic regime. On Ripstein's interpretation, revolutionaries throw into the question the very possibility of legality. It is that claim that I want to put some pressure on.

A state—Ripstein claims that it would not really even warrant the use of the term—is 'barbarous' when those who hold power do so purely for private purposes. They do not even attempt to govern from some 'public' or 'omnilateral' perspective. They comport themselves like private individuals lording it over other private individuals. On Kant's view, this is a state of nature in which some just happen to have achieved a position of (illegitimate) power over others.

A state is republican, at the other end of the spectrum, when it attempts to orient its use of state power with reference to the Idea of the Social Contract. The Idea of the Social Contract makes fully explicit 'the normative structure through which the exercise of public power is consistent with individual freedom' (*FF*, 199). Thus when this Idea is employed as a critical standard through which the manner in which laws are made and their content can be evaluated, a state is both lawful and free.

The intermediate case is that which Kant calls 'despotism'. In despotism, there is law, so that the exercise of political power is in accordance with an at least minimal conception of the public. One can imagine that Kant would consider that it is a condition of there being *law* that it be embedded in certain institutional forms, rather than simply being dictated by a tyrant. The lawfulness that is found in despotisms also fulfils the minimal rule-of-law requirement of securing citizens in their enjoyment of what is theirs.

In Ripstein's reconstruction of Kant's argument, despotism as just characterised bears some relation to both barbarism and to republicanism. Like barbarisms, despotisms display to an unacceptable degree the use of political power for private purposes. The difference is that the private nature of the exercise of state power is in the case of barbarism 'necessary', whereas it is only 'sometimes' used for such purposes in the case of despotisms. That is, the lack of any legal institutions in a barbarism make it the case that the use of political power cannot be otherwise than private, whereas this is a contingent matter in a despotism, and depends presumably on the whim of the political rulers.

Despotism, however, also shares something with republicanism, in that it is lawful. That there is in despotism *law* rather than merely the institutionally unmediated will of the tyrant means that the idea of publicness, or of 'omnimlaterality' is there *in nuce*. We might say that a republic is ominlateral *für sich*, in that the Idea of the Original Contract has been fully brought to consciousness for both citizens and rulers as the critical standard through which the operation of government should be evaluated, though it is always already there in the very idea of publicness, whereas a despotism is omnilateral *an sich*, in that the idea of publicness is operational in the workings of government through the institutional measures that have been put in place, but it does not function as a critical standard for public officials (and perhaps not even for citizens, to the extent that they are habituated to despotic rule). It is present imperfectly in the working of institutions, but not in the minds of people.

Although it therefore shares important features with both barbarism and republicanism, Ripstein justifies Kant's claim that revolutionary action is inappropriate in despotism through the claim that 'despotism is a defective form of a republic' (*FF*, 339). That is, it is conceptually and causally more closely connected to republicanism than it is to despotism. Despotism can be seen because of the germ of publicness that lies within it as a republic *en devenir*, which presumably just requires mutual enlightenment of citizens and rulers to become actualised. Although he does not spell this out explicitly, presumably Ripstein's categorisation of despotism as closer to republicanism is grounded in the tacit claim that the slide back from despotism to barbarism is less likely, both on conceptual and on empirical grounds, than is the slide forward from despotism to republicanism.

Ripstein also claims that despotism is actually on a continuum with republicanism because the deficits present in despotism are also (though presumably to a lesser degree) present in republicanism. On his reading, the claim that 'although people know where they stand, and so can plan their affairs with some level of certainty, the rules that afford them that certainty are imposed from without' is exemplified in every existing state 'to at least some degree'. Were this not the case, ie were there states that were perfectly republican, the duty to improve itself which applies to all states would be *sans objet* (*FF*, 339).

I do not find this view plausible. I think that it rests on an equivocation between two ways in which a state can be imperfect (without being a barbarism). A state can be one in which rulers and citizens all share the belief that the Idea of the Social Contract is the standard against which the functioning of government should be measured. Imperfection creeps in because people fail to see clearly what this criterion—acknowledged by all—actually requires. Thus representatives make good-faith mistakes when they legislate according to the standard, and/or citizens make similarly good-faith mistakes in making use of their freedom of the pen in arguing against for this or that piece of legislation.

Clearly, in situations such as this, unjust legislation, which will inevitably be produced, does not warrant revolution because people on all sides recognise the authority of the Idea of the Original Contract, and because institutions embody omnilaterality. (And to the extent that they do so only imperfectly, the fact that people have taken up the standard of the Idea of Public Reason makes it the case that reform is more likely.)

Despotism as characterised by Ripstein's Kant is imperfect in a different, and deeper manner, which in my view differs qualitatively, and not just quantitatively, from the manner in which republics are imperfect. In a despotism, omnilaterality is not acknowledged as a standard of assessment. It is operative to some degree, because it is latent in the operation of institutions, most notably through the separation of office from office-holder. It is not the case that citizens and rulers in a despotism both share a standard on the basis of which their disagreements can in principle be adjudicated. The lack of a fully acknowledged public standard makes despotism imperfect in a different, and deeper, manner than the way in which real-world republics are imperfect.

Another way of seeing this is by considering how plausible it is that the public use of reason by citizens making use of their freedom of expression to criticise government will improve the working of government in the case of republics and in the case of despotisms. When the Idea of the Original Contract is shared as a standard of evaluation by both citizens and rulers, it can function as a shared standard by which to adjudicate disputes. If both share the standard, it is at least plausible to think that citizens will be able to show that, for example, a given piece of legislation is imperfectly just by demonstrating that it is incompatible with the Idea. Where common standards are recognised on all sides, there is hope for rational discourse.

The thought that the public use of reason might undo despotism's native imperfection—the fact that the Idea of the Original Contract functions *an sich* and not *für sich*—seems much more far-fetched. For here what is required is not that a demonstration be made that this rather than that item of legislation is superior according to a shared standard, but rather, that the standard be acknowledged, to begin with. Publicness plays itself out to some degree behind the backs of despots through their setting up of minimally lawful institutions. Making despots realise the standard that they are rationally committed to without knowing it through having set up those institutions is a much more difficult task than that that awaits the citizen making public use of her reason in a republic.

Now pointing to the difference between the imperfections of despotisms and of real-world republics does not suffice to refute Kant's view that revolution is inappropriate both in the case of despotisms and in that of imperfect republics. But it does show that the argument against revolution cannot be the same in both cases. Specifically, the anti-revolution argument for despotisms cannot simply piggyback on the plausibility of the anti-revolution view for imperfect republics, via the claim that despotisms are potential republics. They may very well be that, but the mechanisms that are likely to make that potentiality eventuate are different from those that are likely to improve already existing republics.

Another way of putting the point (or perhaps a slightly different, but related point) is by going back to the characterisation of despotism as sharing something both with barbarisms and with republics. What warrants the belief that the move forward to republicanism is more likely for despotisms than the slide back into barbarism? While despots may very well become hoist by their own petard as the norms of publicness latent in the lawful institutions they set up become public currency, and begin to inform the expectations of citizens, they may also very well decide to drop the pretence of lawfulness when they realise that the veneer of lawfulness is escaping their control and preventing them from drawing sufficient private advantage from the use of offices of state. And if this is as likely as is the move forward into republicanism, is it reasonable to expect citizens to abstain from overthrowing a government that appears ready, as it were, to drop all pretences of legality in order to bare its teeth?

We thus need an argument for why revolution is inappropriate in despotisms that does not borrow in any way from their potential for reforming into republics. And this argument will, as I suggested at the outset of this section, have to lay a lot of weight on the barest conception of the rule of law. I clearly do not have the time to determine whether such an argument can be made good. But it is important to note, in order to appreciate just how great the burden of proof is, just how minimal the requirement that Ripstein imposes upon regimes to count as despotisms rather than barbarisms really is. In particular, it does not seem to me to contain the minimal elements required to count as a conception of the rule of law. In a recent account of the concept, Jeremy Waldron has included an 'orientation toward the public good' as one of the necessary ingredients for a satisfactory account of the rule of law (alongside such elements that Ripstein's despotisms would arguably present, such as 'positivity', 'courts', 'general public norms' and 'systematicity'). As Waldron puts it:

> [I]t strains our ordinary concept of law to apply it to norms that address matters of personal or partial concern, or to institutions that make no pretense to operate in the name of the whole community, presenting themselves as oriented instead to the benefit of the individuals who control them.[5]

[5] J Waldron, 'The Concept and the Rule of Law' (2008) 43 *Georgia Law Review* 1, 31.

Barbarisms necessarily violate this requirement, and republics usually, but not unfailingly, satisfy it. Despotisms as characterised by Ripstein sometimes satisfy it, but when they do, it is due to some contingent alignment of the will of despots with the general good, rather than in virtue of a shared commitment to the Idea of the Social Contract as a benchmark for evaluating legislation, as in the case of republics. This is just to say that a despotism could be very despotic indeed, and still satisfy the requirements that would make violent resistance illegitimate.

To put the matter another way: despotisms and barbarisms differ formally rather than substantively from one another. That is, we could well imagine a barbarism and a despotism imposing exactly the same requirements upon citizens. The former would justify resistance simply in virtue of its formal characteristics: rules in this case result directly from the will of the ruler, rather than being institutionally mediated in the minimal way required for a regime to count as a despotism. That such substantively identical regimes would, on Ripstein's reconstruction of Kant, warrant such different political attitudes and actions risks making Kant formalistic in an unattractive sense of that term.

I end this section in the form of a challenge, and return a distinction made earlier in this section: while we can all agree that violent revolution would be inappropriate in Canada, even for those who vehemently disagree with the policies of the present government on a range of issues, and while we can all agree that it would be morally justifiable in regions of failed states governed by warlords, are our intuitions as clear in the case of, say, modern-day Iran? China? Guatemala? I am an expert on none of these places, yet it would seem that bare-bones rule-of-law exists in all of them. Would we want to be saddled with a theory that morally condemns revolutionaries in any of those despotic countries?

III

I have suggested in the previous section that Kant's position with respect to the right to revolution might be more difficult to defend than Ripstein believes. It is in fact a much more stringent doctrine than Ripstein allows, one that would permit the victims of warlords and dictators to rise up against their oppressors, but that would somewhat disappointingly deny that right to citizens of authoritarian regimes that have certain minimal institutional trappings that are formally—though not substantively—similar to those that might be found in a republic.

I want in closing to suggest that the stringency of Kant's position on the right to revolution may actually make it more rather than less compatible with the views expressed in the *Contest of Faculties*.

Kant's very stringent view makes it the case that we need not enquire into the historical origins of a state in order to determine whether that state ought to command the obedience of its citizens. On Kant's view, it is the formal rather than the empirical/historical characteristics of a state that are criterial in this regard. As Ripstein himself puts it, 'showing that the state had its historical origins in force and war rather than in some set of peaceable and voluntary arrangements is not relevant to its legitimacy' (*FF*, 335).

What this means is that the fact that a state was generated by revolutionary upheaval does nothing to detract from its legitimate claim to obedience, once it is set up with the requisite institutional trappings. Revolution may very well be wrong, on Kant's view, in all but the most abject cases of barbarous tyranny, but it would also be wrong for anyone to oppose revolutionary force to the revolutionaries, once they have succeeded in setting up a state that is not barbarous.

Thus, it is possible in following Kant both to condemn revolutionaries and to acknowledge their legitimate authority once they take power. But the *Conflict of Faculties* passage requires that we account for more than just acknowledgement. It requires that we view the sympathy that the French Revolution elicited throughout Europe as a sign of a 'moral disposition'.

The explanation that seems to me best suited to account for this would be to state that the observers of a revolution, though they see the revolutionary act as inherently risky, also see it as having the potential to bring about a state that is *better* than the one that will have been overthrown.

My account of Ripstein's reconstruction of Kant envisages two ways in which a state can fall short of fully satisfying the criterion for good government that Kant sees as embodied in the hypothetical social contract device. First, it can fail by falling short of a standard that both it and its citizenry acknowledge as the appropriate standard. Second, it can fall short in that it does not fully acknowledge the standard, though the standard is implicit in certain of the institutional trappings of the state.

The enthusiasm of the educated European public sphere observing events in revolutionary France can thus be explained by the fact that they had good reason to believe that the revolution would give rise to a regime better than the one that it replaced, in either or both of the ways just described. They were thus projecting themselves imaginatively forward in time to when, according to the logic of Kant's argument, they would have no choice but to acknowledge the legitimacy of the state that emerged from the revolutionary upheaval, and were expressing the belief that, though the state that it replaced was formally such as to require the allegiance of citizens, the new one would be better in the degree to which it satisfies the contractarian requirement.

One might see Kant in the final analysis as having put forward something like a precautionary political principle. Given the very great benefits that accrue from the setting up of public political institutions, and the very great risks that accompany the overthrow of even mediocre institutions of this kind, Kant can be seen as arguing that we ought to prescind from overthrowing even very minimally legitimate governments even when the probability of the overthrown regime being replaced by a better one is high, given the very great harms that would befall citizens were the revolution not to give rise to the establishment of public institutions, or perhaps even given the harms that would be generated by a prolonged interregnum. We may not from our present perspective necessarily weigh the harms and benefits in exactly the same way as Kant did. But this does not mean that putative revolutionaries shouldn't attend to the risks of lawlessness. Nor does it rule out the legitimacy of our enthusiasm at the prospect of possible political progress that some revolutionary movements may at times embody.

Part IV

Right and Ethics

8

Right and Ethics: Arthur Ripstein's Force and Freedom

ALLEN WOOD

I. THE INDEPENDENCE OF RIGHT FROM ETHICS

KANT'S *METAPHYSICS OF Morals* divides 'morals' (*Sitten*) into two parts: right (*Recht*) and ethics (*Ethik*).[1] But Kant does not make it clear how right and ethics relate to each other, or how their treatment forms a single whole. It is even unclear, in one basic respect, how the sphere of right can be consistently conceived at all in Kantian terms. Right grounds a set of *duties*—juridical duties or duties of right (*Rechtspflichte*). And all genuine duties for Kant are grounded on categorical imperatives.[2] It is the mark of a categorical imperative, however, that the obligation imposed by it must depend solely on a pure rational incentive, valid for all rational beings as such.[3] Yet Kant distinguishes the legislation of right from that of ethics by saying that with ethical obligations 'the law makes duty the incentive', while the legislation of right 'does not include the incentive of duty in the law and so admits of an incentive other than the idea of duty itself'.[4] By this Kant means that the incentive pertaining to the legislation of right typically involves not a pure rational incentive, but rather incentives provided by external coercion through a public authority. It would apparently follow that duties of right

[1] For all citations to Kant's work, I give page numbers to the relevant volumes from *Immanuel Kants Schriften*. Ausgabe der königlich preussischen Akademie der Wissenschaften (Berlin, W de Gruyter, 1902). The numbers appear in the margins of most translations, but for the purpose of this text, quotations are taken from *Writings of Immanuel Kant* (New York, Cambridge University Press, 1992).

[2] Immanuel Kant, *Metaphysics of Morals* (New York, Cambridge University Press, 1797–98) 4: 222–23 (hereinafter *MM*).

[3] Immanuel Kant, *Groundwork of the Metaphysics of Morals* (New York, Cambridge University Press, 1785) 4: 414–15, 427–28 (hereinafter *Groundwork*).

[4] Kant, *MM*, 6: 218–19.

cannot be (or rest on) categorical imperatives at all, and therefore cannot be duties at all, properly speaking. The expression 'duty of right' would then contain a *contradictio in adjecto*.

Related to this puzzle, there is also a question concerning the ground of right in general, including the ground of the universal principle of right: 'Any action is right if it can coexist with everyone's freedom in accordance with a universal law, or if on its maxim the freedom of choice of each can coexist with everyone's freedom in accordance with a universal law.'[5] One natural way to interpret Kant here is to suppose that the principle of right is somehow even derived from the supreme principle of morality formulated in the *Groundwork*. But Kant never tells us how such a derivation might work. And if it is already questionable how the legislation of right can be based on a categorical imperative at all, it has to be equally questionable whether duties of right, or the universal principle of right, can be based on the principle of morality, which is supposed to be a categorical imperative (and was, in the *Groundwork*, even derived from the concept of such an imperative).

Yet another objection to this natural interpretation is that, on closer inspection, the principle of right does not even directly command us to perform actions that are right, or limit our actions to these, but only tells us which actions count as 'right'. If in addition to this principle of right, there is also a 'law of right' commanding us to perform only actions that are right, then Kant says explicitly that this law

> does not expect, much less demand, that I *myself should* limit my freedom to those conditions just for the sake of this obligation; instead, it says only that freedom is limited to those conditions in conformity with the idea of it and that it may also be limited through deeds *ätlich* by others; and it says this as a postulate that is incapable of further proof.[6]

Kant also adds later that the principle of right is analytic, whereas the principle of ethics is synthetic.[7] It is far from clear how an analytic principle could need, or even admit of, derivation from a synthetic one. And if the principle of right is a 'postulate incapable of further proof', then that too seems to preclude its being derived from the principle of morality.

All these claims might well be seen as requiring the denial not only that duties of right rest on the categorical imperative, but also that the principle or law of right could be proven through, or rest on, any more fundamental principle at all. But if, alternatively, the sphere of right, and of the principle of right and duties of right are independent of the moral principle or categorical

[5] ibid, 6: 230.
[6] ibid, 6: 231.
[7] ibid, 6: 396.

imperative of duty, then Kant seems to be equally silent on what that independent ground could be.

II. RIGHT IS GROUNDED ON EXTERNAL FREEDOM

Among the many achievements of Arthur Ripstein's *Force and Freedom*[8] is that it offers us a reading of the Doctrine of Right that offers a possible path through these difficulties. Specifically, Ripstein shows how Kant rejects the common assumption of many philosophers, that political philosophy (and more generally the area that Kant designates by the term *Recht*) is simply 'an application of general moral principles to the factual circumstances that make political institutions necessary'.[9] In effect, with this claim Ripstein is denying that the principle of right, and duties of right, are grounded on or derived from the principle of morality. And Ripstein's book contains an admirable development of an alternative foundation for right—namely the identification of *right* with the conditions for protecting what Kant calls 'external freedom'—freedom as the independence from constraint by the choice of another.[10] Considering the conditions under which people may have external freedom in accordance with universal law will permit us to see how right might be a separate sphere of morals (*Sitten*), entirely independent of the sphere of ethics, resting on considerations of practical reason that do not depend on the categorical imperative that grounds ethical duties, though the basis of right may have something in common with the basis of ethics, making both of them spheres of morals.

Ripstein's fundamental insight of *Force and Freedom* is that rightful external freedom is the freedom of a person to make choices independently of constraint by the choices of others. For any given person, of course, such freedom must always be limited, merely so that others may also have the same freedom. That, however, is just the point of the universal principle of right: that external freedom, for any given person, is *rightful* freedom only when it can coexist with the freedom of all others according to universal law. The foundation of the entire sphere of right lies in the fact that human beings have good reason to value rightful freedom, and this reason is independent of *ethical* value or the principle of morality grounding *ethical* duties. The remaining problem, not explicitly solved by Ripstein, is to understand this independent ground of rightful freedom, and how it remains independent of ethical value, the value that grounds the categorical imperative of morality that was derived in the

[8] A Ripstein, *Force and Freedom: Kant's Legal and Political Philosophy* (Cambridge, MA, Harvard University Press, 2009) (hereinafter *FF*).

[9] ibid, 1.

[10] Kant, *MM*, 6: 237.

Groundwork. Another way to look at this problem is to see it as providing an interpretation of Kant's claim that rightful external freedom—independence from constraint by the choice of another—is 'the sole original and innate right belonging to every human being by virtue of his humanity'.[11]

III. EXTERNAL FREEDOM AND THE RATIONAL STRUCTURE OF ACTION

The solution to this problem, I believe, lies in Kant's conception of the fundamental rational structure of action. All action for Kant is based on setting an end—an object or state of affairs to be produced. It is the essential characteristic of rational nature to set ends: 'Rational nature discriminates itself from the rest in that it sets itself an end.'[12] An action, by its concept, is that which lies within the power of the agent, and is chosen by the agent as a means to some end.[13] Kant says: 'That which serves the will as the objective ground of its self-determination is the end. … By contrast, what contains merely the ground of the possibility of the action whose effect is the end is called the means.'[14]

Practical reason applies to action in a variety of ways. First, it applies instrumentally: rules of skill tell us the best means to a given end, while a technical imperative of reason, grounding the rational authority of such rules, requires us, on pain of a failure of rationality, to take the indispensable means in our power toward any end we have set.[15] Second, reason applies to action prudentially: pragmatic or prudential reason counsels us to form an idea of happiness, to make it an end, and to give it rational priority over all other ends of inclination.[16] And third, reason applies to action in the form of the moral law: The general basis of all ethical duties is the moral law as presented in the Formula of Humanity as End in Itself (FH). An end in itself is not an end we set or an object to be brought about, but something already existing having a value for whose sake we are required to do or refrain from certain actions.[17] The categorical imperative that grounds our ethical duties commands us to set certain ends—our own perfection and the happiness of others.[18] The moral law also forbids us to set certain ends (eg the unhappiness of others, pursued for its own sake), and it further forbids us to use certain means to our ends

[11] ibid, 6: 237.
[12] Kant, *Groundwork*, 4: 437.
[13] ibid, 4: 417.
[14] ibid, 4: 427.
[15] ibid, 4: 414–15.
[16] ibid, 4: 415–16.
[17] ibid, 4: 427–30.
[18] Kant, *MM*, 6: 385–88.

that are inconsistent with treating ourselves or other rational beings as ends in themselves.

All ethical obligations, all categorical imperatives, rest in this way on rational constraints arising out of ends—ends in themselves, which we are required to treat as ends, or ends we are required by morality to set. All actions required or forbidden by ethics, or by categorical imperatives, are required or forbidden on account of some end—ultimately, the objective worth of humanity as an end in itself, which we are required to respect in our actions. But the ethical imperative treats actions as required, prohibited or meritorious on account of their relation to obligatory ends to be produced: our own perfection and the happiness of others.[19] Envious or malicious actions, for example, are forbidden because they make the unhappiness of some person into an end, while actions that perfect our skills or improve our character are meritorious because they further the end of our own perfection and beneficent actions are meritorious because their end is the happiness of another.

Right, by contrast with ethics, has to do with a class of prescriptions and prohibitions on actions that arise wholly independently of the ends of these actions. Right 'has to do only with the formal condition of choice that is to be limited in external relations in accordance with laws of freedom, without regard for any end (the matter of choice)'.[20] More specifically, right has to do with actions merely insofar as they relate to the freedom of others to choose their own actions in furtherance of ends these others have freely set. Setting an end is an act of freedom. One cannot be compelled (or coerced) to set an end, but one can be coerced to perform actions which are means to ends set by others rather than to one's own ends. 'Another can indeed coerce me to do something that is not my end (but only a means to another's end) but not to make this my end.'[21] External freedom consists in choosing actions that are means to ends you have set, while being forced to act in ways that are means to the ends of others is the absence or violation of external freedom. Right consists in those rational constraints on our actions that have to do not with the ends of those actions but instead with the formal conditions under which your actions are compatible with the external freedom of rational beings in general, according to universal laws that guarantee a like external freedom for all.

The foundation of right therefore consists in a rational ground that all rational beings have for requiring the protection of external freedom of all according to universal law. What could such a ground be? It is this: as a rational being, I necessarily set ends. This implies a rational requirement that I be free

[19] ibid, 6: 385–88.
[20] ibid, 6: 375.
[21] ibid, 6: 381.

to choose the actions by which I pursue those ends. An end is not merely an object I merely desire or wish for; it is essentially an object I pursue through my actions, conceived by me as means to that end. Human beings—beings with practical reason—are not beings who have their desires satisfied merely by the mechanism of nature (eg by the mechanical operation of instincts) or through the beneficent agency of beings other than themselves—such as gods, or robots. For in order to serve the ends of human beings, even gods would have to be prayed to, and robots would have to be programmed and commanded (if only by a remote control device); these actions of praying or commanding would have to be freely chosen as means to the ends the human beings have freely set. Another way of putting it is this: human beings have the privilege—or, if you prefer, they are subject to the curse (Kant recognises that it can be viewed in both ways)—that whatever good they achieve, and whatever happiness they enjoy, must be the result of their own work: it must arise from their setting an end and their selecting, or perhaps inventing, the means necessary to achieve it, and then applying the means through actions chosen by the human being as such means (*MA* 8:111–12).[22]

It follows that as a rational being, I necessarily desire in general, and as far as possible (consistent with other demands of reason) that the actions I perform should serve ends I have set, rather than serving different ends, ends set by others. This is a necessary demand of rational agency, part of its essential structure. It is also a demand entirely independent of whatever particular ends I may have, or even the ends I ought to have. Moreover, I recognise that other rational beings necessarily have exactly the same rational interest that I do in choosing their actions to further their own freely chosen ends, rather than having their actions constrained to promote ends chosen by others. To recognise a being—whether oneself or another—as a rational agent is to view it as lying under the indispensable rational necessity that it wills to be free, as far as possible, consistent with other demands of reason, to pursue its own ends rather than being forced to have its actions serve the ends set by others without its freely given cooperation or consent.

My demand to be externally free is therefore qualified by the demand of reason that others have the same rational claim on external freedom that I do. No one's external freedom can therefore be unlimited if others are to be externally free as well. This is the ground of the qualification 'consistent with other demands of reason' that must be added to the rational demand for external freedom that each rational being must make.

The ends of morality are objective or binding on us because they are ends we recognise as rationally valid irrespective of the particular wishes, desires,

[22] *cf* Immanuel Kant, *Idea Toward a Universal History with a Cosmopolitan Aim* (Cambridge, Cambridge University Press, 1784) 8: 19–20.

ends or interests of individuals. The happiness of each individual has a moral claim on other individuals because it has a value that can be recognised by any rational being. Persons are ends in themselves because they have a value that is not conditional on anyone's empirical wishes or desires but makes an impartial claim on us through a command of reason. Something analogous, but quite distinct, is true of the other constitutive necessity of rational nature I have just identified—namely its requirement that it be free to choose actions in furtherance of ends set by it rather than having its actions forced to serve ends it does not share.

Coercion is a restriction on external freedom: to coerce someone is to force them to act in a way that conforms to your will rather than theirs, and makes their actions serve ends you have set which are not ends they have set. Kant's theory of right is based on the idea that the only way coercion could ever be justified is in the name of protecting external freedom—the very freedom that coercion annuls, infringes or limits. A person cannot be justifiably coerced for the sake of the value of any end whatever: neither the happiness of another, nor the happiness of all, nor even the happiness of the person who is coerced, could provide an adequate ground for the coercion of a free and rational being. Such a reason could consist only in the fact that the coercion in question is required in order to protect the external freedom of rational agents in general—rightful freedom, external freedom according to universal law. Kant takes it to be an analytic judgement that coercion that protects rightful freedom is itself in accord with right.[23] 'Right and authorization to use coercion therefore mean one and the same thing.'[24]

This is the basic reason why right and not ethics can be the source of duties whose fulfilment may be externally coerced. Ethical duties are based on ends—on the rational requirement that we set and pursue certain ends that are also duties—which Kant calls 'duties of virtue'.[25] These ends belong to two categories: our own perfection, and the happiness of others.[26] Because a rational being cannot be externally coerced to set an end, the fulfilment of ethical duties cannot be externally coerced:

> Duties of virtue cannot be subject to external legislation simply because they have to do with an end which (or the having of which) is also a duty. No external legislation can bring about one's setting an end for himself, … although it may prescribe actions that lead to an end without the subject making it his end.[27]

[23] Kant, *MM*, 6: 231.
[24] ibid, 6: 232.
[25] ibid, 6:382–85.
[26] ibid, 6: 385–88.
[27] ibid, 6: 239.

But it would be wrong (contrary to right) to try to coerce the fulfilment of an ethical duty by coercing the agent to fulfil an end that agent has not set. The fulfilment of ethical duties must always be through self-constraint, not external constraint or coercion.[28] The attempt to derive duties of right from the supreme principle of morality must therefore necessarily fail, since the only duties that can be derived from this principle are duties it would be wrong (contrary to right) to coerce anyone to fulfil.

IV. RIGHT AND UNIVERSAL LAW

It is not a requirement of merely prudential reason, still less of merely instrumental reason, that we should will to be free to choose actions that further our own ends. For this requirement applies not only to our self-interested actions, but to all our actions as such. As far as reason permits, we will them to be chosen by us to serve our ends, rather than being forced to serve the ends of others. Further, when we take the standpoint of reason, abstracting from all partiality to ourselves, we also see from this perspective that every rational being equally requires that its freedom be protected from destruction, limitation or usurpation by the choice of another.

And just as morality requires us, when we set our ends and choose means to them, to act on maxims that hold as universal laws from the impartial standpoint of reason, so reason also requires us to recognise every person's equal right to be free from the constraint of the will of others in choosing his actions. This rational requirement of equal freedom consists in having the choice of every rational being protected from external interference to the fullest extent that it can be, consistently with a like freedom of all others according to universal law. The coercion that is consistent with right depends on the claim that everyone's external freedom must be limited in order that all may have external freedom. No one's external freedom should be limited merely for the sake of some end, either of that person or of others. But the external freedom of each of us must be restricted in order that others may be externally free. This is the basis, in Kant's theory of rational action, for right, the supreme principle of right, and all the claims and duties of right. In both ethics and in right, there is a rational constraint imposed by the equal recognition of others, or, as we may also put it, by the requirement that our actions conform to the constraints of universal law. This formal constraint of reason, requiring the recognition of others as having the same claims we do, and limiting permissible actions to those conforming to universal law, is common to duties of right and of ethics. That is what makes these two spheres both spheres of 'morals' (*Sitten*).

[28] ibid, 6: 379.

To put the same point another way: neither ethical duties nor duties of right are based on a selfish calculation to the effect that if I treat others in a certain way, they will treat me in a similar way. Duties of beneficence are not based on the thought that if I help others when they are in need, then they will (be more likely to?) help me when I am in need, or conversely, that if I do not help them, then they (probably?) won't help me either. Likewise, I do not have a duty to refrain from violating the rightful freedom of others because I think that will make it more likely that they will refrain from violating mine. Both cases involve, rather, an impartial claim of reason grounded on the constraint of universal law.

What the two spheres have in common, therefore, is their subjection to 'the categorical imperative, which as such only affirms what obligation is: act upon a maxim that can hold as a universal law'.[29] I speculate that those who interpret right as grounded on the supreme principle of morality that applies to ethics may do so because they are thinking of the moral law as nothing but the requirement of universalisability. But this is only one aspect of the moral principle—the formal aspect (represented by the Formula of Universal Law or Law of Nature)—which needs to be complemented by formulas that provide ethics with its characteristic ends and motivation (the Formula of Humanity as End in Itself), and that represent ethical legislation as uniting the ends of all rational beings into a system (the Formula of Autonomy or Realm of Ends).[30] The merely formal aspect of ethics is indeed present in right as well, but only as a constraint constituting the idea of obligation in general, which finds different applications in right and in ethics.

The constraints of right grounded on the freedom of others, and the constraint of universal law that applies to ethics, are therefore analogous constraints, grounded on the categorical imperative that expresses merely 'the concept of obligation'. But these constraints are not the same, because the application of the concept of obligation (of universal law) is different in the two spheres. The two constraints are also not such that the one constraint could be derived from or be dependent upon the other. The ethical claim that others have on our respect and concern rests on their value as ends in themselves, but their claims of right do not. At most, the ethical value possessed by others as ends in themselves would ground the ethical claim that their rights have on us as moral beings. They could never ground the entitlement of one person to have another person coerced or externally constrained to respect their rights. That last claim, to the coercive enforcement of external freedom as independence of another's choice, is one that belongs to right alone. It could not be derived from ethics, since its claims are never entitled to coercive

[29] ibid, 6: 225.
[30] Kant, *Groundwork*, 4: 436.

enforcement. Right therefore rests solely on the claim any person has on any other, from the impartial standpoint of reason, to be left free to choose his actions in furtherance of his own ends, rather than being forced to choose them to serve the ends of someone else.

It bears emphasising that no ethical duty, as such, carries with it such a right of coercive enforcement: forcibly to compel someone to discharge a duty of beneficence is itself a violation of the right of the person compelled. If duties of right had their basis in the categorical imperative, they too could not be enforced through external constraint. It is only the rational claim that the external freedom of each person has on every other that grounds duties of right. Ethical duties and incentives, therefore, could not belong to the sphere of right as such. They can neither explain why we have duties of right nor determine the content of those duties. The whole idea that right must somehow be derived from ethics, and that the universal principle of right must either be a version of, or derived from, the categorical imperative, involves a projection onto Kant of the basic error that Ripstein exposes as fundamentally alien to Kantian thinking: namely the error that legal and political philosophy is nothing but an application of *ethics* to the specific circumstances of law and politics.

V. RIGHT IS GROUNDED ON OUR HUMANITY

The ethical claim involves the worth of every person as an end in itself. This involves an ethical worth that belongs to the humanity of every person in Kant's technical sense of the term—humanity as the capacity to set ends and choose means to them.[31] The worth of humanity as end in itself provides the end or matter of ethical duty and the motive (*Bewegungsgrund*) for obeying the ethical imperative.[32] This end in itself is an *existent* or *self-sufficient* end (a person having a worth for whose sake we act), as distinct from the ends to be produced that might be set as ends based on this end (eg the ends of our own perfection or the happiness of others). The basis of the innate right to freedom is also 'humanity' in the same technical sense of the term: namely the capacity to set ends according to reason and choose actions as means to them. Each human being has an innate right to freedom, '(independence from being constrained by another's choice), insofar as it can exist with the freedom of every other in

[31] Kant, *Groundwork*, 4: 429. I Kant, *Critique of the Power of Judgment* (New York, Cambridge University Press, 2000) 5: 431. I Kant, *Religion Within the Boundaries of Mere Reason* (New York, Cambridge University Press, 1996) 6:27. I Kant, *Anthropology from a Pragmatic Point of View* (New York, Cambridge University Press, 2012) 7: 322–24, 327.

[32] Kant, *Groundwork*, 4: 426–29.

accordance with a universal law, [which belongs] to every human being by virtue of his humanity'.[33]

This basis, however, is distinct from the worth of humanity as end in itself that grounds ethical duties by providing the motive for obedience to a categorical imperative. For one thing, the worth of humanity as end in itself grounds only non-coercible (ethical) duties, whereas duties of right are subject to external coercion. Also, humanity as end in itself grounds duties on an *end* (humanity as end in itself), whereas claims of right must be independent of every end of action. Ethics places inner (or self-) constraint on the ends-to-be-produced that we adopt (requiring us to include our own perfection and the happiness of others among these ends); but right leaves ends entirely to our free choice, requiring us instead to limit our actions so that they are consistent with the external freedom of others.[34] Humanity is the ground of right in the sense that to recognise a person as having humanity is to appreciate the rational structure of action as a choice of means to an end set by the agent, and thus the rational requirement that the choice of any rational agent be independent of the constraining will of another in choosing actions as means to one's own ends. That rational requirement, impartially regarded (hence subject to universal law), is the foundation of right.

VI. RIGHT AS EXTERNAL CONSTRAINT, AND AS RIGHT AS DUTY

There is even a rather strong sense in which a duty of right does not directly ground my doings or refrainings at all. Recall that the legislation of right does not carry with it duty itself as the legislative incentive. And notice again that Kant states the universal principle of right not as a proposition that tells us what to do, but simply as a proposition that tells us which actions count as 'right'. It tells us, as Kant says, not how we should limit our actions, but how they are limited in accordance with external freedom and hence how they may be rightfully limited by others. A *right* action is one that may not, by standards of right, be coercively prevented, while an action that is *wrong* (*unrecht*), according to those same standards, must be subject to coercive prevention. My duties of right do not, under the legislation of right, exercise rational constraint directly on *me* (this they can do only when regarded under the legislation of ethics); rather, they specify the use of coercive force that others may rightfully use on me, and it is that coercive force exercised on me that constitutes the bindingness on me of a duty of right. It is in that sense only that duties of right fall under a categorical imperative: they do so for a rational being that sees

[33] Kant, *MM*, 6: 237.
[34] ibid, 6: 382.

right actions not merely as actions to which I may be restricted by external compulsion (consistent with the rightful freedom of all under universal law) but also actions to which I must internally restrict myself based on the ethical incentive to do only those actions that conform to the concept of universally binding legislation. That is the sense in which the 'law of right' can be called a 'categorical imperative, which as such only affirms what obligation is: act upon a maxim that can hold as a universal law'.[35]

The concept of a maxim that can hold as universal law is connected, Kant is claiming, with the concept of obligation, but at a level more abstract than either right or ethics, and this concept applies to the obligations of ethics and right in different ways. In ethics, it is applied to the maxims through which individual rational agents ought to govern their own conduct through the motive of duty and with inner (or self-)constraint. As a rational moral agent, I ought to reject maxims as contrary to duty if they cannot harmonise with universal law,[36] and I ought to adopt any maxim that comprehends within the same rational volition itself as a universal law for all rational beings.[37]

As applied to right, however, this concept concerns not individual self-government, but the conditions under which rational beings may be externally constrained by a commanding will with the power to coerce. Every rational being, as a being that sets ends and chooses actions as means to them, wills that as far as possible its actions should serve its own ends rather than being constrained to serve the ends of another. As a rational being acting under the idea of obligation as conformity to universal law, however, it can rationally claim for itself only so much such external freedom as is consistent with a like freedom for all other rational beings according to universal law. This determines the limits of external freedom that are consistent with right. These two applications of the concept of obligation as conformity to universal law are distinct and even disjoint, since the application to ethics concerns inner self-government only, not external constraint, and the latter concerns only what actions may and may not be externally constrained, not the rules for rational self-government.

The universal principle of right, therefore, cannot possibly be based on or derived from the supreme principle of morality—even if what Kant calls 'the universal law of right'[38] commands categorically. This is because a categorical imperative is one which carries the incentive to its obedience within itself, rather than borrowing the incentive from elsewhere.[39] That is what makes the

[35] ibid, 6: 225.
[36] Kant, *Groundwork*, 4: 421.
[37] ibid, 4: 440.
[38] Kant, *MM*, 6: 231.
[39] Kant, *Groundwork*, 4: 414.

moral law governing ethics a principle of inner self-government rather than a principle of external constraint. Since it belongs to the concept of juridical legislation that the incentive must be borrowed from elsewhere, hence allowing for external coercion as an incentive to obedience, no juridical law or duty of right can, *considered as such*, be a categorical imperative. If in fact there is *also* a categorical imperative to comply with duties of right (as Kant holds that there is, in the form of the 'universal law of right'), then this must be because there is *also* an *ethical* incentive to comply with the legislation of right. 'So while there are many *directly ethical* duties, internal legislation makes the rest of them, one and all [ie duties of right], indirectly ethical.'[40]

In other words, either duties of right are always also (indirectly) ethical duties, or there is an ethical incentive, independent of the legislation of right itself, to comply with duties of right. Consequently, duties of right, considered as such, are *not* ethical; they must have a foundation independent of ethics, or the supreme principle of morality. If it is for us a categorical imperative to limit our actions to those that are right (according to the universal principle of right), this is a matter of ethics, not of right. The foundation of that principle, and of duties of right, in fact, the foundation of the entire legislation of right, must be different from and independent of the categorical imperative of ethics. The legislation of right also stands in need of an independent foundation because right makes stronger claims, in one important respect, than any ethical legislation could justify. Specifically, duties of right may be coercively enforced, while the coercive enforcement of ethical duties is always wrong—contrary to right, hence also (if duties of right also make an ethical claim on us) contrary to ethics and to the categorical imperative. Right therefore requires a rational foundation entirely independent of ethics. And it has one, based on the line of reasoning presented above.

VII. RIPSTEIN ON EXTERNAL FREEDOM AS THE GROUND OF RIGHT

This is the only way Kant's theory of right makes sense. It is also the basic idea used by Ripstein in his exposition of Kant's theory of right. In support of the suggestion that my account is substantially the same as Ripstein's, I offer the following set of quotations from early in his book:

> Kant draws a series of sharp divisions between right and ethics. … The inner nature of ethical conduct means that the only incentive consistent with the autonomy at the heart of morality must be morality itself; rightful conduct can be induced by incentives provided by others. Other persons are entitled to enforce duties of right,

[40] Kant, *MM*, 6: 220–21.

> but not duties of virtue. Each of these differences precludes any direct appeal to the Categorical Imperative.[41]

> The idea of independence carries the justificatory burden of the entire argument. … [In the Doctrine of Right] Kant's concern is not with how people ought to interact, as a matter of ethics, but with how they can be forced to interact, as a matter of right.[42]

> Kant's legal and political philosophy starts with a simple but powerful conception of freedom as independence from another person's choice.[43]

> The right to independence is not a special case of a more general interest in being able to set and pursue your purposes. Instead, it is a distinctive aspect of your status as a person in relation to other persons, entitled to set your own purposes, and not required to act as an instrument for the pursuit of anyone else's purposes.[44]

> Your right is that you, rather than any other person, be the one who determines which purposes you will pursue.[45]

VIII. KANT IS SOONER A SOCIAL DEMOCRAT THAN A LIBERTARIAN

Apart from stating this basic idea of Kant's theory of right, the other main virtue of Ripstein's book is the way he develops the idea of rightful freedom as independence of the choice of another, applying it to property, contract, the foundation of political authority, and to the operations of the state that are needed to give reality to the freedom of rational beings regarded as the independence of their choices from being forced to serve the ends of others.

This basic idea of Kant's theory of right, when stated directly and forcefully, has a tendency to sound like a libertarian slogan. No doubt this is why Kant's theory of right was at one time read by people such as FA Hayek, Robert Nozick and Mary Gregor as supporting their libertarian political ideology. But older Kantian theories of right—those of Hermann Cohen, Karl Vorländer and Max Adler, for instance—and also the consensus of more recent treatments of Kantian right—by Wolfgang Kersting, Allen Rosen, Paul Guyer, Leslie Mulholland, Alexander Kaufman and myself—have all defended a very different set of conclusions, arguing that Kantian right would sooner result in a social democratic state than in the state celebrated by libertarians. Ripstein's book is very much within this later tradition, and is to be commended for the

[41] Ripstein, *FF*, 11–12.
[42] ibid, 14.
[43] ibid, 29.
[44] ibid, 34.
[45] ibid, 40.

way it develops Kant's theory so that it encompasses all the recognisable functions of the social democratic state.

Libertarians often claim—thinking that the claim is good Kantianism—that no one's freedom may be restricted by the state for the sake of the welfare of others, or even the welfare of all. And they are right, as far as that one claim goes. But in practice, their ideology advances only the interests of concentrated wealth, capital and corporate power. That is because their way of thinking refuses to acknowledge that it is equally essential to right that the external freedom of the rich and powerful must be restricted by the state in order to protect the external freedom of the less rich and less powerful. If I must either face destitution or else live only by working for you on your terms, then I am not free to choose how I live. If I have nothing to eat, nothing to wear, no place to live, no protection from illness or disease, then I am profoundly vulnerable to the coercion of others and do not have a free life in even the most basic sense of the term. It is therefore the responsibility of the commonwealth (the state) to protect every citizen from such a fate, not in the name of welfare, but in the name of freedom. That is truly good Kantianism.

Kant does say that the rightful equality of citizens, which consists in 'each having coercive rights against every other', is compatible with 'the greatest inequality of in terms of the quantity and degree of their possessions'.[46] So he does not object to economic inequality on any grounds of equality. But he takes the rightful freedom of each to consist in being able to

> seek his happiness in the way that seems good to him, provided he does not infringe upon the freedom of others to strive for a like end which can coexist with the freedom of everyone in accordance with a possible universal law (ie does not infringe on the right of another).[47]

For this reason, Kant also insists that the rightful independence of citizens depends on their having enough property that each is 'his own master' (*sui iuris*); no one must be forced to live only 'by giving others permission to make use of his powers—and hence that, in the strict sense of the word, he serves no one other than the commonwealth' (in its protection of the rightful freedom of all).[48] As Kant sees it, inequality of possessions, therefore, infringes right less often by infringing the rightful equality of citizens than by infringing their rightful freedom and independence. It is to this that libertarian ideology is systematically (wilfully) blind.

[46] Immanuel Kant, *On the Common Saying: That May Be Correct in Theory but It Is of No Use in Practice*, (New York, Cambridge University Press, 1996) 8: 291.
[47] ibid, 8: 290.
[48] ibid, 8: 295.

Kant thinks that duties of right do not require an assignable individual to whom the duty is owed. He holds that rebellion against a tyrant does no wrong to him—since by the injustice of his rule he has forfeited the claim not to be overthrown—but it violates right, by replacing a law-governed civil society (albeit an imperfect one) with rule by mere force.[49] He likewise thinks that it is wrong to make a lying declaration—a statement made in a context requiring truthfulness as a duty of right—even to someone whose misconduct has forfeited any right to be told the truth (this is the issue separating Kant from Constant in Kant's late essay on the right to lie).[50]

Conversely, Kant thinks a person's right can be violated even if there is no assignable individual who has violated it. Thus if the violation of my right by a particular person can be called 'particular injustice', there can also be a 'general injustice' involving a violation of my right, where no assignable individual has wronged me. For instance, a series of economic transactions, none of which in particular involves a violation of anyone's right, can result in someone's being in a position in which they are deprived of what is rightfully theirs, and in such a case, it is the responsibility of a law-governed civil society to make arrangements to rectify the general injustice.

> One can participate in a general injustice, even if one does no injustice according to laws and institutions. Now if one shows beneficence to a wretch, then one has not given anything to him gratuitously, but has only given what one earlier helped to take from him through the general injustice. For if no one took more of the goods of life than another, there would be no rich and no poor.[51]

The wealthy, Kant thinks, are the beneficiaries of such injustice, and should be made to pay in order to rectify it. When the government fails to require them to do this, what such people consider beneficence does not really deserve that name:

> Having the resources to practice such beneficence as depends on the goods of fortune is, for the most part, a result of certain human beings being favored through the injustice of the government, which introduces an inequality of wealth that makes others need their beneficence. Under such circumstances, does a rich man's help to the needy, on which he so readily prides himself as something meritorious, really deserve to be called beneficence at all?[52]

There can be no protection of rightful freedom, Kant holds, without a state authority capable of acting in the name of all, and capable of rectifying

[49] ibid, 8: 382.
[50] Immanuel, Kant, *On a Supposed Right to Lie from Philanthropy* (New York, Cambridge University Press, 1996) 8: 426.
[51] Immanuel Kant, *Lectures on Ethics* (Cambridge, Cambridge University Press, 1997) 27: 416.
[52] Kant, *MM*, 6: 454.

general injustice as well as particular injustice. A person cannot be free—their choices independent of wrongful constraint by the ends of others—unless they have a mode of life capable of sustaining that independence. Welfare or happiness, for Kant, is an ethical value, with which right has nothing to do. People should set the happiness of others as an end on ethical grounds, but may not be coerced to promote this end. But rightful freedom is the right of all; it belongs no more to the wealthy and powerful than to anyone else, and the possession of wealth and power give no one the privilege of taking it away from others. When the social or economic system has such a result, they commit general injustice, which it is the responsibility of civil society to rectify.

Article 25 of the United Nations Universal Declaration of Human Rights holds that:

> Everyone has the right to a standard of living adequate for the health and well-being of himself and of his family, including food, clothing, housing and medical care and necessary social services, and the right to security in the event of unemployment, sickness, disability, widowhood, old age or other lack of livelihood in circumstances beyond his control.

These are rights whose existence is often denied by libertarians, and often represented by libertarians and utilitarians alike under the heading of 'welfare'. However, these rights seem to me best justified, as they are by a Kantian theory of right, as necessary conditions of personal freedom and independence. Their violation may sometimes take place through particular injustices, but most often occurs through the general injustice of social customs—the way women, for instance, are treated in virtually all cultures, or the general injustice of the so-called 'free' market. A society like ours, that denies these rights to millions upon millions of its citizens, cannot call itself a free society just because it leaves the wealthy and powerful free to deny others the freedoms which are theirs by right. It instead comes close to being, in Kant's technical sense of the term, a barbaric society: ruled by force, where most are deprived of rightful freedom.[53]

When human rights in Article 25 are, justified in this way, by being seen as necessary conditions for a free life, those whose wealth and power threatens these rights are not viewed as lacking in 'compassion', missing some virtue which it would be nice if they had, but at least acceptable for them to lack. Instead, they are unmasked as what they really are: wrongdoers, criminals in relation to natural rights, refusing respect to the dignity and freedom of others. On the other side, those who demand what is theirs under these rights are not seen as beggars asking for handouts, but as demanding no more than what

[53] Kant, *Anthropology*, 7: 331.

properly belongs to them. Kant saw these points clearly, and expressed them eloquently, in two memorable unpublished fragments of the 1760s:

> Many people take pleasure in doing good actions but consequently do not want to stand under obligations toward others. If one only comes to them submissively, they will do everything: they do not want to subject themselves to the rights of people, but to view them simply as objects of magnanimity. It is not all one under what title I get something. What properly belongs to me must not be accorded me merely as something I beg for.[54]

> In our present condition, when general injustice is firmly entrenched, the natural rights of the lowly cease. They are therefore only debtors, the superiors owe them nothing. Therefore, these superiors are called 'gracious lords'. But he who needs nothing from them but justice can hold them to their debts and does not need to be submissive.[55]

IX. RIPSTEIN'S APPENDIX ON RIGHT AND ETHICS

Thus far I have been praising Ripstein's approach for the way it enables us to understand right as having a rational foundation independent of ethics, so that duties of right and the principle of right need not be seen as based on or derived from the categorical imperative of morality. But Ripstein devotes his thematic consideration of the relation of right to ethics to an Appendix, in which he says a number of things that seem to me not only inconsistent with his main account, but also deeply confused, and difficult (at least for me) to make sense of. I want to conclude my remarks here by explaining my perplexity, and trying to correct some of what I believe he gets wrong.

In this Appendix, Ripstein asserts that 'the Universal Principle of Right really does follow from the Categorical Imperative, though it is not equivalent to it'.[56] In his later explanation of the argument that it does so, however, he says: 'Such an argument is not a derivation of the Universal Principle of Right from the Categorical Imperative; it only shows the former to be the legitimate extension of the latter.'[57] These remarks might be interpreted sympathetically, in light of what has been said above, as making the point that the universal law, belonging to the concept of obligation, and constituting categorical imperatives, is something that right and ethics share. Right and ethics are equally 'extensions'—applications, to two independent domains (the separate domains of external freedom and of inner self-government)—of

[54] *Writings of Immanuel Kant* (New York, Cambridge University Press, 1992) 145.
[55] ibid, 140–41.
[56] Ripstein, *FF*, 358.
[57] ibid, 372.

that concept. However, if Ripstein's main account of Kant's theory of right is correct, and if my development of it earlier in these comments has been faithful to his insights, then he cannot possibly be correct when he asserts at the beginning of his Appendix that the universal principle of right 'follows' from the categorical imperative. If the principle of right is in any sense a legitimate 'extension' of the categorical imperative (as Ripstein says of it later on), the categorical imperative cannot provide any justification for duties of right as coercively enforceable. At most, what he says might be true if taken to mean that for each juridical duty, in addition to the juridical obligation to comply with it, we have also an *ethical incentive* to comply with it, or perhaps even an ethical duty corresponding to it, which follows from the categorical imperative. Earlier I quoted Ripstein as saying that the differences Kant draws between right and morality preclude any *direct* appeal to the *ethical* categorical imperative in treating of matters of right.

X. WHY DOES THE DOCTRINE OF RIGHT COME FIRST?

Regarding the unity of the metaphysics of morals, Ripstein makes the following remark at the end of the Appendix:

> Textually, the Doctrine of Right belongs in the *Metaphysics of Morals*. It belongs at the beginning, and the principles of right, including public and private right, constrain the means available for agents to use, and *thereby* constrain the maxims on which they may act. The Doctrine of Virtue's discussions of duties owed to others presupposes [*sic*] the individuation of persons as embodied rational beings.[58]

It is true that Kant regards the constraints of right as *also* ethical constraints, but that does not entail that the Doctrine of Right would have to come first: to perform that function, it could just as well have come second.

However, Ripstein's last sentence suggests that he may think Kant cannot be in a position to derive duties of virtue without some sort of deduction of the spatiality of moral persons. But that idea too seems to me without merit. Kant understands the ethical duties derived in the Doctrine of Virtue to be an application of the a priori principle of morality to the empirical facts of human nature in general.[59] The existence of human beings as bodies in space may be one of these facts, but there are many others concerning natural inclinations, self-love, self-esteem and people's attitudes toward themselves and others that are not thematised in the Doctrine of Right and are just as

[58] ibid, 387–88.
[59] Kant, *MM*, 6: 217.

important for the Doctrine of Virtue as the fact that persons are embodied rational beings in space.

The unity of the metaphysics of morals is sufficiently established by recognising that the two legislations of right and morality both concern duties or rational constraints on human conduct grounded, though in two quite different ways, in the nature of rational agency itself and on the constraint of universal law contained in the concept of obligation. The legislation of ethics concerns the categorical principles of volition, which correspond to moral constraints on our ends. The legislation of right concerns the requirement of external freedom built into the structure of rational action itself, as it plays out in the relation between different persons sharing the same external world, and the nature of this requirement when it is viewed from the impartial standpoint of reason.

I speculate that the Doctrine of Right comes first because the rational requirement of rightful freedom is simpler and more abstract than what is involved in setting ends according to reason, and shaping the character and feelings of rational beings so that they will harmonise with the constraints of moral principles. Ripstein would appear to want greater unity than this, and a clearer reason why right precedes ethics. He also wants to see the universal principle of right as following from the categorical imperative, at least in the sense of being a 'legitimate extension' of it. But I find the whole idea that the principle right is an 'extension' of the categorical imperative to be either obscure or plainly false. It might be rescued from obscurity if the notion of 'extension' is explicated as the independent application of universal law (the concept of obligation) to two distinct and independent domains. It is false, however, if it is meant to suggest that duties of right are a class of ethical duties arrived at merely by 'extending' the application of the categorical imperative of ethics to some new domain. For that 'extension' could result only in more *non-coercible* ethical duties, not in the externally coercible duties of right. Ripstein seems to me to acknowledge—but also to understate—this point at the very end of his book when he says that 'Focusing exclusively on the Categorical Imperative …, coercion must seem accidental.'[60] On the contrary, I would say: Focusing on the (ethical) 'Categorical Imperative' makes it impossible to establish any *coercible* duties at all.

Ripstein also appears to associate this notion of an 'extension' with Kant's remark, which I quoted earlier, that the principle of right is a 'postulate incapable of further proof'.[61] But we also saw earlier that what this means is that the principle of right does not have a force analogous to the categorical imperative at all: it does not command us as agents, but is only a principle for

[60] Ripstein, *FF*, 388.
[61] Kant, *MM*, 6: 231.

determining which of our actions count as *right* and which as *wrong*—solely for the purpose of determining what is (and is not) *rightful* external coercion. Further, the fact that the principle of right is presented as a postulate incapable of further proof makes it clear that it cannot possibly be grounded on the categorical imperative at all, whether by way of 'extension' or in any other way.

XI. RIPSTEIN'S AMPHIBOLY

In the Appendix, Ripstein makes a further attempt to relate right to ethics, using a distinction drawn by Kant in the first *Critique*'s Amphiboly of Concepts of Reflection between a comparison of concepts and a comparison of objects.[62] This too I find obscure, perhaps because I simply don't see how the parallel with the Amphiboly is supposed to work. In the Amphiboly, Kant is concerned with what he calls 'concepts of reflection'—concepts that arise when the same object is considered in their relation to different faculties—specifically, the faculties of sensible intuition and discursive understanding. Ripstein tries to develop his idea by offering some analogies between the four concepts of reflection discussed in the Amphiboly and various features of duties of right. He associates 'identity/difference' with the individuation of actions, 'agreement/opposition' with the enforcement of right, 'inner/outer' with the fact that duties of right concern relations between persons, and 'form/matter' with the point that right concerns deeds (actions as the use of means) in abstraction from ends. I can't comment on these associations, except to say that they strike me as both unilluminating and arbitrary, an unedifying exercise in Kantian architectonic Rorschachery (or what Claude Levi-Strauss called *bricolage*).

Beyond that, I do agree with the details of some of the things he said in these discussions, but disagree with others. I will mention, as befits a critic, two of the latter. Ripstein mistakenly says, for instance that 'a wrong is always a wrong against some other person in particular'.[63] That statement directly contradicts the central point of Kant's famous late essay on the right to lie—which is that we can wrong humanity generally through a lying declaration even if we do no wrong to the particular person to whom we lie. Ripstein also succumbs to an extremely common (but not the less deplorable) misunderstanding of the First Section of the *Groundwork* when he suggests that Kant means to reproach the honest merchant for realising that his honesty serves his self-interest. (People often read something sinister into the psychology both of the much-maligned merchant and of the 'friend of humanity' who is

[62] Immanuel Kant, *Critique of Pure Reason* (New York, Cambridge University Press, 1998) A260–63, B316–19 (cited by A/B pagination).

[63] Ripstein, *FF*, 382.

beneficent from sympathy, when doing so involves missing precisely the point Kant is trying to make in these examples, and also supplying themselves with bogus reasons to dispute Kant's supposedly negative judgements about these two perfectly innocent agents. There seems to be no bottom to the abyss of misunderstanding to which this leads.)

XII. IS RIGHTFUL COERCION CONSISTENT WITH THE FORMULA OF UNIVERSAL LAW?

In conversation, Ripstein has told me that his real concern in this Appendix was to respond to a worry expressed by Hermann Cohen, who thought there might be a problem reconciling rightful coercion with the Formula of Universal Law. Apparently, the worry is that since it makes no sense to suppose that someone might will their own coercion, it seems as if any maxim involving coercing me could not be willed as a universal law. But this worry is utterly without substance. If the maxim in question is that of a legitimate authority exercising rightful coercion in order to protect the rightful freedom of all, there would be no problem with willing that as universal law. In so doing, I will a law that involves my being coerced in case I attempt to do wrong. More generally, the rational volition of such laws does not require me to be able to will independently each command or each act falling under the law. If it did, then I also could not will any law that might conflict with my immoral inclinations. There is no sense in which it is true that I cannot will that I be coercively prevented from doing wrong in which it is not equally true that I cannot will that these inclinations be thwarted. Kant himself explicitly rejects the Golden Rule as a moral principle if it is supposed to provide a criminal with grounds for arguing against the judge who punishes him.[64] Any supposed threat of inconsistency between rightful coercion and the categorical imperative would seem to rest on a fairly fundamental misunderstanding of what is involved in the latter principle. In any case, showing that rightful coercion is *consistent* with the moral imperative would not require us to make the stronger claims that the principle of right *follows from* that imperative or represents an *extension* of it (whatever that might mean).

In short, I think Ripstein's otherwise generally sound and extremely insightful book has acute appendicitis. Many of the claims in this Appendix are inconsistent with the principal arguments of Ripstein's book. I believe a proper understanding of Kantian ethics should prepare us to excise the misguided claims in this non-functional, blind-ended detour from Ripstein's generally admirable and highly illuminating treatment of Kant's theory of right.

[64] Kant, *Groundwork*, 4: 430n.

9

Kant's Apparent Positivism

MARTIN J STONE

'POLITICAL PHILOSOPHY', ARTHUR Ripstein writes, 'is often thought of as an application of general moral principles to the factual circumstances that make political institutions necessary.'[1] This statement characterises both Locke and the Utilitarians, different as their teachings are: both posit a self-standing moral principle, one fully graspable apart from the law; and both regard institutions as instruments for bringing about the value they favour—rights or happiness. Kant presents a different view of the relation between morality and law: law makes morality more determinate; it *expresses* a morality of interaction. I will discuss several aspects of this view.

I. LIMITS OF POLITICAL AUTHORITY

Without political authority, the interaction of independent persons on the basis of equal freedom would be impossible, Kant maintains. This account of political authority (as a condition of freedom) also marks its limit: public institutions can force people to cooperate only as required to sustain a system of equal freedom.[2] Can the contemporary liberal commitment to social and economic equality find a footing within this account? Many have worried that it cannot. Wolfgang Kersting, for example, writes:

> The area of application of [Kant's] principle of equality is strictly confined to the legal interrelations of citizens. … Consequently, Kantian equality is totally indifferent towards the economic structure of society and the distribution of goods, means and socio-economic power laid down by it. Kant's legal and political equality lacks

[1] A Ripstein, *Force and Freedom: Kant's Legal and Political Philosophy* (Cambridge, MA, Harvard University Press, 2009) (hereinafter *FF*).

[2] See ibid, 295, 265; see also xi, 26–27, 31; *cf* S Byrd and J Hruschka, *Kant's Doctrine of Right: A Commentary* (Cambridge, Cambridge University Press, 2010) 185.

> all economic implications and social commitments; it cannot be used to justify the welfare state and to legitimize welfare state programs of redistribution. The promotion of social equality and the increase of economic justice is not considered as a legally necessary political aim.... Kant has no genuinely philosophical interest in clarifying and grounding the concepts of social equality and economic justice. This limitedness of his political philosophy should not be interpreted away.[3]

But to 'interpret away' the political limitations of Kant's theory is just what Ripstein has sought to do: social and economic inequalities come within the purview of the Kantian state, Ripstein argues, because they threaten people's independence, not just their welfare.[4]

To see the thought at work here, consider first Ripstein's account of a fairly uncontroversial instance of public power—the power to build and manage roads. A road is a public right of way, and only a network of such rights of way, Ripstein argues, could ensure that commerce and communication do not become dependent on the choice of any private owner: without roads, A might become landlocked—his access to B might depend on the permission of C. This example illustrates the way *personal* subjection isn't the only threat to Right. Since relations of Right are to form a public system, the state must worry about the overall effects of this system—and specifically about its tendency to undermine the 'independence' which is the basis of ownership in the first place. Building roads comes within the state's mandate not because people are better off with roads, but because a system of independent proprietors is impossible without them.

Now someone's being landlocked (as might happen in a roadless system of private property) and someone's being poor or homeless (as might happen without public provision) are both, in Ripstein's view, conditions of dependence on others. This is more than a metaphor: the landlocked can rightfully move from place to place—and the poor or homeless might rightfully *be* in a place—only by the leave of other proprietors. On this account, 'poverty' and 'homelessness' characterise one's normative relation to others, not just the state of one's material resources. When Kersting says that Kant cannot justify 'redistribution', he is apparently thinking that the grounds of redistribution could only be a concern with people's welfare.[5] But if the poor and

[3] W Kersting, 'Kant's Concept of the State', in H Williams (ed), *Essays on Kant's Political Philosophy* (Chicago, University of Chicago Press, 1992) 143, 153.

[4] See Ripstein, *FF*, chs 8, 9.

[5] On this assumption, Kant's talk of a public duty to support the poor looks like a textual anomaly. See Immanuel Kant, *Metaphysics of Morals* (Cambridge, Cambridge University Press, 1996) 6: 326 (hereinafter *MM*). Cf E Weinrib, 'Poverty and Property in Kant's System of Rights' (2003) 78 *Notre Dame Law Review* 795.

the homeless fare badly, this is a consequence of their normative standing in a system of property, and this standing characterises what they are, not just what befalls them as a result. Hence, for Ripstein, there is a public obligation to alleviate or to prevent these conditions of dependence—just as there is an obligation to build roads.

On this account, poverty is an impersonal or systemic analogue of the condition of dependence that characterises slavery or serfdom.[6] Just as master and slave do not share a united will, so too—Ripstein argues—a regime of (privately) rightful relations that left some dependent for their subsistence on the choices of others could not be a regime to which all could consent. In Kant's terms, the 'duty of rightful honour' negates the possibility of such consent—just as it negates consent to one's own servitude. If consent is impossible, so is a united will; and if a united will is impossible, so is any actualisation of Right-as-independence.

Ripstein's argument shows that the Kantian state need not be a libertarian one, but does it go far enough to allay Kersting's concerns? Today's states are expected to do many things: to protect health and the environment, regulate risks, provide for the handicapped, fund education and research, support the arts, create parks, preserve history—to name a few. Can all of this really be considered part of the sustaining conditions of a system of reciprocal freedom? If it can, what limits on public power *are* implied by Kant's view? I have two specific worries.

First, Ripstein's main examples (roads and poverty) involve remedies to dependencies arising from a system of private property rights. This suggests *one* principled way to extend Right-based public powers. But it is obviously implausible to think that public regulation of health or the environment is entirely a matter of countering the systemic effects of property rights. Ripstein agrees, for he mentions a more general ground for public regulation: 'The State's mandate to protect public health follows from its mandate to see to its own preservation.'[7] This makes good sense—a system of rights wouldn't count for much if it couldn't preserve itself—but this still seems too limited. After all, even the libertarian will agree to it, as long as it is understood in a way that doesn't sweep away the general distinction he cares about: between state action to preserve public life (the state might respond to pandemics, as it might respond to foreign aggression) and state action to promote *good* life or flourishing. A contemporary state's mandate concerning public health looks like it requires the latter, a mandate to see that life goes well. But it needs to be explained

[6] See Ripstein, *FF*, 274.
[7] ibid, 261.

how this is possible as a principled extension of Right-as-independence—ie without recourse to exogenous notions of 'welfare'.

Second, in those cases where it clearly succeeds, Ripstein's argument shows that the state has not just a mandate but an *obligation* to address interpersonal dependencies such as poverty and homelessness. But many powers of a contemporary state are in fact matters of discretion. It would be odd, for example, to say that a state lacked the power to create parks, support the arts or preserve history; but it would also be odd to say that such actions were constitutionally required. Is there room in an argument like Kant's—an argument from the sustaining conditions of a system of private freedom—for the existence of public powers that are discretionary or essentially deliberative?

A different response to libertarianism says that valuing *freedom* involves a commitment to creating the social conditions of flourishing agents, and that this encompasses sufficient material resources, educational opportunities, health, a range of life choices and so on. This response isn't available here because the Kantian notion of freedom (ie the one that grounds public authority) is a relational one—independence from the choice of others. Its opposite is servitude or domination. Freedom as 'the conditions for autonomous choice' is, in contrast, a monadic notion—an interpretation of the agent's welfare. So Kantian Right should be indifferent to such freedom: it can't respond to Kersting's worries by considering people's real capacities or their opportunities to pursue a sufficient range of options.[8]

II. RIGHT'S DEPENDENCE ON JUDGEMENT

Kant's Law of Right says: 'So act externally that the free use of your choice can coexist with the freedom of everyone in accordance with a universal law.'[9] How do I know whether I'm complying with this? There is a sense in which Kant champions a naïve answer: if you're not sure, ask a lawyer—an expert in the law. The Law of Right has application only as it is articulated through public laws. This seems obvious in many cases: whether my walking across a field is a wrong to you depends on whose field it is, and that is a matter of the law of property, of a deed that is a matter of public record. But on Kant's account, we need law in every case where concepts of Right are applied—for two different reasons.

First, judgements of Right (eg instantiations of the schema '*x* wrongs *y*') are often uncertain: either the answer in a particular case isn't obvious or there

[8] External freedom is not autonomy: See, eg, Ripstein, *FF*, 11, 15, 34, 36, 38, 380, 384.

[9] Kant, *MM*, 6: 231.

isn't a single right answer. On some versions of 'law as applied ethics' (eg utilitarianism), morality *is* fully determinate and has all the answers, at least in principle: uncertainties in legal judgment are due only to our limited information about what will lead to what. In contrast, Kantian Right is realised through application of abstract categories. These categories perhaps make clear that I must stay out of your field and not take your apples, but they are vague and indeterminate in a variety of circumstances. They don't answer—or yield any methodology for answering—such questions as whether I may take some of your apples in a particular emergency, or what you need to do to acquire possession of those apples in the first place, or how much you thereby acquire, or what happens if you leave your field unoccupied for a long time, and so on. Such indeterminacies won't be resolved by adverting to a full set of empirical facts. Rather, some constitutive decisions are needed, a choice of rules or standards from among a range of options that are equally reasonable—or at least equally reasonable before the choice is made.

Second, even if the indeterminacies of Right *were* just a matter of the right answers being non-obvious, this wouldn't mean that we could do without law and leave things up to the private judgement of each. For then the reality of your rights would depend on my goodwill and judgement: you would enjoy independence only according to what *seems* right to me[10]—and that isn't independence at all. Right-as-independence requires *rightful ways* of determining and enforcing rights, and this couldn't be a matter of unilateral action by you or me: an institution entitled to apply and enforce the rules on behalf of everyone is needed.[11]

In sum, Right depends on positive law in two ways: to authoritatively *determine* the content of rights; and to *authoritatively* determine the content of rights—ie to give rights a public (legal) form so that they aren't left up to private will and judgement.

What more might be said a priori about how Right is to be legally specified? What are legal judgements aiming to get right? That is the topic of Kant's reflections on Private Right, but I want to focus on one of Ripstein's glosses on this topic as a whole. Right-as-independence requires systematic application of a distinction, Ripstein says, between my innocent frustration of your

[10] *cf* ibid, 6: 312.

[11] This is part of what leads Kant to say that his Postulate of Public Right can be 'explicated analytically from the concept of Right in external relations, in contrast with violence' (*MM*, 6: 308). To similar effect is GWF Hegel, *Elements of the Philosophy of Right*, trans A Wood (Cambridge, Hackett Publishing, 2002) s 212: '[O]nly what is *law* has binding force as *right*.'

purposes on the one hand, and my interfering with your powers of choice (your *purposiveness*) on the other. Here is one of his illustrations:[12]

> (1) I grab the last quart of milk from the store shelf before you get to it. I have frustrated your *purposes* by changing the context in which you act; but I haven't interfered with your purposiveness—your ability to pursue your own ends using the means you have. I haven't, for example, taken or destroyed any of your means of acting.
>
> (2) I wrench the quart of milk out of your hands. I have wronged you, because I have affected something which is yours to dispose of as you wish—your body. (Legally, this is the tort of battery.)

This example illustrates two points at once. First, Right does not relate our choices in terms of 'the end each has in mind':[13] in terms of your (frustrated) end, the two cases are indeed identical. Second, to relate our choices on a basis *other* than our ends, the law must ubiquitously work out the content of the proposed distinction (between frustrating your purposes and interfering with your purposiveness). It is easy to see why. If you could constrain me to provide a favourable context (ie the one you'd prefer) for your pursuits, I would be your subordinate. My right to frustrate your purposes is the incidence of my own (equal) freedom. (The same principle is involved when I decline to enter into a contract with you.) Hence, Ripstein's distinction (purposes/purposiveness) makes explicit the form of judgement involved in a consistent set of rights to freedom: we do wrong by using or destroying the other's means or powers; but short of that, each of us is free to affect the environment in which everyone acts. Rights to do what one wants or to realise particular ends, in contrast, notoriously form no consistent set, since anything I might want to do conflicts with something you might want.[14]

Is Ripstein's gloss on the Principle of Right any more determinate than the Principle itself? There is no reason to think it is. Does building a large box around you interfere with your powers of choice or merely affect the context in which you exercise them? Lawyers will recognise this as a case of 'false imprisonment'—a paradigm case of interfering with your powers. But this idea is vague, and variations can be imagined in which there is uncertainty about how to apply it: does the size of the area to which you are confined matter, for example?[15] Similarly, although my grabbing the last quart of milk

[12] See Ripstein, *FF*, 16, 101; see also 39, 41, 45, 47–49, 51, 153.

[13] Kant, *MM*, 6: 230.

[14] Hence such conflicts of liberties can only be resolved in terms of some other value. See Ripstein, *FF*, 32.

[15] See *Shen v Leo A Daly Co*, [2000] 222 F3d 472: 'Although it is difficult to define exactly how close the level of restraint must be, in this case the country of Taiwan is clearly too great an area within which to be falsely imprisoned.'

may be a paradigm of mere inconsideration (without infringement of right), notions of 'having possession' vs 'being merely on the way to taking possession' come into play here, and it is easy to see that these notions will present casuistic difficulties in other cases. Just when might your reasonable expectation of possessing something create a right to exclude others? And must the answer be exactly the same for, say, buying milk, hunting whales and hunting foxes?[16] Not surprisingly, there are also many cases in which the law finds no other means of drawing the distinction Ripstein proposes (between choices that infringe a right and those that merely change the practical environment) than to ask whether you acted 'reasonably under the circumstances'.[17] (As a term that mediates between our respective rights, 'reasonableness' is, of course, itself indeterminate and requires further applicative judgements in particular cases.)

All of this points to the significant role which legal judgements must play in a system of Right. In general, it might be said: (1) that application of Ripstein's categories depends on casuistry and the analogical comparison of particular cases; (2) that shared judgements about paradigm cases anchor the content of these categories; (3) that sometimes there may be conflicting but equally acceptable applicative judgements; and (4) that positive law must sometimes authoritatively choose among different ways of continuing the legal scheme. In short, Ripstein's distinction elucidates the *form* of legal judgement (in terms of its most abstract categories) but doesn't thereby supply a blueprint for classifying particulars under these categories.[18] Hence legal judgement in particular cases must bear a considerable burden; the categorical framework—the metaphysics of Right—affords no independent test of when a judge has got things right.

III. LEGAL POSITIVISM

Kantian 'Right' is a division of morality, but the forgoing remarks explain why positive law is indispensable to it: to conform to Right is to follow what is publicly laid down as Right. Perhaps it is no surprise, then, that Kant has been classified as a 'legal positivist'. Jeremy Waldron writes:

> If … there are reasons for thinking that society needs just one view on some particular matter to which all its members are to defer, then there has got to be a way

[16] See *Person v Post*, [1805] 3 Cai R 175.
[17] A choice that *accidentally* injures others is one such case. See chapter 1, Section III above.
[18] *cf* Ripstein, *FF*, 264.

> of identifying a community view and grounds for one's allegiance to it that are not predicated on any judgment one would have to make concerning the view's moral rectitude. That is the positivist position and Kant's contribution is to have linked that position conclusively … to the idea of a set of property rights, secured and assured as a system.[19]

The 'positivist position'–namely, that the content of the law-in-force is identifiable on the basis of its institutional sources (without measuring its moral rectitude)—today finds an opponent who holds that moral truths *do* play a role (either always or just sometimes) in determining the law's content. Kant didn't discuss this matter, but it does seem that his doctrine would be friendly, for the reasons Waldron suggests, to the positivist position: if the law were such that moral discernment were needed to identify its content, it couldn't play the role (of replacing private judgement) that Right-as-independence requires.[20]

And yet, the classification of Kant's views in terms of our contemporary debate about positivism doesn't seem quite so straightforward. For Kant's emphasis on legal positivity occurs in the context of an argument which—by envisioning a progression from Private Right (a priori moral principles) to Public Right (institutionally based laws)—goes against the spirit of positivism. The Principle of Right belongs to morality, but not to morality as something standing over and against law: the Principle is *proprietary* to law (it is useless apart from its public specification and enforcement) and *dependent* on law for its determinate content.

Should this package be characterised as positivism? It *can* be; the present point isn't to legislate the use of a word. What matters is just that two points be kept in mind. First, all legal theories acknowledge a role for positive law—a role for legal norms identifiable merely on the basis of their sources. What characterises traditional 'natural law' theories is that positivity does not exhaust the concept of law—law has also a critical, moral part—and by this standard, Kant continues the natural law tradition: he endeavours to situate the law's positive aspect *within* morality, to exhibit it as a moral requirement.[21] Second,

[19] J Waldron, 'Kant's Legal Positivism' (1996) 109 *Harvard Law Review* 1535, 1566. Cf A Ryan, *Property and Political Theory* (Oxford, Blackwell, 1984) 79 (quoted in Waldron): 'Kant asserts as vigorously as any legal positivist that men only have property in external things when a legal order gives them that property and provides remedies for its loss.'

[20] *MM*, 6: 312. For a similar argument for positivism (but without the moral background of Right), see J Raz, *The Authority of Law* (Oxford, Oxford University Press, 2009) ch 3; and J Raz, 'Authority, Law and Morality' in *Ethics in the Public Domain* (Oxford, Clarendon Press, 1995) ch 10.

[21] *cf* the introduction to *MM*, where Kant describes his task as that of exhibiting the '[a priori] basis' (or "immutable principles") for "any possible giving of positive laws." 6: 229-30; *cf* 6: 224, 237, 242.

a contemporary positivist is typically arguing with someone who claims that independent or *self-standing* moral truths can or must determine the content of the law. But Kant's version of the continuity of law and morality isn't a matter of the law taking marching orders from self-standing moral principles. As I have emphasized, the Principle of Right is proprietary to law and dependent on law for authoritative specifications of its content.

None of this will be news to Waldron, who lucidly set out Kant's theory of property as an argumentative progression from natural (but 'provisional') rights to the conclusive titles backed by positive law. But why doesn't this progression make Waldron hesitate about the thesis 'Kant-as-positivist'? Waldron's answer goes as follows:

> The conjecture that natural property rights might operate as constraints on positive law is reflected in Kant's view that provisional acquisitions of external resources may be made in the state of nature, which it will subsequently be the function of civil society to ratify and to make conclusive. But one cannot … treat provisional acquisitions in any sort of Lockean way. … The idea of such acquisitions is incapable … of playing the sort of role in our thinking that Nozick wanted the principle of justice in acquisition to play. The idea that acquisition in the state of nature is provisional walks onto the stage of Kantian theory hand-in-hand with the idea that a system of positive law is going to have to modify most acquisitions, privilege others, and abrogate some of them altogether in the name of a single, unified approach to justice.[22]

In this passage, Waldron emphasizes the contrast between Kantian Right and moral theories (such as Locke's and Nozick's) that *do* purport to offer moral blueprints for legal institutions: since Kantian Right is abstract (rather than such a blueprint), it walks 'hand-in-hand', as Waldron says, with a 'system of positive law'. This seems exactly right. But does it make Kant a positivist? Isn't this way of law and morality *holding hands*–or of making positive law morally indispensable—rather what *distinguishes* Kant from the views characteristic of legal positivism? The point might be put like this. Historically, positivism originates with a new picture of morality: morality as fully directive and self-standing (apart from legal institutions). (Utilitarianism is the most developed version of this picture). This new idea about morality may not precisely *entail* legal positivism, but neither is its role in motivating positivism merely accidental. For if one does think of morality as fully directive and self-standing, it may come to seem urgent (as it did to the first positivists) to represent law as merely an instrument for securing morality's independent results and hence urgent to

[22] Waldron (n 19) 1565.

limit the domain of legality (as John Austin proposed) to positive law.[23] Locke and Nozick aren't utilitarians, of course, but they do (as Waldron, in effect, stresses) share the same general picture of the self-standing role that morality can play. Hence their 'rights-based' views are (like utilitarianism) conducive to legal positivism—precisely on account of how much independent work such views take morality to do. In contrast, where the legal part of morality isn't self-standing but rather dependent on legal institutions and official judgement, this motivation for drawing a sharp boundary between morality and law is absent. In other words, Kantian Right might be consistent with positivism, but it does undercut at least one historically important motivation for limiting the domain of legality to positive law.

Someone might wish to say that Kantian Right isn't merely dependent on positive law but so abstract as to rest almost everything of substance on it. This isn't wrong, but it doesn't follow that the categories of Right do no moral work at all. The Legal Realists—who made heavy weather of the indeterminacy of legal concepts—did often come to this stronger conclusion: they reasoned from the correct observation that legal concepts need further specification to the conclusion that legal officials must apply such concepts on the basis of whatever policies seem best to them.[24] If such reasoning (from indeterminacy to 'policy') were sound, then Kantian Right might indeed be dismissed, given its indeterminacy, as inert or superfluous. But the Realist's inference, however familiar it has become, is mistaken: abstract legal concepts may not 'decide concrete cases', as Holmes put it,[25] but they do give legal reasoners a distinctive question to ask. For example, tort law's standard of 'reasonable care' is (I've argued elsewhere)[26] a specification, for situations of unintended harm, of the Kantian question 'whether the action of one can be united with the freedom of the other'[27]—and it is obviously not just *any* further reasoning (about how

[23] Here I'm summarizing part of M Stone, 'Legal Positivism as an Idea about Morality' (2011) 61 *University of Toronto Law Journal* 2, 313–41; and M Stone, 'Legal Positivism as an Idea about what Morality Might Be' (forthcoming).

[24] Waldron himself does not express or favour such views. For examples in legal scholarship, see OW Holmes, 'Privilege, Malice, and Intent' (1894) 8 *Harvard Law Review* 1; and L Green, 'Tort Law: Public Law in Disguise' (1960) 38 *Texas Law Review* 257. For judicial examples, see *Spartan Steel & Alloys Ltd v Martin & Co*, [1973] 1 QB 27, 37; *Petitions of the Kinsman Transit Co*, [1964] 338 F2d 708, 725 (2d Cir); *Lamb v London Borough of Camden*, [1981] 2 All Eng Rep 408 (CA).

[25] *Lochner v New York*, 198 US 45 (1905).

[26] See chapter 1, Section III above. See also M Stone, 'The Significance of Doing and Suffering' in G Postema (ed), *Philosophy and the Law of Torts* (Cambridge, Cambridge University Press, 2001); and E Weinrib, *The Idea of Private Law* (Cambridge, MA, Harvard University Press, 2012) ch 6, which influenced me.

[27] Kant, *MM*, 6: 230.

to apply the standard of 'reasonable care') that successfully engages *this* question. (To endeavor to reach a decision by asking what rule would maximise wealth or spread accident losses is, at best, to change the topic, since—unlike 'reasonable care'—such economic notions don't describe any relation between the parties.) The law's abstract standards may not determine uniquely correct answers, but that doesn't mean they don't set perfectly good questions: on the Kantian view, legal indeterminacy invites concretising judgement, not diversions into policy.[28]

IV. PROVISIONALITY

My overall theme has been the way Kant's morality of interaction ("Private Right") goes 'hand in hand' with an outsized role for positive law and legal judgement. A methodological remark of Ripstein's is relevant to this: 'Kant approaches the question of the legitimate use of force through *a sequence of arguments*.'[29] Yes—and not just in the anodyne sense that there are different arguments, so of course you encounter them in sequence, but in a stronger sense which bears a likeness to Hegel's 'dialectical' procedures.[30]

Kant's argument starts from (1) Innate Right (the independent purposiveness of each) and moves to (2) Private Right (which introduces the possibility of acquiring 'external things') and then to (3) Public Right ('From private law in the state of nature proceeds the postulate of public law')[31] which describes a constitutional state. Each stage builds on what came before. The opening idea of Right as independent purposiveness leads—in light of people's *object*-using purposes—to the question: can others ever be constrained from using objects not in my physical possession? Kant's answer—'yes'—makes space for claims to private property but only by creating a further problem (an apparent inconsistency with the 'authorisations' of Innate Right): property claims would unilaterally bind others in non-reciprocal ways. And this problem can only be resolved (Kant argues) through Public Law, conceived as our common ('omni-lateral') legislation and enforcement of the scheme of rights.

[28] See M Stone, 'Formalism', in S Shapiro and J Coleman (eds), *The Oxford Handbook of Jurisprudence* (Oxford, Oxford University Press, 2004); M Stone, 'Focusing the Law: What Legal Interpretation is Not', in A Marmor (ed), *Law and Interpretation: Essays in Legal Philosophy* (Oxford, Oxford University Press, 1998).

[29] Ripstein, *FF*, 6 (my emphasis); *cf* 13–14.

[30] Compare what Hegel said about philosophy: 'the result [isn't] the actual whole, but rather the result together with the process through which it came about'. GWF Hegel, *Phenomenology of Spirit*, trans AV Miller (Oxford, Clarendon Press, 1977) s 3.

[31] Kant, *MM*, 6: 307.

Many of Kant's commentators take this sequential method of argumentation for granted and focus on explicating its details.[32] But I think that understanding its details requires asking what (if anything) makes it *necessary* to represent Right in this sequential way and (relatedly) why the inadequacy of each argumentative stage compels a further step forward rather than suggesting that a wrong start had been made. In particular, when Kant introduces Public Law as a necessary condition for application of 'concepts of Right'[33] why doesn't this imply that Right was misrepresented ab initio, when it appeared *apart* from the public conditions of its application?

These questions are pertinent to the general issue I have been discussing: the relation between morality (Private Right) and positive (Public) law. For these questions arise because Public Law isn't meant, in Kant's argument, to *add-on* to something already complete without it but to *unfold* something that was latent from the start. Suppose that, on some island, we divided up the land, but then discovered that our scheme didn't work very well without someone to settle disputes and enforce it. This needn't suggest that we had a wrong *conception* of what we were initially doing; its only a question of removing troubles by adding a means of implementation. It is in such ways that some of Kant's modern predecessors argue for public authority: to leave the state of nature would cure the 'inconvenience' (as Locke said) of everyone judging about rights for themselves. In contrast, the idea of 'rights left up to private judgement' is, for Kant, an inadequate *conception* of rights, a flouting of Right's own requirements, for you can't be 'independent' where the actuality your rights depends on my ('unilateral') will and judgement. This is why the later stages of Kant's argument implicate its starting point: if Right is, by its very nature, something publicly established and enjoyed, doesn't this mean that, in starting with Private Right—with merely unilateral claims to property—it wasn't really *Right* we had in view at all?

According to Ripstein, Kant's argument is structured in terms of a logic of *defect* and its removal, and this is what we are to understand by Kant's claim

[32] In some accounts, like Kersting (n 3), we hear Hegel's idiom: 'The point [of Kant's talk of provisionality] is that Private law in the state of nature becomes aware of its own imperfection and understands the necessity of a legislative determination of its contents'—as if Kant were writing a phenomenology of legal consciousness. According to Weinrib (n 26) ch 4: 'The postulate of practical reason with respect to rights allows us provisionally to hold the notion of external property in place until thought of it can be completed in a further phase that establishes the conditions under which external property is conclusively rightful.' These accounts are faithful to Kant's thought, but they don't ask why an account of Right must be a sequence that posits and cancels something temporarily 'held in place'.

[33] ibid, 6: 312.

that property rights without public law are merely *provisional*. 'Provisional right' isn't the name of any existing right—like, eg, a 'conditional right' in the lawyer's sense. As Kant stresses, there is no genuine title, apart from public law, to constrain others: 'human beings do no wrong' in proceeding, in the state of nature, as if there were no rights at all.[34] Hence, a provisional right, Ripstein says, is a 'title to coerce that nobody is entitled to enforce coercively'.[35] Of course, that's as much (or as little) any real title to coerce as a provisional right is a right, but this needn't seem paradoxical. It is to be understood on the (privative or defectual) model of a 'bad argument': that, after all, is an argument for a conclusion that that nobody is compelled to accept.

But the question I am asking can be stated in terms of one of Ripstein's elaboration of this idea:

> If I believe in good faith that the boundary between our property is in one place, and you, equally in good faith, believe that it is somewhere else, neither of us has any obligation of right to yield to the other.… To yield in such circumstances is … to fail to stand on our rights. … More generally, neither of us needs to give in to the unilateral judgment of the other as to how to classify particulars. Unilateral judgment cannot be a law for another person. The solution … is the judiciary: a body that has omnilateral authorization to apply the law to particular cases. The highest court's decision is final, not because it could not make a mistake, but because it has a public authorization to decide for everyone.[36]

Since the necessity of public authority is represented here as (1) a defect of Private Right (ie its indeterminacy)[37] together with (2) the impossibility of curing this defect through private judgement ('unilateral judgement cannot be a law for another person'), someone might ask: why don't (1) and (2) undermine Ripstein's initial description of you and me having a good-faith dispute about property? How could we so much as take ourselves to be asserting genuine claims to property, given our knowledge of the truth that rights can't, in the nature of the case, be unilaterally established? I take these questions merely to bring out what is peculiar to Kant's 'sequenced' account: it asks that we both accept an initial description of Private Right *and* recognise this description as flouting Right's own conditions of possibility.[38] But how could our

[34] *cf* ibid, 6: 255–57; 6: 307–08.

[35] Ripstein, *FF*, 165. Ripstein adds that in the state of nature 'neither of us has a title to coerce consistent with our respective independence under universal law, so neither of us has a right, properly speaking'. On 'defect', see also 181: 'three defects … make … application [of purely private right] merely provisional'; *cf* 146.

[36] Ripstein, *FF*, 172.

[37] *cf* Kant, *MM*, 6: 266.

[38] *cf* Kant, *MM*, 6: 312.

commitment to the initial description of Private Right be any greater than what is warranted by our subsequent reflections which reveal this description to be conceptually 'defective'? What, in other words, propels us onward to a 'defect-remedying' stage (Public Right) rather than backward to a rejection of the starting point?

Returning to the idea of Kant as *positivist*, Kant's argumentative sequence is just what makes this classification seem one-sided. For when the contemporary positivist argues that moral truths never determine the content of the law-in-force, no prior 'stage' informs this argument: no morality of private interaction that is proprietary to law.[39] Certainly, Kant shares the positivist's thesis that the law won't serve its purpose (of authoritatively determining morality) if legal content were sensitive to moral truth. But, unlike the positivist, Kant doesn't suggest that this is the main thing to be said about law's relation to morality; the main thing, for Kant, occurs in the antecedent stages, which present the a priori principles of Innate and Private Right.[40]

Yet this same argumentative sequence also makes it difficult to regard Kant as a *non-positivist*, at least if this means—what the contemporary positivist sets his face against—that independent moral truths *do* determine the content of the law. As Waldron observes, Private Right is not equipped to play that sort of (Lockean) role. And 'provisional' property rights are no ordinary 'rights' since they don't—apart from their articulation through public law—morally constrain others. Hence, the nature of Kant's doctrine seems well captured by Fichte when the latter wrote: 'There is no natural right at all in the sense often given to that term, ie, there can be no rightful relation between human beings except within a commonwealth and under positive laws.'[41] Of course,

[39] *cf* Kant, *MM*, 6: 230: the Doctrine is to establish 'the [moral] basis for any possible giving of positive laws'. Expressed historically, Kant is rejecting not just Locke's teaching that property rights are only externally related to public law, but also Hobbes's teaching that property is impossible in a state of nature. See Hobbes, *Leviathan*, ed CB Macpherson (Harmondsworth, Penguin, 1968) 188: in the state of nature 'there be no … *Mine* and *Thine* distinct'. Contrast Kant, *MM*, 6: 256 and 6: 313 ('provisional' mine and thine is the basis of the obligation to leave the state of nature). See also 6: 306; *cf* 6: 312–13; *cf* 6: 256–57.

[40] Hence, Kant could embrace the modest legal positivism proposed in J Gardner, 'Legal Positivism: 5 1/2 Myths' (2001) 46 *American Journal of Jurisprudence* 199: 'Legal positivism is not a whole theory of law's nature after all. It is a thesis about legal validity, which is compatible with any number of other theses about law's nature, including the thesis that all valid law is by its nature subject to special moral objectives and imperatives of its own.' I develop this contrast (between modest and robust positivism) in my 'Legal Positivism as an Idea about What Morality Might Be' (forthcoming).

[41] JG Fichte, *Foundations of the Science of Right*, ed F Neuhouser, trans M Baur (Cambridge, Cambridge University Press, 2000) 132; see also 101–02: 'An original right … is a mere *fiction*, but one that must necessarily be created for the science of right.'

what Fichte rejects is not natural right *as such*, but only a mistaken *conception* of it ('the sense often given to that term'): namely, right as something determinately available without institutions. Public laws, he says in another passage, are 'nothing other than natural right realized'.[42]

I conclude that the interest of Kant's doctrine lies partly in its power to suggest an alternative to the positions that inform contemporary debates about positivism. Indeed, Kant combines two theses that some might think of as mutually exclusive: (1) that law expresses a part of morality and (2) that legal norms are valid only on the basis of their institutional sources, not their moral merits. The second of these is the thesis of contemporary positivism; but the first means that an account of the nature of law isn't merely an account of its positivity.

Sequencing appears closely connected to the matter of Kant's philosophical thought, and not just when it comes to Right: that there are 'pure forms of understanding' which, nonetheless, apply only to objects of experience presents an analogous structure.[43] Am I making too much fuss about this form of philosophical representation? Isn't it enough that various political phenomena *are* illuminated if we adopt it? I don't think so. Many of the interpretive disputes about the *Doctrine of Right* reflect uncertainties about how to understand its unfolding stages. 'Kant as positivist' is one example, and there others, such as the dispute between those who see Kant as starting out from pre-political notions of private freedom and those who see him as writing in critique of such notions.[44] And isn't there something strange in itself in Kant's representation of pre-institutional claims to property as unilateral, violent assertions, which are then to be made-Right (rather than rejected), to be redeemed as part of the history of peace (ie 'mine and thine secured under laws')?[45] These questions point to the need for some account of what makes Kant's 'sequential' form of representation necessary (and not merely optional) for his philosophy of Right. That is, it would be worthwhile to ask: do Kant's ideas about the nature of rights and the basis of political authority require such a sequence of arguments? Or would talk of argumentative 'stages' be, in some more perspicuous representation, dispensable?

[42] Fichte, ibid, 133.

[43] I am indebted to a conversation with James Conant about this.

[44] See, eg, the chapters by Pallikkathyil and Flikschuh above.

[45] Kant, *MM*, 6: 355: '[E]stablishing this universal and perpetual peace is not simply a part but rather the entire final purpose of the doctrine of right....'

Part V

Reply

10

Embodied Free Beings under Public Law: A Reply

ARTHUR RIPSTEIN*

I AM GRATEFUL to all of the contributors for their careful and sustained engagement with my work, and, delighted that it has provoked such outstanding scholars to engage so deeply with Kant's *Doctrine of Right*. I am also grateful to Sari Kisilevsky, Martin Stone and Sergio Tenenbaum for their work in organising the symposia on *Force and Freedom* for which many of the chapters were first written, and to Sari and Martin for their work in organising and editing the volume.

In these replies, I will take up some, but not all, of the issues that they raise. My responses are organised by some general themes: I begin with innate right and private right, considering the arguments of Flikschuh, Pallikkathayil, Julius and Sangiovanni. In very different ways, each of these critics takes up the issue of the formal and relational nature of right. I then turn to public right, responding to Pavlakos, Weinstock and Stone as well as one argument from Flikschuh. Each of their chapters engages the relation between the Postulate of Public Right and the Idea of the Original Contract. The third section looks to issues of Right and Ethics, where I will focus on Wood's challenge, as well as some residual issues raised by Stone and Pavlakos.

I. INNATE AND PRIVATE RIGHT

Kant divides the *Doctrine of Right* into Private Right and Public Right. The Introduction to the doctrine of right, which contains both Kant's formulation of the Universal Principle of Right and his discussion of the innate right of humanity that each of us has in his or her own person is 'not part of the

* I am grateful to Sari Kisilevsky, Martin Stone, Jacob Weinrib and Ariel Zylberman for comments on an earlier version of this reply.

division'. In *Force and Freedom*, I take Kant's organising structure seriously, and suppose that the Universal Principle of Right has its primary though by no means exclusive application to the innate right of humanity. Flikschuh challenges the primacy of innate right; Pallikkathayil questions its distinctiveness. Both endorse its formal nature, though they have different views of its relational nature. Julius and Sangiovanni focus more on the Universal Principle of Right, but they question its relational, formal nature.

A. Innate Right and the Body

Both Pallikkathayil and Flikschuh question my claim that the body occupies a distinctive place in the justification of public authority. Flikschuh questions the emphasis I place on the connection between a person's body and that person's innate right of humanity; Pallikkathayil raises doubts about the body from a different direction, arguing that each person's relation to his or her own body is much more property-like than I am prepared to concede.

First, it is worth noting the way in which Kant characterises innate right in terms of the body, and, in particular, the way in which he identifies your person with your body. Kant's view is that your body is your person, considered spatially, so it is also your person considered in terms of external relations. The body is that through which you act; the only way you do anything in space and time, and so the only way you do anything in relation to others is with your body. Kant makes this point explicit in his opening remarks about the difference between a property right and the right of humanity in your own person, which he calls your right to freedom.

Kant writes:

> For someone who tried in the first case (of empirical possession) to wrest the apple from my hand or to drag me away from my resting place would indeed wrong me with regard to what is internally mine (freedom); but he would not wrong me with regard to what is externally mine unless I could assert that I am in possession of the object even without holding it. I could not then call these objects (the apple and the resting place) mine. (6: 248)

The same contrast appears when Kant offers his deduction of the concept of merely rightful possession by showing that the concept is distinct from the concept of right itself.

> An a priori proposition about right with regard to empirical possession is analytic, for it says nothing more than what follows from empirical possession in accordance with the principle of contradiction, namely that if I am holding a thing (and so physically connected with it), someone who affects it without my consent (eg, snatches an apple from my hand) effects and diminishes what is internally mine (my

> freedom), so that his maxim is in direct contradiction with the axiom of right. So the proposition about empirical possession in conformity with rights does not go beyond the right of a person with regard to himself. (6:250)

The contrast here between property right and the right to internal freedom is the contrast between a right with respect to something that could belong to another and something that could not. My 'internal freedom' is not internal in the sense that it is a matter of my thought, or of anything non-relational; it is not even the sort of internal freedom that is the subject of Kant's *Groundwork*. It is freedom, understood as 'independence from being constrained by another's choice' (6:237), as my person standing in certain relations to the freedom of others. What is internally mine can only be understood in terms of the external relations between us. It consists in my independence of the choice of others while holding something with my hand, or my body resting in some place. Non-physical possession 'goes beyond' the right of a person with regard to himself because it makes it possible to wrong another without interfering with that person's body and, just as importantly, makes it rightful to wrest an apple from another person's hand or to drag someone away from his resting place, if doing so is the enforcement of a property right. Relations of right are always external, because they relate the choice of one human being to the choice of another, but the objects of those rights differ; the object of an internal right could not just as well be the object of some other person's right, whereas the object of an external right could just as well be the object of some other person's right. If you had not bought your hat and I had bought it instead, it would be my hat. No such structure applies to your right to your own body or your reputation. The ins and outs of this enable Kant to say that the 'axiom of outer freedom' covers what is 'internally mine', and explain why he writes that occupying a place on the earth with my body is 'concerned only with my outer freedom, hence only possession of myself, not as something external to me, so that it is only an internal right' (6:254).

Pallikkathayil's essay seeks to blunt Kant's sharp distinction between property rights and our rights with respect to our own bodies. She raises fascinating examples and puzzles in order to suggest that our relation to our bodies is more property-like, and our relation to our property more body-like, than Kant supposes. At the same time, I suspect that the root of our disagreement is not to be located in different conceptions of the nature and moral significance of each person's body, but rather in different ways of characterizing the problems of the state of nature, and in particular, in Pallikkathayil's rejection of Kant's argument about unilateral acquisition.

I will come to what I take to be the primary challenge that Pallikkathayil raises in a moment, but before doing so I want to say something about the way in which she thinks about rights in general, when she describes rights as protecting a discretionary space. I think there is something right about this, but I have misgivings about the way in which she understands it and the relation between assurance and the existence of that discretionary space. Part of the difficulty, as I will explain in more detail in my responses to Flikschuh and Sangiovanni, is that I do not suppose that rights are instruments for protecting something the significance of which can be characterised without reference to the concept of right. As a result, I am not sure about the idea of a discretionary space. The same point applies to her characterisation of innate right in terms of concepts of control and agency. These are non-relational concepts. As such, they cannot be made to explicate Kantian concepts of right. Indeed, it may be that Pallikkathayil's position is vulnerable to Flikschuh's arguments about purposiveness. On the view that I defend, however, rights are relational: you have a right to something if it is not up to others how to use it. In many but by no means all cases,[1] this gives you a certain amount of discretion over the object of the right, but in those cases, any such discretion follows from the discretion you have over the conduct of others. As I will explain in more detail below, the discretion follows from the right; it does not underwrite it.

This difference has a significant implication with respect to Pallikkathayil's characterisation of the problem of assurance. She represents assurance as a factual guarantee of security. She puts it this way:

> If I must abandon my leisurely morning walk to run away from you or to stop and hurl rocks at you, I do not enjoy the discretionary space that my right entitles me to. In this way, even if I am able to thwart or deter any attempted aggression, I am still not able to rely on my rights. Instead, I rely on my power as measured against your unilateral choices. In order to be able to rely on my rights, they must somehow be enforced apart from the choices that either of us makes.

On this understanding, without assurance, rights are not enforced, and this problem is common to rights to person and to property. Kant understands assurance as something more ambitious; without assurance, property rights are not enforceable. Strikingly, Pallikkathayil does not include this among the defects in the Kantian state of nature. Yet it is of the first importance to Kant's argument. It also frames Kant's conception of assurance. When Kant writes 'a unilateral will cannot serve as a coercive law for everyone with regard to possession that is external and therefore contingent, since that would infringe upon freedom in accordance with a universal laws' (6:256), his claim is that neither of us is bound by the unilateral acts of others, and so nobody is bound to avoid interfering with things others have acquired (when the possessor is not in physical possession of it). Without assurance that you will do likewise, I do no wrong if I do not defer to your unilateral acts or claims.

[1] Most notably, because you cannot sell yourself into slavery, you have no discretion over whether others may enslave you. They may not.

The point is not that assurance lets you rest easy that I will not attack; whether the state will do better than individuals on that dimension is an empirical question, which may have different answers for different people. Worse, if rights are understood in terms of discretionary space, attacks by others are hardly alone in compromising it. Instead, Kant's point about assurance is exclusively concerned with rights: either of us may rightfully resist the attempts by others to enforce their property rights in a state of nature, because neither of us needs to defer to the unilateral claims of others. Conversely, neither of us is entitled to enforce our claims to external objects except within a system that protects all of us.

Pallikkathayil's challenge to my example of casting a shadow over your land reflects the same misconception: nobody could deny that whether I cast a shadow changes (and perhaps reduces) your range of options for your land. The question of whether it is a wrong, however, is not equivalent to the question of whether it changes your option set. Anything that others do that changes the context in which you use what is yours affects your discretionary space, as indeed do many natural events. If the problem of assurance is understood in the empirical way that Pallikkathayil suggests, nothing could solve it. Her examples sometimes suggest that assurance is a problem specific to acts of aggression. Yet the focus on discretionary space provides no principled way of isolating aggression (or the act of others, for that matter) as requiring a separate solution.

Pallikkathayil's reduction of assurance to predictions about success in whatever you have decided to do leads her to reject Kant's argument about the distinctiveness of acquisition, and to replace it with a problem of indeterminacy with respect to procedures. She argues that the requirement of equal freedom is sufficient to authorise the unilateral acquisition of property. Pallikkathayil takes herself to be disagreeing with Kant as well as with me, so I will not point to the textual difficulties of her approach. Instead, I will suggest two related grounds for supposing the Kantian approach to be superior. The first concerns the limitations of the part of Kant's argument on which Pallikkathayil does rely. She notes that the Postulate of Practical Reason with Regard to Rights seeks to show that human beings can rightfully have external objects—property—as their own. She questions whether anything further is required to justify acquisition: 'The need for a public lawgiving authority is not generated by the need to confer authority on us to acquire property but rather by the need to confer authority on the procedures that specify how property acquisition is to take place.' This way of setting things up overlooks the fundamental feature of the nature of ownership: to own something is to have a kind of authority over others, because an owner gets to decide the terms on which others may enter a piece of land or use a chattel. The Postulate of Practical Reason with Regard to Rights shows that this form of authority can be consistent with everyone's freedom. Acquisition is different, however, because it involves what appears to be a unilateral extension of authority; by acquiring something, I expand the scope of my authority. Thus, acquisition appears to be a case in which one person's choice can expand that person's own authority; by acquiring an object, entirely at my own initiative and without your consent, I put you under new duties with respect to it. By contrast, when I move my body, all that changes is which region of space I currently occupy; the amount of space from which you are excluded remains exactly the same. That transition in the case of acquiring property is the core of the difficulty. As a general matter, no unilateral act of mine is a law for you, but the acquisition of property seems to make my act a law for you.

This brings me back to Pallikkathayil's characterisation of rights as discretionary spheres. Her emphasis appears to be on what it is for a property owner to own property. Yet Kant's theory of property, and I think any fully defensible theory of property, concerns itself with the way in which property constrains the conduct of others, rather than the benefit it provides to its owner.[2]

Understood as a constraint on non-owners, rather than as benefit to owners, or even as a constraint-on-non-owners-for-the-benefit-of-owners, the acquisition of property generates a special problem. It also generates a further problem about enforcement; in a state of nature you do not need to defer to my proprietary claims; if the problem of unilateral acquisition were somehow solved, the problem of unilateral enforcement would remain.

B. Removable Parts

Pallikkathayil offers a related but distinct argument when she writes: 'We need rules for property acquisition, which involve acquiring a right and hence imposing obligations on others, and we need rules for bodily alienation, which involve renouncing a right and hence relieving others of obligations.' This framing makes the issues morally, conceptually and legally more difficult than they need to be. It also has the odd implication that the fundamental problem that the state is required to solve about bodies could not arise until techniques were developed for reattaching or culturing detached parts.

Consider Pallikkathayil's example of the detached finger. We think of human hands as capable of grasping, and this is so even if they have been damaged; we think of the damaged hand as a defective one. My own view is that Kant supposes your relation to your animal form is your relation to it as it functions as that through which you act. An interruption in the continuity

[2] I develop this argument in detail in 'Possession and Use', in J Penner and H Smith (eds) *Philosophical Foundations of Property Law* (Oxford, Oxford University Press, 2013).

of your animal form does not deprive it of its unity, just as an interruption in the continuity of an action does not undermine its unity. 'I spent the morning working on my reply' is not shorthand for a detailed description that mentions each time I looked out the window or answered the telephone. Instead, the action is characterised in terms of its organised use of the means in pursuit of an end, not as a series of individual muscular contractions, which are then aggregated to produce a whole. When Kant claims that the body is 'a perfect unity', he is not appealing to controversial metaphysics so much as capturing the familiar thought that to think of something as a person (or animal) is to think of it as a whole, not a collection of accidentally connected parts. The same idea underwrites the thought that a part that has been separated from you and can be reattached continues to be a part of you. That is why it does not spend a period of time being unowned, or require an affirmative act on your part to make it yours (again.) If it was unowned, someone else might just as well take it, and, having acquired it as property, refuse to return it to you unless you paid a fee. That is not how we think of these examples, because we suppose that the person who picks up the detached body part does so on your behalf, in pretty much the same way that we think that someone who administers medical care to you when you are unconscious, or rescues you when you are in danger, acts as your agent. That is why neither your own empirical act of picking up your fingers nor your agent's empirical act of doing so counts as an affirmative act establishing a right in the relevant sense. These familiar ideas help explain our reaction to Pallikkathayil's example of someone else claiming a patent on Henrietta Lacks's cell line. It is that it is up to her, rather than her physician, to determine how these cells are treated, and what is done with them. Whatever we might think about people holding patents on a cell line, we want to say that if what was formerly part of a person's body becomes the kind of thing that can belong to another, the person whose body it is from has a better claim to it than anyone else does.

Pallikkathayil's other examples, such as that of the prosthetic limb, also have easy answers, over which legal systems have not troubled themselves. It is no answer to a charge of battery (unauthorised touching) to say that you touched the victim's clothing, not her body, but while the clothing is not being worn, to interfere with it is theft or conversion but not battery. The prosthetic limb has the same structure: while you are using it, anyone who interferes with it thereby interferes with you; to remove it while in use is *both* theft and battery. Interfering with a prosthetic limb or wheelchair while it is in use is like Kant's example of interfering with the apple that someone grasps. To interfere with it is to interfere with the person using it. That does not mean that such objects cannot be property, only that some instances of interfering with them are also wrongs against the person. Combining these examples, we can characterise its use as extended. But we do not need to, because the question of the nature of the wrong is not the same as the extent of it. The person who interferes with the prosthetic device that is not in use does not commit a battery, even if the extent of that wrong is severe. These contrasts show that a property right concerns something that can be separated from you or belong to another; your bodily right to your own person is only at issue when someone interferes with your body, which can be done by interfering with things you own only when you are in physical possession of them. Again, why do I abandon my hair at the barbershop? Not because of anything a priori, but because the law begins with the normal course of events, which in this case means that there is a 'opt-in' system for keeping your hair when it is trimmed. The same point applies to implanted medical devices. Once it is inside me, others wrong me if they interfere. Drug couriers who swallow condoms filled with cocaine put it beyond the rightful reach of others by incorporating it into a body that other private persons are not allowed to touch or interfere with. There is no new right created, no place that others are no longer allowed to go. All that has happened is that the incorporated substance is out of the rightful reach of others while it is inside the courier's body.

I mention the simple and boring way in which legal systems process this type of question to cast doubt on Pallikkathayil's claim that the issues of acquisition and abandonment are fundamentally about indeterminacy. Insofar as the problem is cast in terms of indeterminacy, all the law needs to provide is a determination. Yet each of her examples gets its force from the assumption that there is a principled way of drawing distinctions. No doubt there will be hard cases the courts need to adjudicate, but the examples themselves suggest that the moral concepts themselves are capable of doing rather more than she claims.

Alienation is slightly different; abandoning body parts is in some ways like abandoning property. We can know a priori that there must be some appropriate standard for them. We need positive law to supply the standard. You do not abandon your coat by putting it down for a moment, but if enough time passes (as specified by positive law) you do. The need for these types of line-drawing exercises for both bodies and property does not, however, show any difficulty with the fundamental distinction between them. It merely shows something that Kant always insisted on, namely the difficulty of classifying particulars, and the need for procedures to do so.

I suspect that the issue here reflects the deeper disagreement with which I began. For Kant, a property right is fundamentally a right to exclude others; it constrains the conduct of others with respect to the use of the thing, and because others are constrained, leaves things subject to my choice as against theirs. If that is how we think about property, then the question of whether your particular use, or even the effects on you of my use, governs the ways in which I may permissibly use my land has a simple answer: no. You cannot require me to provide a path for (or build a tower to block) light, because you have no right that the extent to which I occupy the space that makes up my land depends on whether it enables you to use your land the way you would most prefer.[3] At most, you can restrict the ways in which the effects of my use of my land render your land unusable, for example by making loud noises that interfere with your use, releasing foul odours or digging a hole too close to the boundary so that your land collapses. The point reflects the deeper disagreement because Pallikkathayil's description of a zone of discretion seems to be focused on making sure that property and body parts are useful to their owners. So understood, blocking the sun from reaching your land makes your land less useful to you. The difference between these cases may seem illusory: either way, you still have your land; either way it is not as useful to you. The difference is that you are entitled to restrict the ways in which my use of my land changes your land, but you are not entitled to require me to use mine in specific way that best suits you. Requiring me to restrict sound or smell leaving my land from reaching yours is protecting what you have; requiring me to provide a path for you or the sunlight you require demands instead that I refrain from occupying the space that makes up my land so as to better enable you to use yours as you see fit.

Private right does not protect preferred uses. It protects your right to what you already have as against others. That is why the rightfulness of people having things as their own does not, without more, guarantee their rightfulness of acquisition. It is also why it makes the distinction between wronging someone and failing to confer a benefit central in a way that Pallikkathayil's focus on security and the ability to continue with your plans cannot. If I change the context in which you use what you have, the effect on your plans may be the same as, or greater than, it would have been had I damaged your property. Nonetheless, private right treats these as fundamentally different.

Pallikkathayil's attempt to assimilate bodily rights and property rights turned on three claims: that each involved assurance because of factual vulnerability in the absence of the state; that each involved indeterminacy with respect to procedure; and that there was no special issue about unilateral action for property. None of these is successful. The problem of acquisition is not just a problem of indeterminacy, and so the need for positive law to clarify abandonment does not establish the required equivalence; assurance is not merely a matter of being certain that you will be able to follow through on your plans.

[3] Of course, this basic principle requires application in many specific cases. But it is not an indeterminate principle that might have gone the other way. Flikschuh misreads the same example in a different way, supposing that because public right regimes can regulate land use, basic distinctions of private right are just matters of positive law.

C. Innate Right and the Division of Rights

Where Pallikkathayil collapses the distinction between theft and battery in one direction, supposing human beings to own their bodies piecemeal, Flikschuh eliminates it in another, when she contends that 'innate Right is empirically non-instantiable' because it 'specifies a purely formal, purely juridical relation between persons as possible bearers of rights' to which 'no substantive entitlements attach'. This appears to leave no space for the idea of wrongs against the person. By conceiving innate right as merely preparatory for public right, Flikschuh not only has difficulty explaining Kant's contrast between dragging someone's body from its resting place and taking that person's land; she also appears to reach the conclusion that the wrongfulness of the former is a question of 'public policy making', a matter for a public authority to decide, rather than the rights of the parties. Thus she supposes that in dealing with it, a public authority may not be 'preoccupied with questions about individual freedom'. However one might finally evaluate such a view, it is not Kant's position. Your innate right is a right to what you have already, prior to any act.

The other aspect of innate right—the right to 'be a human being beyond reproach'—has the same structure of entitling you to have others avoid interfering with something that you have without having done anything to acquire it. Your good reputation is something that you have—indeed necessarily have—prior to anything that you do. Flikschuh objects to my characterisation of innate right in terms of the body. Kant's emphasis on the right to 'be beyond reproach'—the right to be presumed to have done no wrong prior to any act—reflects the idea that what is innately yours is yours is a matter of right, without requiring an affirmative act to establish it. Like your right to your own body, your right to your reputation is something with which you are born, and provides the basis for any further rights you might acquire. Kant explains:

> [T]he aim in introducing such a division within the system of natural right (insofar as it is concerned with innate right) is that when a dispute arises about an acquired right and the question comes up, on whom does the burden of proof fall, either about a controversial fact or if this is settled, about a controversial right, someone who refuses to accept this obligation can appeal methodically to his innate right to freedom (which is now specified in its various relations), as if he were appealing to various bases for rights. (6:238)

Innate right thus forms the basis of right as a system of imputation; it can be appealed to in cases of dispute about acquired rights. It structures each human being's entitlement to avoid being held to account for something he or she did not do, by structuring the way in which particular standards of conduct are brought to bear on specific deeds. Prohibitions on battery, negligence or breach of contract regulate the ways in which human beings are permitted to conduct themselves in relation to others. They determine the form of the basic rights and obligations that individual human beings have as against each other and the manner in which new obligations can be undertaken. These primary norms of conduct make up the law of obligations. The primary norms also generate secondary norms of repair in cases of wrongdoing. As Kant observes, if someone has wronged me 'and I have a right to demand compensation from them, by this I will still only preserve what is mine undiminished' (6:271).

In order to govern interaction and structure remedial norms, however, primary norms also require the framework principle that you are accountable for what you have done. That principle, in turn, can only operate if you innately have the right to be beyond reproach, the right to your own good name, which is, as Kant remarks, an innate external possession. It is innate because the system of imputation must begin with each person having his or her own good name; it is external because it resides only in what other people think and say.

Once the connection between innate right and rights to body and reputation is in focus, Kant's decision to 'throw' innate right into the prolegomena can be seen to reflect the systematic structure of the prolegomena, and the structuring role of its concepts in the remainder of the work.

Innate right needs to be addressed in the prolegomena because it provides the basis for the introduction of the idea of acquired right. To so characterise it is not to suppose that the system of rights rests on something outside of it, but rather to draw attention to its structuring role within a system of rights. Kant's examples of snatching the apple and moving the resting person show what is distinctive about acquired rights by contrasting them with your innate right to your own person. They also show that acquired rights go beyond innate right. Innate right itself could not be not a member of the set of private rights that go beyond it, and so cannot be included in their classification. It must lie outside the classification, and so its exposition must lie outside the exposition of the classification of acquired rights. Nor could acquired rights be subject to a division unless the distinction between persons (as bearers of rights) and things (which lack rights) has already been established. This distinction produces a threefold classification: a bearer of innate right can acquire a right to a thing, a right against another person, or a right to a person akin to a right to a thing. Only a bearer of rights can acquire these rights. So not only does innate right lie outside the division because it requires no affirmative act; it is also the presupposition of that division. It is internal because it cannot exist apart from the person whose right it is.

This structuring role for private right does not show that innate right structures public right. It does, show, however, why innate right must be at the heart of an answer to the question that Flikschuh and I agree is the central concern of the *Doctrine of Right*: how can positive (i.e. chosen) law be binding? That question gets its interest from the fact that public law involves authority: had the legislature made a different law, it would have been the law instead. Authority, in turn, is a question for Kantian political philosophy precisely because no person is by nature in charge of another. Instead, each of us has an innate right of humanity in our own person.

D. Purposiveness

Flikschuh also objects that my use of the vocabulary of purposiveness suggests that the innate right is supposed to protect something that matters independently of it. As I hope my response to Pallikkathayil made clear, that is not the way I understand innate right, but innate right is a right to set and pursue your own purposes, consistent with the right of others to do the same under universal law.

Your innate right of humanity in your own person is your entitlement to be treated in a certain way, to stand in certain types of relations to other human beings. It is not in the service of anything that can be usefully described as a basis apart from the relation. So although it is true that there are certain ways that others may not treat you because you are a human being, and so that they must always treat you as an end and never merely as a means, the force of the word 'because' in this formulation does not flow from the idea that humanity has value apart from your innate right to be treated in certain ways, or that your innate right is in the service of protecting or promoting something. It is not that there is some respect, which can be characterised without reference to innate right, in which you and every other human being are equal. Nor is it something that comes in degrees, in which you participate in the same degree or, in Rawls's formulation, in the same 'range' of degree. Instead, your right to equality reflects the fact that no person is subject to another.

Given the relational structure of right, why does purposiveness figure in my reading of Kant? Although the normativity of innate right is entirely relational, it governs non-relational features of the things that it relates. In particular, only a being with a certain set of capacities could stand in such a relation. That does not mean that the relation is somehow a recognition or acknowledgement of the value of those capacities; only that the relation presupposes them. To put the point in terms of an analogy: nobody is an uncle or aunt to any degree whatsoever except in relation to some niece or nephew; the concepts in question are purely relational. At the same time, these relations have presuppositions: only members of a species that are biologically capable of having offspring and siblings can be aunts, uncles, nieces, and nephews. In the same way, only beings capable of standing in the relevant relations, that is, beings capable of choice, can stand in relations of dependence on the choice of another, and so in relations of independence. But it does not follow from this that each human being's entitlement to independence of the choice of others is a reflection of the value of those capacities. Such a reductive explanation goes wrong because any attempt to ground innate right in something non-relational opens up conceptual space in which it is coherent to ask whether the capacity for choice might be better served through a violation of innate right. The reason that you do wrong by imposing your choice on another human being is that that person is not your subordinate. That is the basic moral thought, which cannot be expressed except in terms of relational concepts of right.

From this it follows that although your entitlement to freedom is a constraint on the conduct of others, it also entitles you—means you do no wrong—to set and pursue your own purposes, restricted only by the entitlement of others to do the same. That is, we stand in relation to each other with respect to our capacity to set and pursue purposes. My independence of your choice, and your independence of mine, cannot be specified except in terms of relations between us; it also cannot be specified without reference to the concept of choice, that is, of setting and pursuing our respective purposes. It does not follow from this that we must conclude that the ground of our independence is something called the value of choice or purposiveness. The ground of independence is independence itself, but that, in turn, is a concept that can only be characterised by contrast with the dependence of one person's choice on the choice of another; only beings capable of setting and pursuing ends can be dependent or independent of the choice of others. Independence is a principle of their consistent exercise of freedom; if there were only one being capable of choice, the principle would have no application. The Universal Principle of Right governs the coexistence of everyone's freedom, in accordance with a universal law because it takes the actions of free beings as its object. Kant does not explicitly say that your entitlement is to set and pursue purposes, but his conception of what it is to choose entails that a reconciliation of the power of choice of a plurality of persons is a reconciliation of their purposiveness. In the same way, when Kant describes the innate right to equality, he is not saying that human beings are entitled to equivalent treatment because of some respect in which they are all alike. Instead, he supposes that they are equal in the sense than none is the master of another. Equal freedom is a single relational idea.

I should reiterate that in talking about the entitlement to set and pursue your own purposes, I am not claiming that the value of people doing so somehow provides a foundation for innate right, or that you are your own master because that is the best way to enable you to set and pursue your own purposes. Instead, the order of explanation goes in the opposite direction: because others are not entitled to set purposes for you, because you have no master, you are entitled to set and pursue your purposes as you see fit. The basic norm of right is relational. The basic norm of right is for that reason external; for Kant, the concept of relation and the concept of externality are the same.

I should note also that Flikschuh's endorsement of the relational interpretation of innate right stands in tension with her contention that 'no substantive entitlements attach to it'. I would have thought that the whole point of the Kantian enterprise is to show how relational and formal ideas attach to substantive things. So I do not understand her claim that 'innate Right is empirically non-instantiable—it specifies a purely moral, hence intelligible rights relation between persons'. For it to be relational is for it to govern how people stand in relation to each other, and so to cover what she dismisses as irrelevant—'material claims about innate powers and capacities, or about persons' unilateral use of them'. Perhaps she is concerned to reject the possibility that anything non-relational could provide a constraint on what she calls the 'dignity of public lawmaking'. I want to insist, however, on Kant's view, according to which innate right is relational and always constrains public lawmaking. In discussing punishment, Kant notes that no punishment that would violate the humanity in the person of the wrongdoer can be authorised by public law (6:363) None of 'public policy-making', or 'positive effects on … social matters of state more generally' or even the state's 'continued survival' in the face of a perceived terrorist threat, could underwrite practices such as torture, which do not respect the humanity in each person's own body, or detention or punishment without trial, which violate the right to be beyond reproach. Kantian right forbids such 'policies' as inconsistent with the innate right of humanity in each human being's own person.

E. Relational Rights and Interests

Sangiovanni takes issue with the formalism of Kantian right in a different way. He does not deny that my presentation of Kant's argument is formal, and he explicitly endorses the relational conception of rights, but he charges that it cannot deliver any results without presupposing a material characterisation of the relevant interests. The material aspect of the interests enters into determining whether there is a right; how bad something is for a person must figure in any characterisation of its wrongfulness.

Sangiovanni's argument centres on a pair of examples. He contends that the Kantian view cannot distinguish between rape and looking at or drawing a person's hands as she sits in the library. His development of the argument is ambiguous on a crucial issue, and I will respond by considering both interpretations. On one of these, both rape and drawing another person's hands in the library are cases of using, and the objection is to the formalism of Kant's account, on the grounds that it is unable to distinguish between more and less serious wrongs. On the other, Sangiovanni hopes to show that the concept of one person using another is not significant, and that only interests fundamentally matter. On the first understanding, drawing a picture of your hands in the library is obviously not wrongful; on the second, talk about using you is a pointless detour to a conclusion that can be captured more directly and forcefully through the idea of a person's interest.

Sangiovanni's objection does not succeed on either interpretation. On the first, it turns on collapsing the distinction between the question of whether one person has wronged another, which is not a question of degree, and the question of the degree of wrong. The Kantian view has resources to conclude that some wrongs are more serious than others, without supposing that whether something is a wrong is a matter of degree, as Sangiovanni seems to insist. It is certainly possible to argue that there is a wrong that consists in invading a person's privacy, or misappropriating that person's image. In so far as that is a wrong, we can talk about its degree of seriousness, and question where particular examples fall within the category of that wrong, just as we judge that among bodily injuries, a minor scratch is less serious than a deep gash, which is in turn less serious than the loss of a limb. Such matters of degree will figure in determining the extent of enforcement of a right, whether defensive, remedial, or punitive. Any such questions of degree only arise, however, with respect to what can be shown to be a wrong.

On the second interpretation of Sangiovanni's examples, somebody drawing another's hands in the library is presented as so obviously not wrongful as to cast doubt on the idea of using. This formulation of the objection reflects inattention to Kant's organizing idea of a system of rights under universal law, and its essential distinction between wronging a person and changing the context in which that person acts. Not every action that takes advantage of another person's activity, or, in this case, location, counts as using that person. I do not use you if I position myself so that your shadow protects me from sunlight. So too, if I entertain myself by watching for couples in Central Park who look alike, I do not use them, I merely take advantage of where they happen to be and what they happen to look like. Could the right to be in a public place really encumber the liberty of others to look at or draw (using their own materials) what is around them? The Kantian response must be that merely by being where you have a right to be does not, as such, constrain others to avert their gaze. The Kantian view draws a sharp distinction between interfering with you and changing the context in which you act. Not only do you not wrong me by changing the context in which I act; having changed that context through your choice, you cannot exclude me from the effects of that change. Of course, you could change it another way—perhaps you could put a booth up around yourself in the library so that I cannot see your hands. If you did so, I would not wrong you by drawing a picture of the booth.

Now it might be thought that drawing your hands in the library is different, that I do use you by doing so. That just brings us back to the first interpretation; if it is using you, it is less serious than other cases.

Regardless of which interpretation he intends, Sangiovanni's examples do not pose a problem for the Kantian approach. Either both are wrongs, differing in degree, or they differ in kind. It is only because he shifts between these possibilities that Sangiovanni supposes there is a gap that needs to be filled by appeal to interests.

Still, my response might be thought to be successful against Sangiovanni but in another way evasive, as I still have not said which is the correct interpretation. But the real difficulty is that they are both mistaken. Taking advantage of the effects of a person's appearance or location is not, without more, a case of using that person. So there is no need to focus on the relative seriousness of use in the library example, because there is no use.

Sangiovanni thinks that the concept of an interest must be brought in to solve the problem of seriousness he claims to find in the examples, but in fact the problem is an artefact of his presupposition that rights must be based on interests, which generates the thought that a Kantian view must suppose people have an interest in others not reaping benefits from them. If that were the Kantian view, the two examples would indeed be indistinguishable. But it is not; you have a right that others not use you, not that they not benefit from your presence. Generally speaking, I can only use you by touching you or by getting you to participate in my plans without proper consent (eg by lying to you). If I stalk you or crowd you, these things can be assimilated to touching; perhaps the same thing can be said of spying on you, or other invasions of your privacy. But if I derive some benefit from you happening to be where you happen to be, that isn't even a candidate; it isn't a mild form of invasion of privacy.

Sangiovanni's positive account proposes to address the issue he identified by bringing in an interest in sexual integrity, but the introduction of such an interest only appears to connect relational wrongs to interests because the interest in question is an interest in being free of a certain type of rights violation. When Sangiovanni appeals to each person's 'deep and important interest in sexual integrity' he seeks to explain it in terms of 'the central place that a free sexuality plays at the centre of any flourishing life, given the way we are as human beings'. In so doing, he fails to notice that has conceded the precise Kantian point: the word 'free' discloses that the interest in question is not in being in a certain condition; it is an interest in being free of a certain type of conduct by others, that is, the interest is in standing in a certain relation of independence of others. That is just to say that the interest cannot be conceived except in terms of the right that protects it. It cannot do any work in explaining the wrongfulness of rape, because it presupposes that wrongfulness. Despite his suggestion that the Kantian account is circular, Sangiovanni is the one who is moving in a circle.

Sangiovanni offers two further arguments. He attempts to cast doubt on the idea that rights can be irreducibly relational in this way. Although he explicitly concedes that rights are non-comparative, Sangiovanni retreats from this concession, asking

> In what sense is it true that a system of entitlements in which harmless rapes are permitted 'could not' be realized under universal law? If we take the constraint of universal law in a thinner sense, such that a system of entitlements is consistent with the idea of equal freedom as long as each person's rights are consistent with everyone else having the same rights, then the system of entitlements that permits harmless rapes is compatible with universal law, since it gives everyone an equal right to rape others.

For Sangiovanni, 'equal' must mean 'the same as', that is, it must be understood as comparative. For Kant, by contrast, a system of equal freedom is in the first instance a system of equal status. The formality of the Kantian approach reflects its conception of human beings as entitled to be independent of each other's choices. Nobody is the subordinate of another. Now Sangiovanni does not address this conception, but I find it difficult to grasp the intuitive pull that is supposed to attach to his thought that getting to decide what happens to another person's body is not the central example of subordination. As I explain in my replies to Flikschuh and Pallikkathayil, your body is your person; to take it upon myself to decide how our bodies will interact is to subordinate you. Sangiovanni also seeks a more abstract and general philosophical vindication for his position when, picking up on a remark I made in an unpublished paper on which he commented,[4] he rejects the idea that the irreducibility of spatial relations could provide a model for the irreducibility of right. He contends that a spatial relation, such as 'to the left of'

> depends, or more precisely, *supervenes on* nonrelational facts about spatiotemporal location (while not being reducible to them). And that is exactly what I am claiming with respect to interests: while I accept that relations of freedom are not *reducible* to relations of interests, relations of freedom must be a *function of* relations of underlying interests.

The point of my use of the spatial example is that there are no non-relational facts about spatial location. You can impose an origin and provide coordinates

[4] The paper has since appeared as 'Means and Ends' (2015) 6 *Jurisprudence* 1–23.

of particular locations, but those coordinates are all specified in relation to the origin, which is an arbitrary point, the identity of which consists in its spatial location at the intersection of axes specifying other possible locations. That is, there are no non-relational facts about spatiotemporal location on which relational facts supervene. In the same way, there are no non-relational facts about your right to independence as against others. It neither supervenes on, nor is a '*function of* relations of underlying interests'. I do not know how broadly Sangiovanni understands the term 'function' but his contention does not hold even if he intends it in what David Lewis once called its 'most general set-theoretic sense'.[5] The difficulty comes with providing an interpretation on which rights are a function of something other than other rights. Supervenience provides no further assistance; rights and interests do not satisfy the requirement that 'there cannot be an *A*-difference without a *B*-difference.'[6] You and I may be exactly alike with respect to some interest (*B*), but only one of us has a right to it (*A*); your interest in your property counts, but my interest in your property does not. The only way to avoid this result is to characterise the concept of an interest in terms of rights, saving the supervenience claim by collapsing it into 'there cannot be a difference in rights without a difference in rights'. Rights can change without interests changing, and the set of possible relations of right in which people can stand does not depend upon their actual interests, even though they cannot change without particular human beings doing various things in accordance with various procedures. Sangiovanni's contention requires something stronger than the familiar suggestion that the moral supervenes on the non-moral, because it supposes that interests in particular fix rights. The weaker idea would require only that any two situations that differ with respect to rights differ in some factual way, not that they differed with respect to the interests of those concerned. I conclude, then, that Sangiovanni has failed to find any work for the concept of interest to do in a theory about rights.

F. Equal Freedom without Law

Julius comes at the right to freedom from a different direction. Taking up the Kantian approaches both to private property and traffic laws as developed in

[5] D Lewis, 'General Semantics', in *Philosophical Papers*, vol I, 194. Lewis continues 'in which the domain of arguments and the domain of values may consist of any entities whatsoever, and it is not required that the function be specifiable by any simple rule'.

[6] B McLaughlin and K Bennett, 'Supervenience', in *The Stanford Encyclopedia of Philosophy*, ed EN Zalta (Winter 2011 edn), http://plato.stanford.edu/archives/win2011/entries/supervenience/.

Force and Freedom, he suggests that an alternative to formal rights of possession and explicitly codified rules can be found in the form of mutual accommodation through which people regularly reconcile their separate directions while negotiating public spaces such as sidewalks. If you and I are going in opposite or perpendicular directions, there may be no general rule about who has the right of way, but we can avoid collision with each other, and so reconcile our separate pursuit of our separate (directional) purposes, simply through the skills of ordinary human interaction:

> We can obey the law, when we reach those points, by spontaneously cooperating for freedom there. Faced with an intersection we can decide for a particular interpersonal pattern of externally compatible movements through it. We can take this up as a way in which each will do what she's already set out to do—travel consistently with the other's freedom.

Julius characterises this sort of skilful interpersonal performance as the way in which 'we can obey the law', but it is not clear that this is a law at all. Instead, the thought seems to be that we can do without a law so long as each of us sets the end of travelling consistently with the other's freedom. If all of us share this end, we can reconcile our separate pursuits without either formal rights or general rules. From this, Julius concludes that the idea of avoiding wronging others is better interpreted in terms of an internal motive, rather than in the austere and external manner in which I suggest Kant interprets it.

Working with this conception of equal freedom as mutual accommodation, Julius also suggests that a principle governing the rightful use of things, but short of full exclusive property rights, can be generated. In particular, he contends that there is space for a narrower notion of usufruct. Just as you and I can avoid bumping into each other by sharing the end of travelling consistently with the other's freedom, so, too, he suggests each of us can use things by adopting the end of using things in ways that are consistent with the freedom of others. Thus we do not need to go all the way to exclusive property rights in order to satisfy the Postulate of Practical Reason with Regard to Rights and have the possibility of using usable things in order to set and pursue our respective purposes. Julius puts the point this way:

> A law of this generality can't be a timetable. It can't be an antecedent assignment of rights of way and rights of access to objects, determined before we ever interact. We will have to set its particular terms as we go along. But our improvisation will obey a general law that has force independently of our activity and that was there before we started: the law of freedom requiring that we pursue our particular space-occupying and means-using ends consistently with others' freedom.

As appealing as the idea of making things up as we go along may initially appear, Julius's proposed principle suffers from two related difficulties. The first is that, although it is presented as formal and a priori, 'a single law that has force independently of our activity and that was there before we started', the proposed law is formal in the wrong way and makes each person depend on another's choice. Although he contends that this form of dependence is the inevitable concomitant of human interaction, his case for this does not succeed. The second is that on closer inspection, the model presupposes an antecedent assignment of rights. I will take these up in turn.

First, Julius's proposed 'law' is presented as though it is perfectly formal, and antecedent to the particularities of our interactions. However, the law is material rather than formal; rather than constraining the ways in which we interact, it demands that each of us adopt an end, namely that of accommodating the pursuits of others. That end looks formal, insofar as it makes no reference to what those other specific pursuits of others might be. Despite this apparent formality, however, it is material instead, just in an open-ended way; it must take up particular content supplied by the choices of others in order to appeal to the specific though indeterminate end of accommodating the specific pursuits of others. Its application in every case depends on the content of their ends. It is thus only formal in the sense in which the instruction 'do what Simon says' is formal: it lets someone else's choice be the rule. Applied to our mutual path adjustment on the crowded sidewalk, the idea is clear enough, because it really just tells us to get out of the other's way and becomes increasingly fine-grained as we get closer and we make our respective best guesses about just where the other is about to go. You and I may each move in the same direction trying to get out of the way of the other, but with wit and goodwill, it will not take long for us to sort things out and each continue on our respective way.

So understood, the model of mutual accommodation appears appealing and, at least initially, to admit of much more general application, and to stand in contrast with the Kantian claim that law is required 'no matter how good and right loving human beings might be'. However, closer inspection reveals that the difficulty about its generality casts doubt on its ability to provide an adequate model of even the simple sidewalk example. The question of the extent to which I need to accommodate your plans depends on what counts as what you are already doing, and thus, on the distinction between what you are doing and the context in which you are doing it. That distinction, in turn, is just an instance of the more general distinction between each person's entitlement to his or her means and the context in which those means are used, and so to the concomitant distinction between wronging someone and merely changing the context in which that person acts.

If the only question we face is which direction to move in so as to avoid colliding with another, each of us can do so in light of the end of pursuing our space-occupying activity consistent with the freedom of others. The ease with which we can do this reflects the fact that we can also do it without having a material end of that sort at all. Instead, we can achieve exactly the same thing by having the simpler end of avoiding collision. That end is simpler because it is not really an end it all, but rather a restriction on the way in which we use our bodies. 'Do not bump into other people' does not recommend an end, only a restriction on the ways that means can be used in pursuing other ends: 'move your body in ways consistent with others moving theirs'. In application, this restriction may be subject to indeterminacy and dispute. Like any interpersonal obligation, it can also be incorporated into my principle of action as one of my ends. That is why Kant says that duties of right are indirectly duties of virtue. But it does not need to be an end.[7]

This brings me to my second point, which I will explain in relation to the usufruct/property examples that Julius hopes to illuminate. What would it be for me to make it my end to use things consistently with your thing-using activities? The issue is complicated by the fact that unlike the location of your body, which is specific at any fixed time, your particular uses of things often takes place over an extended period of time. An object can only be subject to your choice if others may not interfere with it even when you are not currently in physical possession of it. Julius's proposal that each of us accommodate the other only looks appealing if it can provide some sort of proxy for this formal idea; we must not only accommodate what the other is actually using at a given time, but rather what others are planning to use. A norm instructing us to take account of the complete plans of others would be informationally demanding, but the informational demands are themselves a symptom of the difficulty, rather than the difficulty itself. Some writers about property, such as Henry Smith, have argued that with perfect information, we would not need the right to exclude, because people could negotiate between themselves the full details of their terms of interaction.[8] The difficulty with this approach, however, is that any such negotiation would seem to presuppose that the negotiating parties already had determinate rights with respect to the things that they are using, that is, that there is a distinction between the things over which you need to negotiate and those over which you do not. Replace negotiation with goodwill, and the problem reasserts itself. The question of the extent to which I need to accommodate your plans depends on what counts as what you

[7] Goodwill does extra work in Julius's principle for another reason: the possibility of mutual adjustment and accommodation that he notes applies even when someone lacks goodwill or is violating a rule or a conventional expectation. As I ride my bicycle around a one-way roundabout, if another cyclist is coming in the opposite direction, I try to figure out where the cyclist is likely to go, so as to avoid a collision. This is not mutual accommodation, but rather the basic requirement of right. The cyclist is a wrongdoer, but has not forfeited the right not to be injured. The cyclist is hardly being accommodating. Neither am I, I want to say.

[8] H Smith, 'Property as the Law of Things' (2012) 125 *Harvard Law Review* 1691.

are already doing, and thus, on the distinction between what you are doing and the context in which you are doing it. But that distinction, in turn, is just an instance of the more general distinction between each person's entitlement to his or her means and the context in which those means are used, and so too of the concomitant distinction between wronging someone and merely changing the context in which that person acts.

Julius's resistance to this distinction leads him to say that even in a system of private property, what you are entitled to do depends in part on the acts of others. Neither Kant nor I meant to suggest otherwise. The point of developing a formal account of reciprocal limits on freedom is to explain how this could be so. The key is to recognise that not everything that changes your ability to use what is yours—whether the location of your body or your bodily powers or the use of objects outside of your body—interferes with what is yours. That is also the point of the distinction between wish and will, and of the Kantian emphasis on the priority of having means over setting ends. Julius is correct that I can set an end for myself without having secured means sufficient to ensure its realisation. The ordinary way of setting an end is to take up initial means, through which you position yourself either to acquire further means or to use means that you are ready have but are not yet specifically useful towards that end, and so on, until you are able to achieve the end. You walk to the subway to buy a token to get on the train, to get to the airport, to use your ticket to get to the plane, to get on the freeway, to get to Los Angeles. You can do all of these things, and others wrong you if they interfere with some but not others. Moving out of your way on the sidewalk is a way of accommodating you at that moment, but does not depend on why you are walking or where you are going. The constraint on my conduct that stops me from bumping into you or blocking you is just your innate right to your own body. As each of us are converging on a single point, each of us does wrong by bumping into the other, but neither does wrong by arriving first. If we are about to arrive at the same time, then we each potentially do wrong, and so each of us must accommodate, but if one accommodates, the other need not. All of this is a matter of the formal rights each of us has toward our own person, not any end of mutual accommodation.

Julius's attempt to raise broader issues for the distinction between property and usufruct, and to seek a formal principle that focuses on the need for everyone to accommodate everyone else, fails to capture adequately the idea that each of us is entitled to set and pursue our own purposes, consistent with the entitlement of others to do the same. Julius's material principle says that pursuing a purpose takes primacy; Kant's formal principle says that right is not about the particularity of purposes, but rather about the fact that each person is independent of all the others, that no person is in charge of another. Julius's material principle permits every person to be in charge of every other one. Perhaps if everyone shares the end of accommodating others within such a system, human beings could live peaceably in this way. Kant's objection is not that this is an unrealistic possibility, but rather that it is material, and so inconsistent with the freedom that each of us has, and with the thought that nobody is in charge of anybody else.

II. PUBLIC RIGHT

A. The Omnilateral Will

Pavlakos argues that the concept of omnilateral willing cannot be made to do any real work in the Kantian account of public right. Taking great pains to distinguish my view from cruder conceptions of the relation between law and morality, Pavlakos nonetheless concludes that my focus on omnilateral willing rests on the indefensible idea that obligation must ultimately be grounded in some form of exercise of will. He puts the challenge this way:

> And here is how the standard picture of moral obligation might impose its form of thinking on Ripstein's account: in morality, where the motivation of the agent is relevant, the one who wills is the agent. In law, where only the external behavior of agents is of any relevance, a different type of willing would be required. This expansion, by analogy, of the role of willing to the case of moral obligation would have an important consideration going for it. Coercive imposition, on its own, could with difficulty meet the main requirement of the rational determination condition, one that we took to apply minimally to any obligation. Recall the rational determination condition: its key requirement for the existence of an obligation is that it appear before the agent qua obligation. When it comes to legal obligation, the standard picture purports to meet that condition through coercive imposition. However, this might seem too weak for meeting the constraint of rational determination. It is precisely this demand—that is, to explain the normative pull of legal obligation—which Ripstein's idea of omnilateral willing purports to meet.

I agree with some of what Pavlakos says, especially about the irrelevance of willing understood as an empirical psychological state. But that is not the point of the omnilateral will in the *Doctrine of Right.* That would make psychology generate obligation in a way that is inconsistent with the general priority of norm over fact in Kant's critical project. Instead, the omnilateral will is introduced as the precondition of everyone enjoying their rights. The basic requirement of a rightful condition is that it satisfies the Postulate of Public Right, by having public officials make, enforce and apply law on behalf of everyone. This omnilaterality is often imperfectly realised; the Idea of the Original Contract specifies the ideal of a will that is fully omnilateral.

Pavlakos correctly notes that the intended contrast is with merely unilateral willing. But I do not reason from the suppressed premise that obligation always requires some sort of will, and a unilateral will won't do, to the conclusion that an omnilateral will is required. Instead, the idea of an omnilateral will doesn't perform a fundamental grounding function. As I make clear in my response to Flikschuh, Kant is resolutely antifoundationalist, in that the basic normative principles all come from the concept of right.

On this understanding, the idea of the omnilateral will captures the thought that the state must act on behalf of everyone, because anything narrower would be an arbitrary imposition because unilateral, and so not be a coercive law for everyone. Why, then, call it a will? On Kant's understanding of action, action must be imputed to an agent. To characterise state action as the expression of an omnilateral will is to characterise the state as an artificial moral person, to which actions can be imputed. It is not a private person, but rather a public one, something that can only be thought if it can be thought of as acting on behalf of everyone.

Recall the puzzle of positive law, as stated in the introduction to the *Metaphysics of Morals* as a whole: 'One can therefore conceive of external lawgiving that would contain only positive laws; but then a natural law would still have to precede it, which would establish the authority of the lawgiver (ie, his authorization to bind others by his mere *choice*)' (6:224). How can the lawgiver's choice be a law for anyone else? That question, in turn, resolves itself into the question of how the bindingness of the lawgiver's choice can be consistent with the freedom of everyone. The omnilateral will binds because omnilaterality is required if human beings are to interact rightfully, not because wills are the key to binding.

Put differently, Kant's rejection of the idea that bindingness must be located in willing grows out of his analysis of where it is to be found. A free being can only be bound by another in a way that is consistent with the freedom of each, that is, the independence of each of the other's choice. The question of whether we all will something is not crucial; the question is whether you can be bound by some other person's say-so, consistent with your independence as a human being.

B. Revolution and the Omnilateral Will

Weinstock's essay engages with the idea of omnilateral willing in a different way. He seeks to soften Kant's anti-revolutionary claims, arguing that, finally, the most difficult questions about the permissibility of revolution must be questions about what can be expected to work. In *Force and Freedom*, I framed the issue of revolution in the sequenced way in which Kant does, distinguishing between the Postulate of Public Right which requires citizens to unite themselves into a rightful condition in order to provide their private rights, and that Idea of the Original Contract, which is the regulative ideal for a rightful condition. The organizing idea of Kant's opposition to revolution is that a bad government, including a despotic one, satisfies the Postulate of Public Right, even though it is gravely defective from the standpoint of the Idea of the Original Contract. Resolving everyone's disputes in accordance with procedures is a necessary condition of right. In a rightful condition, only public law can authorise the use of force. A revolution is a rejection of a rightful condition in the hope of subsequently re-entering a better one. It necessarily violates the Postulate of Public Right. To overthrow public institutions and officials can only be a unilateral act of creating a condition in which all acts are merely unilateral. A condition of public right thus contrasts with a condition of barbarism, where there is force without freedom or law. The use of force against organised violence is permissible.

Weinstock frames the issue in a very different way:

> Though he does not spell this out explicitly, presumably Ripstein's categorisation of despotism as closer to republicanism is grounded in the tacit claim that the road back from despotism to barbarism is less likely, both on conceptual and on empirical grounds, than is the road forward from despotism to republicanism.

Weinstock acknowledges the distinction between the Postulate of Public Right and the Idea of the Original Contract, for example, when he seeks to contrast despotism with an imperfect republic in terms of what he calls '[t]he lack of a fully acknowledged public standard'. This, he suggests 'makes despotism imperfect in a different, and deeper manner than the way in which real-world republics are imperfect'. I agree that this is a difference; the question concerns what follows from it. Weinstock continues: 'When the Idea of the Original Contract is shared as a standard of evaluation by both citizens and rulers, it can function as a shared standard by which to adjudicate disputes.' That cannot quite be correct, if by 'shared standard' Weinstock means a standard that can be applied directly by all of those who share it. The difficulty is that the Idea of the Original Contract is not available as a shared standard. The point of the Postulate of Public Right is that a standard can only be shared by means of public procedures that give effect to it. That does not mean that whatever the institution does is beyond criticism; it only means that nothing can be fully public except via institutions. This point also applies to the Idea of the Original Contract; it can only serve as a shared standard if there are procedures and institutions for giving effect to it. Without pubic procedures in place, no question of their content has any bearing on the possibility of right. Weinstock appears to presuppose that the Idea of the Original Contract can function as a public judgement ('a shared standard'), but makes the public character of such judgement implicitly private: an aggregate of what individuals happen to think about how well the state matches up to the ideal.

It is this role of procedures in creating a public standpoint that stands in the way of Weinstock's suggestion that 'the anti-revolution argument for despotisms cannot simply piggyback on the plausibility of the anti-revolution view for imperfect republics, via the claim that despotisms are potential republics'. No piggybacking is involved: actual republics are defective from the same normative standpoint as are despotisms; indeed, the relevant defect consists in the elements of despotism that are to be found in them. So understood, however, actual governments all include elements of despotism, and all despotisms also act for the most basic public purpose of providing a rightful condition. Weinstock's characterisation of despotism as purely private turns it into barbarism, however, because the mark of barbarism is that all action is merely unilateral.

Weinstock also appeals to Kant's philosophy of history with its supposition that we have moral grounds for assuming that the world and particular institutions within it are improving. But for Kant, the philosophy of history is a basis for hope, not an empirical hypothesis about the projected direction of history. Nothing 'warrants the belief that the move forward to republicanism is more likely for despotisms than the slide back into barbarism', because that belief is no part of Kant's account. Indeed, the very same grounds that impose the requirement that we hope that existing despotisms will improve demand also that we see in every revolution hope for human freedom. The basis of those hopes, however, is not empirical; nor does the possibility of such hopes serve to justify any particular act of insurrection. In the same way, Kant insists that we see wars through the lens of hope, and so see them as leading eventually to peace. Such hopes do not, however, justify going to war.

None of this is to deny that some cases, such as the 1789 French Revolution, are thrilling because they present an example of human beings acting under the idea of their own freedom and equality. The awe it inspires, however, does not amount to a justification of it.

Weinstock's approach, by contrast, would not only regard the French Revolution as justified prospectively; more surprisingly, it would seem to be forced to conclude that no rightful condition existed anywhere before it, because only with the French Revolution did the idea emerge of the people holding rulers to an independent idea of the public good.

C. Public Purposes

Stone takes up the Idea of the Original Contract in yet another way, focusing on the idea that a rightful condition is only supposed to act for fully public purposes. His discussion points to a conceptual issue that arises for any theory of limited government. Kant's account takes this thought further, restricting state action to properly public purposes that can be connected to the state's duty of creating, sustaining and improving itself as a rightful condition. This seems to leave no space for discretionary public purposes. Stone remarks on the oddness of this, observing that: 'It would be odd, for example, to say that a state lacked the power to create parklands or to preserve its history; but it would also be odd to say that it was constitutionally *obligated* to do so.' He then asks exactly the right question: 'Is there room in an argument like Kant's—an argument from the necessary conditions of the possibility of a system of private freedom—for the existence of public powers which are discretionary or essentially deliberative in this way?' Kantians often follow Rousseau in dismissing such questions as wrongly put, but in this case I want to draw attention to the extent to which the question is *rightly* put: the key to understanding a variety of important and familiar state activities is not to ask 'should (or must) a liberal state support arts, preserve nature, celebrate its history, etc,' but instead to focus on the source of the public power under which any of these things might properly be carried out. Flikschuh asks a similar question about public health:

> Public health schemes with their ever-rising costs and related hard social and medical choices are a further example: are we after a regime of equal private freedom here, or concerned with the maintenance of a reasonably healthy population overall, given the positive effects of public health on social matters of state more generally?

These questions raise a puzzle for Kant's position, and a much more serious challenge for much writing in political philosophy, which often supposes that the only question of whether something should be enforced through law concerns its moral value (or balance of value and disvalue), without any attention to the question of whether public officials could have the power to make the relevant law. The point, I shall suggest, is that the state is neither an unfortunate expedient for the protection of private rights, nor an ideal form of organic collective, the thriving of which is of independent moral concern (as Hegel advocates and Flikschuh's formulation in terms of 'external freedom claims as a means to establishing the state' might be taken to suggest). Instead, the fundamental issue must be formal, and concern the form of lawgiving. The organising thought is that the ideal case of freedom is the citizens ruling themselves through their lawmaking institutions.

In *Theory and Practice* Kant regards such powers as unproblematic, but also as barely meriting comment, except to note what their basis is not: making people happy or contented with their lot. Instead, the purpose must be indirect and make a rightful condition easier to govern. (8:298) When Kant speaks of indirect means, it is easy to misread him as making empirical claims, to the effect that citizens will be more manageable if happy. Yet Kant's discussion of indirect duties in the *Doctrine of Virtue* makes it clear that he thinks that indirect duties are not merely empirical, even if their particulars are sensitive to empirical factors. The duty to develop your moral sensibility is part of what it is to make the happiness of others one of your ends. A similar structure applies to the duties of the state, especially its duty to bring itself more fully into conformity with the Idea of the Original Contract. This duty bears important similarities to duties of virtue, as it requires the setting of an end rather than any specific act. On the understanding of such duties that I am sketching here, they include an a priori account of the basis of public power, but also charge public officials with the exercise of judgement in light of a principle of politics, which brings 'empirical cognition of human nature' to bear on its exercise. The thought is this: a state is always subject to a duty to bring itself into ever greater conformity with the Idea of the Original Contract, and so see to it that the citizens rule themselves more fully through their institutions. Flikschuh fails to distinguish this idea from two others. The first of these, which she appears to endorse, is that the state has a sort of freedom that lets it decide on its purposes and 'make public policy' for example, by taking account of a wide range of competing values, weighing freedom more heavily in religious schooling than elsewhere. Her reservations about the moral value of purposiveness do not extend to its exercise by a state; the only constraint on state action appears to be 'reminding public legislators not to transgress against the idea of the juridical equality of each in relation to everyone else'. Indeed, her characterisations of 'public policy making' in terms of its 'function' carry with them a disdain for 'what is in fact often the *public nuisance* of individual choice'. Her endorsement of 'subtle incentive schemes that do exert pressure for policy-confirming behaviour on non-consenting citizens' appears indifferent to Kant's warnings against despotism more generally or paternalism in particular. The other position, which she mistakenly attributes to me, is that examples such as poverty relief and public roads are attempts to perfect private freedom. My own view, which I take Kant to share, traces public powers to the need for citizens to share a united will. Individual relations of dependence are inconsistent with sharing a united will. That is the sense in which the state must 'ensure its own survival'.

In order to make the survival and omnilaterality of its united will its end, the state must take up means adequate to doing so. What means are adequate? That is partially, but not entirely, an empirical question. The formal aspect of making greater conformity with the Idea of the Original Contract its end has two parts. First, as a perfectly general matter, if the state is to make anything its end, it must take up appropriate means. The only means available to it are the development of procedures and the empowerment of officials, because those are the only two ways in which the state can do anything at all. Thus its setting itself an end consists in taking up the means of developing procedures and empowering officials.

Second, an essential part of the end of bringing the state more fully into conformity with the Idea of the Original Contract is for the citizens to be active rather than passive, to rule themselves in a way that they can recognise themselves as doing. The requirement that they recognise themselves as doing so is not a Hegelian add-on that sits uncomfortably with the cold Kantian system; citizens are only active if they satisfy this standard Kantian criterion for choosing rather than wishing: citizens themselves must be conscious of their ability to bring about their object through their action (6:213). Thus, citizens must be able to suppose themselves to be using their political power to rule themselves, that is, they must be able to regard its exercise as something within their control. They must be able to see the state as in an important sense their own. So the state must have the power to create procedures that enable citizens to regard themselves as ruling themselves, and so to regard the state as their own.

How does this relate to Stone's examples? Not every way in which the state might bring good into the world counts as a public purpose. Stone's examples of preservation of cultural and natural history can be brought under the idea of public purposes insofar as they can be represented as ways in which citizens can regard the state as their own. Particular states may put differing degrees of emphasis on each. The same can be said about at least some forms of art. But the particulars depend on a principle of politics, that is on 'empirical cognition of human nature' (8:429). In a particular state at a particular time, that might include support for the arts, the preservation of natural beauty, or the celebration of a nation's history or achievements. The Kantian account says only that the state has the power to make such decisions. No doubt many states make them badly, celebrating history through jingoism and worse, or pouring huge amounts of money into an attempt to bring about athletic achievements. At the same time, interpretation and expression of the state's discretionary purposes must always be limited by the rights of the citizens.

The example of public health, which both Stone and Flikschuh mention, can be explained in more than one way. Illness leads to dependence and poverty, and the state's power to protect against it can be justified on those grounds. Alternatively, in many democratic political cultures, public protection against the depredations of illness has become fundamental to the ways in which many citizens identify with the state.[9]

Thus Kant's account contains resources to distinguish between the mandatory acts a state must perform, such as setting up courts, maintaining public

[9] It is interesting to speculate about whether this form or identification would have arisen in other democratic countries had the United States also adopted comprehensive medical insurance.

roads and defending itself against attack, from worthwhile but discretionary ones such as supporting the arts, celebrating its history, or preserving its natural environment. In deciding among these possible endeavours, all the state can do is empower officials to exercise judgement. Part of how they will do so is through considering popular opinion, but another part is by empowering panels of experts. In making such judgements, a state has broad discretion about means, constrained by the demand that power be exercised consistently with everyone's innate right, but it has no discretion about its fundamental end of being a rightful condition.

D. Right and Ethics

One ordinarily associates appendicitis with an inflammation of the appendix, not that others should find the appendix inflammatory. In responding to Allen Wood's generous but probing remarks about the relation between the Universal Principle of Right and the Categorical Imperative, I hope to address the problem therapeutically, rather than through the full appendectomy that Wood prescribes. I will also engage with Stone's question 'What is the genus of which [consistency of will and consistency of choice] are the species?' and Pavlakos's quest for a 'unified account of obligation'.

Let me begin by noting that the Categorical Imperative appears five times in the Introduction to the *Metaphysics of Morals*,[10] three times in Private Right,[11] twice in Public Right,[12] and once in the Appendix, in which Kant replies to Bouwerk's review in the *Göttingen Journal*.

Strikingly, it does not occur in the Introduction to the *Doctrine of Right*, where the Universal Principle of Right is introduced. When it occurs in the *Doctrine of Right* no reference is made to any of the three formulae of the *Groundwork* or to the *Doctrine of Virtue*.

I begin with this fragment of a concordance because at least part of the issue here concerns the different ways in which Kant uses the term 'categorical imperative'. Later he writes: 'The supreme principle of the doctrine of morals is, therefore, act on the maxim which can also hold as a universal law. Any maxim that does not so qualify is contrary to morals.' Only later (at least according to Bernd Ludwig's edition of the *Doctrine of Right*, which is followed in the translation edited by Wood)[13] does Kant distinguish the incentives of

[10] At Ak 221, 222, 223, 225 and 227.
[11] At 252, 273 and 280n.
[12] At 318 and 331.
[13] See Immanuel Kant, *Practical Philosophy*, ed A Wood, trans M Gregor (Cambridge, Cambridge University Press, 1996) 383.

different types of lawgiving, noting that the incentives of right are limited to pathological determining grounds of choice, aversions in particular 'for it is a lawgiving, which constrains, not an allurement which invites' (6:219). This is a distinction between forms of lawgiving, and not, strictly speaking, between imperatives, since Kant has already told us that:

> An imperative differs from a practical law in that the law indeed represents an action as necessary but takes no account of whether this action already inheres by an inner necessity in the acting subject (as in a holy being) or whether it is contingent (as in the human being); for where the former is the case there is no imperative. (6:222)

These textual issues are important in distinguishing the question that I sought to answer in the Appendix to *Force and Freedom*, from two I did not. The question I did seek to answer can be put this way: The *Groundwork* and *Critique of Practical Reason* purport to show how the Categorical Imperative, understood as a rule for maxims, could indeed be categorically valid for any being with a free will. The Universal Principle of Right is also supposed to be categorically binding. Much of *Force and Freedom* is taken up with exploring its implications, and putting to one side questions about whether it requires or could receive any kind of further vindication. Nonetheless, all of this raises a question: if the Categorical Imperative, as formulated in the *Groundwork* and Second *Critique*, really is a rationally binding principle, how could the superficially similar but nonetheless distinct Universal Principle of Right also be rationally binding? Many readers might reject the antecedent of this question, but Kant did not. So how are they related? When I wrote that the Universal Principle of Right is an extension of the categorical imperative, I meant to answer this question. In the Introduction to the *Metaphysics of Morals* as a whole, Kant first defines an imperative as 'a practical rule by which an action in itself contingent is made necessary', and then says that: 'A categorical (unconditional) imperative is one that represents an action as objectively necessary and makes it necessary not indirectly, through the representation of some end they can be attained by the action, but through the mere representation of this action itself (its form), and hence directly.' He continues: 'The ground of the possibility of categorical imperatives is this: that they refer to no other property of choice (by which some purpose can be ascribed to it) but simply to its *freedom*' (6:222). The Universal Principle of Right is presented as categorically binding in this sense, through its form, rather than through some end it will achieve.

There are two questions that have proved distracting in the literature on the *Doctrine of Right*, which I was not hoping to answer. The first of these is whether external lawgiving can be derived from internal lawgiving, simply as such, that is, whether the concept of an enforceable obligation for which the incentive doesn't matter can be derived from the concept of an obligation that serves as its own incentive. I do not think there is any hope of any such derivation, and I agree with Wood that a lot of the literature has been deformed by the assumption that some such derivation must be possible if the *Doctrine of Right* is to succeed on its own terms. The second is whether the permissibility of external incentives makes the concept of right an instance of heteronomy. I suspect that this question has also distorted understanding of Kant. Wood and I agree, again, that the domain of right is ultimately a domain of freedom, even though it admits of contingent incentives.

The claim that I was trying to make in the Appendix is that if Kant's broader defence of morality as categorical, and the Categorical Imperative as the regulative principle for a free will is accepted, then the Universal Principle of Right is the categorical norm governing finite rational beings who occupy space. That is the sense in which the Universal Principle of Right requires an extension—a postulate—to apply to the case of external freedom, since the concept of a free will, though synthetic, does not comprehend the distinction between inner and outer. It remains categorical rather than hypothetical, because it does not depend on an end, even though it has a condition of application, namely the occupation of space. If the Categorical Imperative is the regulative principle for a free will, it regulates the will's own activity only, evaluating maxims of action for their consistency with the idea of a free will. External freedom is different because it comprehends choice exclusively in terms of actions in space. A moral principle governing spatially embodied beings requires a 'postulate incapable of further proof' because nothing could count as a proof of spatiality from concepts of inner freedom alone. A restriction on conduct is only at issue where inconsistency is possible, and external purposiveness is only potentially inconsistent with respect to means. So the *Doctrine of Right* makes no reference to ends for private persons, but only to means; it talks about how you may use your means to set and pursue your own purposes, consistent with the entitlement of others to do the same. It says nothing about the ends for which you are using those means. It says this not because ends cannot be compelled (though of course they cannot) but simply because ends neither conflict nor fail to conflict externally. Only the ways in which means are used can come into external conflict, in the ways that I outline in the parts of my book that Wood liked.

In place of my argument via the postulate, Wood seeks to locate the source of the Universal Principle of Right in the value of rational nature. He puts it this way:

> Moreover, I recognise that other rational beings necessarily have exactly the same rational interest that I do in choosing their actions to further their own freely chosen ends, rather than having their actions constrained to promote ends chosen by others. To recognise a being— whether oneself or another—as a rational agent is to view it as lying under the indispensable rational necessity that it wills to be free, as far as possible, consistent with other demands of reason, to pursue its own ends rather

> than being forced to have its actions serve the ends set by others without its freely given cooperation or consent.
>
> My demand to be externally free is therefore qualified by the demand of reason that others have the same rational claim on external freedom that I do.

A full engagement with this argument would take more space than I have here. One issue concerns Wood's proposed inference from recognizing my own purposive nature to the recognition that others have exactly the same rational entitlements as I do. I am not confident that this transition can be made, and that it does not fall into what Kant characterises as a paralogism, moving, as it does, from a monadic feature of my own case to a relation with others. The monadic feature—having what Wood calls a 'rational interest'—is not binding on others, and so cannot establish that their rational interest is binding on me. Putting that issue aside, however, Wood's argument faces an obstacle that can be stated more succinctly. If the inference can be made out, the question arises as to whether its conclusion is a principle of virtue or a principle of right. If it is a principle of virtue, it does not give others the standing to compel conformity with it; if it is a principle of right, others can enforce it, but it is difficult to see how it is supposed to follow from its premise, which appears to be a principle of virtue, focused exclusively on the necessary content of a rational being's will. So either the argument is restricted to virtue, and fails to justify the Universal Principle of Right, or it reproduces the very problem that was supposed to be at issue, namely explaining how *any* claim about the necessary content of a rational being's will could have implications for the use of force either by or against that being. This difficulty is exacerbated by the fact that, were the argument to succeed, it would certainly prove too much. Each rational being also has a 'rational interest' in his or her own virtue, but that interest does not entitle one person to constrain another to provide for the conditions of the development or realisation of that virtue. Right and virtue do not just differ in the fact that force cannot be used to make another person virtuous; just as fundamentally, they differ in that force cannot be used against others to enable the development or exercise of one's own virtue.

It is also difficult to see how Wood's formulation—'This formal constraint of reason, requiring the recognition of others as having the same claims we do'—is supposed to operate in a framework of Kantian right. Right does not demand that we recognise others as having the same claims as we do; it authorises enforcement of a certain set of claims, whether or not these are recognised by others.

I should reiterate that the point I am making here concerns the structure of right. You are entitled to compel me to act in conformity with right because each of us is entitled to be independent of the other. That is, you are entitled to hold me to the conditions of our reciprocal freedom. That is very different from the claim that Wood seems to want to make, according to which enforcement is legitimate because all you are doing is holding another person to *his own* rational commitments. The same thought seems to underlie Pavlakos's search for a 'unified principle'. Kant explicitly rejects this idea when he writes in the *Doctrine of Right*:

> [W]hen it is said that a creditor has a right to require his debtor to pay his debt, this does not mean that he can remind the debtor that his reason itself puts him under obligation to perform this; it means, instead, that coercion which constrains everyone to pay his debts can coexist with the freedom of everyone, including that of debtors, in accordance with a universal external law. (6:232)

A common requirement that people recognise certain claims as the principle unifying right and ethics would undo the distinction between them, because ethics also imposes rational requirements on people. The *differentia specifica* of right, namely that it concerns external freedom, is reduced to a contingent feature, imposed because of the impossibility of successfully compelling someone to adopt an end.

Finally, as far as the motivation of the Appendix goes, I fear I did not express myself as clearly as I should have in the conversation that Wood recounts. I meant to provide a path between two objections to the independence of right from ethics. The first of these is the thought that the only possible ground for respecting the rights of others, or for exiting the state of nature, must itself turn on the Categorical Imperative, understood in ethical terms. Proponents of this view often take the first Ulpian precept of rightful honour and claim it to be a duty of virtue, which they see as carrying the full burden of the *Doctrine of Right.* This reading turns the entire *Doctrine of Right* into an exercise in applied ethics, which has the surprising consequence that beings capable only of instrumental reasoning, such as the 'Race of Devils' that Kant mentions in *Toward Perpetual Peace*, would be exempt from all claims of right, and so could not be compelled to enter into a rightful condition. The second is Hermann Cohen's argument that insists that coercion is accidental in relation to Kantian morality, and that there cannot be a moral principle specific to coercion. If Cohen's argument is successful, the Universal Principle of Right is not redundant but simply mistaken, and the correct Kantian path moves directly from the Categorical Imperative to principles of politics.

Most of the book constructs an alternative to Cohen's argument, and the Appendix seeks to establish that the Universal Principle of Right does not require ethical underpinnings of the sort that some have supposed to be required. The status of every human being as *sui juris* is sufficient to generate the *Doctrine of Right.* No further or internal incentive is required to ground duties of right, or to authorise human beings to compel each other to enter a rightful condition. Against Cohen, the argument of the Appendix is supposed to show that someone committed to Kantian ethics must incorporate the Universal Principle of Right into his or her maxims of action, even though the Universal Principle of Right cannot be derived from any of the *Groundwork* formulations of the categorical imperative.

I may have I misled Wood with my characterisation of the Universal Principle of Right as 'following from' the Categorical Imperative. Perhaps a better way to put the point would be to say that the only way to bring the conceptual structure of the Categorical Imperative to bear on a plurality of rational beings who occupy space is by means of the Universal Principle of Right.

The strategy for responding to Cohen's argument is what led me to a discussion of the Amphiboly. The point of that discussion was to show that a principle for maxims alone does not generate a category of plurality or of external relation, and so cannot figure in the sort of argument that Wood puts forward in his attempt to unify right and ethics. Wood characterises that discussion as Rorschach; all I can say is that it looks very different to me.

That leaves us, then, with the question of the relation between the *Doctrine of Right* and the aspects of Kant's moral philosophy developed of the *Groundwork* and *Critique of Practical Reason*. No argument can be made from inner morality to outer morality, because no argument from the inner (understood without reference to the form of the outer, that is, space) to the outer could ever be successful. Instead, the only place to look for guidance on the alignment between inner and outer freedom is in Kant's official discussions of the differences between inner and outer in the Amphiboly in the *Critique of Pure Reason*. As I tried to explain in my responses to Flikschuh and Sangiovanni, the irreducibility of spatial relations provides the basis for the irreducibility of all concepts of right.

Index